Strategic Planning For Dummies®

D0573147

Your Planning Framework

By placing all the parts of a plan into the following three areas, you can clearly see how the pieces fit together.

- ✔ **Where are we now?** Review your current strategic position vision, and values.

- ✔ **Where are we going?** Establish your competitive advantage your organization is headed.

- ✔ **How will we get there?** Layout the road to connect where you are now to where you're going. Set your strategic objectives, goals, and action items, and then decide how you want to execute your plan.

Major Pieces of a Strategic Plan

An effective strategic plan includes all of the following pieces. It's easy to get confused with all the different parts of a strategic plan. If you're feeling lost, use this list as an outline for putting your strategic plan together.

- ✔ **Mission statement:** To define the organization's core purpose. Why do we exist?

- ✔ **Vision statement:** To explain where you are headed, your future state. To formulate a picture of what your organization's future makeup will be and where the organization is headed. What will your organization look like 5 to 10 years from now?

- ✔ **Values statement or guiding principals:** To clarify what you stand for and believe in.

- ✔ **SWOT:** To assess the particular strengths, weaknesses, opportunities, and threats that are strategically important to your organization.

- ✔ **Competitive advantage:** To define what you are best at. What can your organization potentially do better than any other organization?

- ✔ **Strategic objectives:** To connect your mission to your vision. Strategic objectives are long-term, continuous strategic areas that get you moving from your mission to achieving your vision. What are the key activities that you need to perform in order to achieve your vision?

- ✔ **Strategies:** To establish a guide that matches your organization's strengths with market opportunities to position your organization in the mind of the customer. Does your strategy match your strengths with how you will provide value to and be perceived by your customers?

- ✔ **Short-term goals/priorities/initiatives:** To set goals that convert the strategic objectives into specific performance targets. Effective goals clearly state what, when, how, and who and are specifically measurable. What are the 1- to 3-year goals you are trying to achieve to get to your strategic objectives?

- ✔ **Action items/plans:** To set specific action plans that lead to implementing your goals. Are your action items comprehensive enough to achieve your goals?

- ✔ **Scorecard:** To measure and manage your strategic plan. What are the key performance measures you can track in order to monitor whether you are achieving your goals?

- ✔ **Financial assessment:** To determine whether your strategic plan makes financial sense. Do the estimated revenue projections exceed your estimated expenses?

For Dummies: Bestselling Book Series for Beginners

Strategic Planning For Dummies®

Cheat Sheet

Planning Pitfalls

Strategic planning is as much about planning as it is about execution. Avoid these planning pitfalls and you'll have a strategic plan that is a living, breathing document:

- ✔ **Lack of ownership:** The most common reason a plan fails is lack of ownership. If people don't have a stake and responsibility in the plan, it will be business as usual for all but a frustrated few.
- ✔ **Lack of communication:** The plan doesn't get communicated to employees, and they don't understand how they contribute.
- ✔ **Getting mired in the day-to-day:** Owners and managers, consumed by daily operating problems, lose sight of long-term goals.
- ✔ **Out of the ordinary:** The plan is treated as something separate and removed from the management process.
- ✔ **An overwhelming plan:** The goals and actions generated in the strategic planning session are too numerous because the team failed to make tough choices to eliminate non-critical actions.
- ✔ **A meaningless plan:** The vision, mission and value statements are viewed as fluff and not supported by actions or don't have employee buy-in.

- ✔ **Annual strategy:** Strategy is only discussed at yearly weekend retreats.
- ✔ **Not considering implementation:** Implementation is not discussed in the strategic planning process. The planning document is seen as an end in itself.
- ✔ **No progress report:** There's no method to track progress. No one feels any forward momentum.
- ✔ **No accountability:** Accountability and high visibility are needed to help drive change. This means that each measure, objective, data source, and initiative must have an owner.
- ✔ **Lack of empowerment:** While accountability may provide strong motivation for improving performance, employees must also have the authority, responsibility, and tools necessary to impact relevant measures. Otherwise, they may resist involvement and ownership.

The Guidelines for a Good Strategy

Need a quick gut check to see if your strategy is sound? Here are the guidelines for a good strategy. Make sure that your strategy . . .

- ✔ Establishes unique value proposition compared to your competitors
- ✔ Is executed through operations that provide different and tailored value to customers
- ✔ Identifies clear tradeoffs and clarifies what *not* to do
- ✔ Focuses on activities that fit together and reinforce each other
- ✔ Drives continual improvement within the organization and moves it toward its vision

Make Strategy a Habit

Your strategic planning process isn't linear; it's circular. Strategic planning isn't just a one-time event, so you need to make it a habit. Use the following suggestions to embed the concepts into your organization.

- ✔ Get ready for the strategic planning process
- ✔ Articulate your mission and vision
- ✔ Review your strategic position
- ✔ Agree on priorities
- ✔ Organize the plan
- ✔ Identify next actions
- ✔ Roll out the plan
- ✔ Hold everyone accountable

For Dummies: Bestselling Book Series for Beginners

Strategic Planning

FOR

DUMMIES®

by Erica Olsen

Wiley Publishing, Inc.

Strategic Planning For Dummies®

Published by
Wiley Publishing, Inc.
111 River St.
Hoboken, NJ 07030-5774
www.wiley.com

Copyright © 2007 by Wiley Publishing, Inc., Indianapolis, Indiana

Published by Wiley Publishing, Inc., Indianapolis, Indiana

Published simultaneously in Canada

For general information on our other products and services, please contact our Customer Care Department within the U.S. at 800-762-2974, outside the U.S. at 317-572-3993, or fax 317-572-4002.

For technical support, please visit www.wiley.com/techsupport.

Wiley also publishes its books in a variety of electronic formats. Some content that appears in print may not be available in electronic books.

Library of Congress Control Number: 2006932688

ISBN-13: 978-0-470-03716-4

ISBN-10: 0-470-03716-4

Manufactured in the United States of America

10 9 8 7 6 5 4 3 2 1

1O/RS/RQ/QW/IN

WILEY

About the Author

Erica holds a BA in Communications and an MBA in International Management from Thunderbird. She's frequently tapped to lecture at the University of Nevada in Reno and the University of Phoenix in Reno on management and planning topics. She hosts workshops and has spoken at conferences nationwide.

As one of the developers of MyStrategicPlan, Erica has stripped strategic planning of its fate as a static document. With her online strategic planning system, any organization, regardless of size and budget, can build a plan in a matter of weeks (or even days). Once completed, the online system actually helps organizations execute the plan instead of just shoving it on a shelf.

MyStrategicPlan is just one of several services offered by Erica's company, M3 Planning. M3 also does onsite strategic planning facilitation and retreats as well as market research consulting. Over the last several years, M3 has developed and reviewed hundreds of strategic plans for organizations across the country.

In addition to *Strategic Planning For Dummies*, Erica has co-authored *Strategic Planning Made Easy: A Practical Guide to Growth and Profitability,* and contributes regular columns to local, regional, and national business publications.

When Erica is not lecturing, writing, or planning, she's alternately kayaking, backcountry skiing, rock climbing, biking, running, or bagging peaks around the Western Hemisphere with her husband Gregor.

Erica always enjoy hearing from her readers. If you have questions about your strategic planning or if you have a success story to share, please contact her through any of the methods below:

E-mail: erica@mystrategicplan.com
Web site: www.mystrategicplan.com
Blog: Strategically Speaking, www.mystrategicplan.com/blog

Dedication

To all the business owners, executive directors, and managers in this world who have a big vision. May you successfully reach that big, hairy, audacious goal.

Author's Acknowledgments

My sincere thanks and appreciation goes out to everyone who had a hand in putting this book together. The journey was an amazingly wonderful and enlightening experience, and I am grateful for the remarkable opportunity to author this book. I must recognize a few specific people.

To my book brain trust, who provided ideas, recommendations, and suggestions at every turn — thank you for making this book as good as it could be. I want to specifically thank Carol McClelland, Tim Gallan, Michael Lewis, Carrie Burchfield, technical editor Ann Bastianelli, and Jan King for all your help. I would also like to thank the graphics and layout teams at Wiley Publishing who made this book come to life and the marketing teams who brought this book to business owners and managers everywhere. And a special thanks to Howard Putnam, author of *The Winds of Turbulence*, for his kind words.

To our strategic planning clients, who've all contributed to this book through their examples, questions, suggestions, and experiences — thank you for the opportunity to work with your organizations. Working with you is a pleasure and gift to everyone at my company.

Thank you to my great friends for sticking by my side even when I was buried in my writing. You're a continual source of encouragement. Special thanks go out to my friends and colleagues who gave me creative inspiration when I got stuck, specifically Greg Fine, Michael-Anne Hougland, and Chris Champagne.

To my family, who's the best family in the world, thank you for supporting me in everything I do. My brothers Ryan and Brett, you provided needed distractions in between my deadlines. Grandma and Grandpa Olsen (aka G & G), you instilled the entrepreneurial spirit in our family; to you I am eternally grateful. Aunt Marlene, you're an amazing mentor; thank you for sharing your knowledge and wisdom with me. Mom, you're a one-of-a-kind business partner and mentor; thank you for taking care of the business and our clients when I was facing looming deadlines. Dad, you added needed clarifications, answers, and content ideas whenever I needed them; thank you for dropping everything to help me. You are as much the author of this book as I am. You're the best.

Most importantly, I want to thank my husband, Gregor. Your unfailing support for everything I do doesn't go unnoticed. I couldn't accomplish any of what I do without you.

Publisher's Acknowledgments

We're proud of this book; please send us your comments through our Dummies online registration form located at www.dummies.com/register/.

Some of the people who helped bring this book to market include the following:

Acquisitions, Editorial, and Media Development

Senior Project Editor: Tim Gallan

Acquisitions Editor: Michael Lewis

Copy Editor: Carrie A. Burchfield

Technical Editor: Ann Bastianelli

Editorial Manager: Christine Meloy Beck

Editorial Assistants: Erin Calligan, David Lutton, Leeann Harney

Cartoons: Rich Tennant, www.the5thwave.com

Composition Services

Project Coordinator: Adrienne Martinez

Layout and Graphics: Claudia Bell, Lavonne Cook, Lauren Goddard, John Greenough, Denny Hager, Stephanie D. Jumper, Barry Offringa, Heather Ryan, Erin Zeltner

Proofreaders: Brian H. Walls, Techbooks

Indexer: Techbooks

Publishing and Editorial for Consumer Dummies

    Diane Graves Steele, Vice President and Publisher, Consumer Dummies

    Joyce Pepple, Acquisitions Director, Consumer Dummies

    Kristin A. Cocks, Product Development Director, Consumer Dummies

    Michael Spring, Vice President and Publisher, Travel

    Kelly Regan, Editorial Director, Travel

Publishing for Technology Dummies

    Andy Cummings, Vice President and Publisher, Dummies Technology/General User

Composition Services

    Gerry Fahey, Vice President of Production Services

    Debbie Stailey, Director of Composition Services

Contents at a Glance

Table of Contents

• •

Introduction

• •

*B*asically, you have two choices when it comes to running your organization: Be intentional about the path your organization follows or turn on autopilot. Turning on autopilot is kind of like hopping in your Hummer, turning on the satellite navigation system, and following the directions from your home to Las Vegas. Computers aren't the best at making decisions, so you may get to Las Vegas eventually, but are you going to Las Vegas, New Mexico, or Las Vegas, Nevada. If you plot your course before you set off, you're a lot more likely to get to your destination.

Many people deliberately plan their personal lives, but when it comes to business, they don't take the same approach. If you're running your organization without a plan, you're just using the navigation system. This concept may seem rudimentary, but the facts state that 90 percent of businesses are running without a plan. Ninety percent is hoping that the navigation system doesn't fail. But because you're reading this book, you're ready to run the show, and you're close to joining the elite ten percent that know a strategic plan is important.

About This Book

This book is about getting from Point A to Point B more effectively and efficiently and having more fun along the way. Part of that journey is the strategy and part of it is the planning, development, and execution.

Strategic planning isn't about taking on additional work; it's about taking all those numerous daily decisions and making them part of an integrated process. Whether you want to be more effective and efficient or you want to make more money, have a bigger community impact, or move your company from good to great, this book is for you! No more thinking that strategic planning is daunting. This book makes the process easy, straightforward, rewarding, and fun. Did I already mention that it's fun?

Strategic Planning For Dummies brings everything business owners, executive directors, or managers need to take their organizations to the next phase of business growth. The book presents a practical set of strategic planning tools and guides you through an integrated strategic planning process. Each part contains relevant content, real-world examples, and useful worksheets. Discover how strategic planning is the key element to your growth through this no nonsense approach.

Strategic planning is a subject that has been overcomplicated by jargon, competing semantics, and consultants of the world (me included!). In reality, strategic planning is a business concept that's useful to all businesses and organizations, no matter its size or resources. Strategic planning is incorrectly positioned as a tool only available to big businesses. With the help of a practical and realistic approach to strategic planning, *Strategic Planning For Dummies* helps you reap the benefits of strategic planning, whether you're a big boy or a small fish.

Conventions Used in This Book

The following conventions are used throughout the text to make concepts consistent and easy to understand:

- ✔ All Web addresses and e-mail addresses appear in `monofont`.

  Some Web addresses may break across two lines of text. If that happens, know that I haven't put in any extra characters (such as hyphens) to indicate the break. So, when typing these addresses into your Web browsers, type exactly what you see in this book, pretending as though the line break doesn't exist.

- ✔ New terms appear in *italic* type and are closely followed by a definition.

- ✔ **Bold** is used to highlight the action parts of numbered steps.

- ✔ The text in gray boxes, what the Dummies folks refer to as *sidebars,* is optional reading. I use sidebars to go off on tangents or present extended examples. You can skip them if you want.

Foolish Assumptions

As I wrote this book, I made some assumptions about you, my reader:

- ✔ You're a decision maker. You hold the position of business owner, manager, executive director, department head, or team/group leader.

- ✔ You can influence change in your organization. Whether you have the final say, you have a strong enough position to influence the course of your business.

✔ You want to see your organization grow! Growth is different for every organization. But the underlying premise is you want your organization to do more.

✔ You can see the edges of your strategy, but you need to fill in the detail. Most organizations know what general direction they're headed in, but they need to turn the generalities into specifics.

✔ You have a plan, but it's sitting on the shelf gathering dust. Or you have a plan, but it's half-way completed.

✔ You want to get everyone on the same page. I hear this phrase with almost every client I work with, so I assume this applies to you too. The need to get your whole company focused and pulling in the same direction is a great motivator to do strategic planning.

Although all these assumptions may not apply to you, am I at least close? I wish I could predict the future of your business, but alas, I haven't been granted that power. A strategic plan helps to take out the uncertainty and allows you to shape the future *you* want. And I'm here to help you with your steps along the way.

How This Book Is Organized

Strategic Planning For Dummies is divided into five parts. A quick review of the Table of Contents and the following description of the parts gives you a solid overview of the entire book. If you want information about a particular topic, the Index can also help you locate it.

Part I: Laying the Foundation for Your Strategic Plan

The chapters in this part are packed full of who, what, how, and why you should care. You look at a number of concepts in this part:

✔ The strategic planning process

✔ Who should be involved

✔ How long the process takes

✔ How you facilitate a strategic planning process

✔ When the right time for planning is

> ✔ The differences between business plans and strategic plans
> ✔ When your organization shouldn't embark on strategic planning

If you're looking to convince your boss or team members about the importance of strategic planning, look no further than Chapter 2.

Part II: Looking Backward to Move Forward

Hold on a second. Don't move past this part too quickly. I know you want to. Whether your organization has been around for two years or 200 years, you have important knowledge to build your strategic plan on. I like to call that knowledge *tribal knowledge.* Chapter 4 asks you to bring that tribal knowledge into the forefront of your planning. Chapter 5 digs into the hard subject of what you do best and is about identifying, developing, and sustaining your organization's competitive advantage. Additionally, Part II provides you with advice on making sure that the foundation of your business is solid. Chapter 6 includes a discussion about mission, vision, and values.

Part III: Sizing Up Your Current Situation

Part III focuses on collecting information that's critical for your strategic decision making. Organizations can't plan without gathering the right data, so Chapter 7 looks at internal data collection and analysis; and Chapters 8 and 9 extend past your business to external data collection on the environmental, customer, industry, and competitive levels. A set of tools is provided for synthesizing the data so it's more useful in strategic decision making.

Part IV: Moving Your Organization into the Future

The main reason you need to do strategic planning is to look into and plan for the future. In this part, you determine how you grow by looking at the different types of value-creating strategies as well as the more specific strategies surrounding growth, integration, and diversification. Most importantly, you identify and evaluate opportunities and then select a strategy to move in that direction.

Part V: Creating and Making the Most of Your Plan

No matter how good the plan, if it sits on the shelf, it's going to be useless. In this part, you put all the elements of the plan together in an organized fashion. You develop strategic objectives, goals and tactics, and scorecards. After your plan is organized, you assess the financial viability of the plan, how to communicate the plan, methods to hold people accountable, and how to adapt the plan to an ever-changing environment. This part provides a wealth of information about strategy execution and performance management.

Part VI: The Part of Tens

Need some quick tips, a shot in the arm, or just a good laugh? The Part of Tens is a collection of hints, reminders, observations, and warnings about what to do and not to do. These chapters focus on giving you a quick set of guidelines for three key areas: facilitating strategy meetings, getting your plan done, and executing the strategy.

Icons Used in This Book

Throughout the book, icons appear in the left margins to alert you to special information.

When you see this icon, the text includes an example of how the idea is used in other organizations — big and small.

This symbol marks an important truth that's worth repeating. Taking note of these ideas can help you make progress with your strategic plan.

The information next to the tip icon always includes a helpful hint to keep your strategic plan moving forward as smoothly as possible. Whether the tips are time savers or step savers, these hints help you move forward.

Any information next to this icon is something you want to be wary about. Watch your step when you see a Warning. The information can include mistakes made by others that you can learn from or moments where you have to weigh the cost of doing one thing over another.

This symbol indicates a concept or work area where the outcome goes into your strategic plan.

Are you an experienced strategic planner? If so, these icons are for you. Take your planning to the next level by employing the ideas highlighted with this icon.

Where to Go from Here

This book is as much about strategy development and execution as it is about the plan itself. If you want to spend time on strategy development, go to Parts II, III, and IV. On the other hand, if you just want to put your plan together, go to Parts I and V.

Another approach to tackling this book is to consider your own thinking and education style. What gets you excited? How do you like to think?

- ✔ **Big picture thinkers:** You may love Chapters 5, 6, and 10 because they focus on what's possible and are future oriented.

- ✔ **Analytical minds:** Chapters 4, 7, 8, 9, and 15 are for those of you who always look at the what ifs. These chapters look at how to use data from your internal and external environments to develop a list of possible strategies.

- ✔ **Detail-oriented folks:** If you're thinking, "How are we going to do this?" then head to Chapters 13 and 14 to put the pieces together.

- ✔ **Social butterflies, team builders, and crowd pleasers:** Check out Chapters 2, 3, and 19 for ideas to build consensus and get everyone's input.

However you approach your plan, I recommend you start a strategy notebook to capture your thoughts as you move through your planning process. I guarantee you'll stumble across a section of text or an idea that you don't want to lose, so if you jot it down in your notebook, you won't have to go back and find it. In several places, I refer to the notebook as a place to work through some actions and exercises.

Regardless of how you find your way around *Strategic Planning For Dummies,* I'm sure that you can develop a strategic plan that fits your team's approach and organization's style. Please share your stories, experiences, vision, and successes with me and other readers on my blog at www.mystrategicplan. com/blog. I look forward to hearing from you! Happy strategizing!

Part I

Laying the Foundation for Your Strategic Plan

"Einstein over there miscalculated our start-up costs and we ran out of money before we could afford to open a 24-hour store."

In this part . . .

Having a strategic plan is the best way to bring focus and direction to your organization. The chapters in this part make you a strategic planning convert. In this part, you discover what strategic planning is and why it's important. You also dive into the steps of the strategic planning process, including who should be involved along the way.

Chapter 1

What Is Strategic Planning Anyhow?

*W*hat will your business be like in three years? Do you have a roadmap to get from today to your envisioned tomorrow? Will you be a few steps closer to realizing your vision by next year? No one can predict the future. But if you don't change anything, the future won't be any different than the past.

One sure-fire way to impact your company's future (and profitability) is to dust off a timeless tool — the strategic plan — and intentionally drive your organization forward. No one strategic model fits all organizations, but the planning process includes certain basic elements that all businesses can use to explore their vision, goals, and next steps of an effective strategic plan. A good strategic plan achieves the following:

  ✔ Reflects the values of the organization

  ✔ Inspires change and revision in products and target markets

  ✔ Clearly defines the criteria for achieving success

  ✔ Assists everyone in daily decision making

No one can predict the future. But effective leaders aren't sitting around and waiting for it to happen either. They're anticipating what lies ahead. Managers and business owners aren't waiting for their competitors to swoop in and put them out of business. Instead, they're using their strategic plans to get ahead of the game. So it's odd to think that many people avoid strategic planning because they consider it complex, costly, and time-intensive. Most of the time the plan is shelved before it's implemented, even knowing the fact that some other company can invade your market!

But strategic planning doesn't have to be mysterious, complicated, or time-consuming. In fact, it should be quick, simple, and easily executed. And strategic planning isn't just something you cross of your list of to-dos — you must create a culture of strategic thinking, so your strategic planning doesn't become an annual retreat but, instead, a part of daily decision making.

Clearing Up the Confusion about Strategic Planning

Many people are confused by the terms *strategy, strategic plan,* and *strategic planning.* Well, I am here to help you get a clear picture. For the moment, forget what you've heard about this subject. I promise that strategic planning makes a huge difference to your organization both tangibly and intangibly, so keep reading!

What is strategy?

Strategy means consciously choosing to be clear about your company's direction in relation to what's happening in the dynamic environment. With this knowledge, you're in a much better position to respond proactively to the changing environment.

The fine points of strategy are as follows:

- ✔ Establishes unique value proposition compared to your competitors
- ✔ Executed through operations that provide different and tailored value to customers
- ✔ Identifies clear tradeoffs and clarifies what *not* to do
- ✔ Focuses on activities that fit together and reinforce each other
- ✔ Drives continual improvement within the organization and moves it toward its vision

Surprising strategic-planning stats

Consider the following statistics from the Balanced Scorecard Collaborative (covered in Chapter 12):

✔ 95 percent of a typical workforce doesn't understand its organization's strategy.

✔ 90 percent of organizations fail to execute their strategies successfully.

✔ 86 percent of executive teams spend less than one hour per month discussing strategy.

✔ 60 percent of organizations don't link strategy to budgeting.

So what's the upshot of these surprising revelations? Strategic planning matters to the life of your business.

Knowing what strategy is can also be explained by looking at what strategy is *not*. Dr. Michael Porter, the leading strategy guru and professor at Harvard, had this to say at the 2006 World Business Forum in Chicago. Strategy is not

✔ Best practice improvement

✔ Execution

✔ Aspirations

✔ A vision

✔ Learning

✔ Agility

✔ Flexibility

✔ Innovation

✔ The Internet (or any technology)

✔ Downsizing

✔ Restructuring

✔ Mergers/Consolidation

✔ Alliances/Partnering

✔ Outsourcing

What is a strategic plan?

Simply put, a *strategic plan* is the formalized roadmap that describes how your company executes the chosen strategy. A plan spells out where an organization is going over the next year or more and how it's going to get there. Typically, the plan is organization-wide or focused on a major function such as a division or a department. A strategic plan is a management tool that serves the purpose of helping an organization do a better job, because a plan focuses the energy, resources, and time of everyone in the organization in the same direction.

So, you may be thinking, "Hey I've got this great book on business plans, so I'll just use that to form my strategic plan." But be aware that strategic plans and business plans aren't the same concepts.

A strategic plan

- ✔ Is for established businesses and business owners who are serious about growth
- ✔ Helps build your competitive advantage
- ✔ Communicates your strategy to staff
- ✔ Prioritizes your financial needs
- ✔ Provides focus and direction to move from plan to action

A business plan, on the other hand,

- ✔ Is for new businesses, projects, or entrepreneurs who are serious about starting up a business
- ✔ Helps define the purpose of your business
- ✔ Helps plan human resources and operational needs
- ✔ Is critical if you're seeking funding
- ✔ Assesses business opportunities
- ✔ Provides structure to ideas

What is the strategic planning process?

In order to create your strategic plan, you have to go through the strategic planning process. The planning process typically includes several major activities or steps. People often have different names for these major activities. They may even conduct them in a different order. Strategic planning often includes use of several key terms as well. See Chapter 3 for specific guidelines and checklists to help you with your process.

Don't be concerned about finding the perfect way to conduct a strategic planning process. (Perfection doesn't really exist, does it?) Modify the information in this book to fit with your organization's culture and timing.

What are the big planning pitfalls?

Strategic planning can yield less than desirable results if you end up in one of the possible pitfalls. To prevent that from happening, here's a list of the most common traps to avoid:

- ✔ **Relying on bad information or no information:** A plan is only as good as the information on which it's based. Too often, teams rely on untested assumptions or hunches, erecting their plans on an unsteady foundation. Chapters 7, 8, and 9 cover collecting good information for your plan.

- ✔ **Ignoring what your planning process reveals:** Planning isn't magic: You can't always get what you want. The planning process includes research and investigation. Your investigation may yield results that tell you not to go in a certain direction. Don't ignore that information!

- ✔ **Being unrealistic about your ability to plan:** Put planning in its place and time. It takes time and effort to plan well. Some companies want the results but aren't willing or able to make the investment. Be realistic about what you can invest. Find a way to plan that suits your available resources, which include your time, energy, and money. Chapter 3 helps you decide what kind of planning process to embark on.

- ✔ **Planning for planning sake:** Planning can become a substitute for action. Don't plan so much that you ignore the execution. Well-laid plans take time to implement. And results take time to yield an outcome. Chapter 14 is all about action.

- ✔ **Get your house in order first:** Planning can reveal that your house isn't in order. When an organization pauses to plan, issues that have been buried or put on the backburner come to the forefront and can easily derail your planning efforts. Make sure that your company is in order and that there are no major conflicts before you embark on strategizing. Chapter 3 and 7 help you to identify if you have any organizational issues that will derail your planning.

- ✔ **Don't copy and paste:** It's easy to fall into the trap of copying the best practices of a company similar to yours. Although employing best practices from your industry is important, other organizations' experiences aren't relevant to your own. Organizations are unique, complex, and diverse. You need to find your own path instead of following a cookie-cutter approach.

What are the components of a strategic plan?

There are several different frameworks to think about and use while you're developing your strategic plan. Think of the frameworks as different lenses through which to view the strategic planning process. You don't always look through two or three lenses at once. Normally you use one at a time, and often you may not know that you're using certain frameworks that are embedded in your process. If you're trying to explain to your planning team how pieces of the puzzle fit together, first you must understand the following components of the strategic plan:

- ✔ **Strategy and culture:** Your organization's culture is made up of people, processes, experiences, ideas, and attitudes. Your strategy is where your organization is headed, what path it takes, and how it gets there. You can't have strategy without culture or vice versa. Your culture is like your house, and if it's not in order, the best strategy in the world can't take your company anywhere.

- ✔ **Internal and external:** Similar to the strategy and culture framework (previous bullet), you have an internal and external framework. The strategy is external. You gather information from your customers, competitors, industry, and environment to identify your opportunities and threats. Through employee surveys, board assessments, and financial statements, you identify your company's strengths and weaknesses, which are internal.

- ✔ **The Balanced Scorecard perspectives:** The Balanced Scorecard is a framework used to develop goals and objectives in four areas (instead of departments): financial, customers, internal business processes, and people. The financial, internal business processes, and people areas are internal. The customer area is external. Chapter 12 elaborates on this framework and the Balanced Scorecard.

- ✔ **Market focus:** Growth comes from focusing on your customers and delivering superior value to them consistently year after year. Built into your strategic plan is a market-focus framework because of how critical this is to your organizational growth.

> ✔ **Where are we now? Where are we going? How will we get there?:**
> Because it's easy to confuse how all the elements of a plan come
> together and where they go, this framework is a simple, yet clear way of
> looking at the whole plan. This framework is explained in Chapter 3.

What are the most frequently asked strategic planning questions?

Strategic planning can create a ton of questions. You're not alone if you have
a long list. The following sections cover the answers to the most commonly
asked questions.

Who uses strategic plans?

Everyone — or at least every company and organization that wants to be
successful. Companies in every industry, in every part of the country, and in
most of the Fortune 500 use strategic plans. Organizations within the nonprofit, government, and small to big business sectors also have strategic
plans. See Chapter 3 for statistics for how widely strategic planning is used
as a management tool.

Does every strategic plan include the same elements?

A strategic plan should include many elements:

- ✔ A mission statement and vision statement
- ✔ A description of the company's long-term goals and objectives
- ✔ Strategies the company plans to use to achieve general goals and
  objectives
- ✔ Action plans to implement the goals and objectives

The strategic plan may also identify external factors that can affect achievement of long-term goals. Plans may vary in detail and scope (depending on
how big the organization is), but for the most part, a strategic plan includes
the basic elements listed above.

Just exactly what is strategic planning?

The term *strategic planning* refers to a coordinated and systematic process
for developing a plan for the overall direction of your endeavor for the purpose of optimizing future potential. For a profit-making business, this process
involves many questions:

> ✔ What is the mission and purpose of the business?
>
> ✔ Where do we want to take the business?
>
> ✔ What do we sell currently? What could we sell in the future?
>
> ✔ To whom shall we sell it?
>
> ✔ What do we do that is unique?
>
> ✔ How shall we beat or avoid competition?

The central purpose of this process is to ensure that the course and direction is well thought out, sound, and appropriate. In addition, the process provides reassurance that the limited resources of the enterprise (time and capital) are sharply focused in support of that course and direction. The process encompasses both strategy formulation and implementation.

What is the difference between strategic planning and long-range planning?

The major difference between strategic planning and long-range planning is in emphasis. Long-range planning is generally considered to mean the development of a plan of action to accomplish a goal or set of goals over a period of several years. The major assumption in long range planning is that current knowledge about future conditions is sufficiently reliable to enable the development of these plans. Because the environment is assumed to be predictable, the emphasis is on the articulation of internally focused plans to accomplish agreed-on goals.

The major assumption in strategic planning, however, is that an organization must be responsive to a dynamic, changing environment. Therefore, the emphasis in strategic planning is on understanding how the environment is changing and will change and on developing organizational decisions that are responsive to these changes.

Does every company need a strategic plan?

Every endeavor or enterprise already has a strategy. These range from some vague sense of the desires of the owner to massive, overly sophisticated master plans. So the question shouldn't be whether every company needs a strategy but instead whether the company's strategy needs to be well thought out, sound, appropriate, and do-able. The answer is yes.

We are highly successful already, so why should we plan?

Success is strong evidence that a company has had a sound and appropriate strategy. Note the past tense. There's absolutely no guarantee that yesterday's sound and appropriate strategy will continue to be successful in the future. Indeed, there's great danger in assuming so without adequate study.

Can a smaller company afford the time for strategic planning?

Experience shows that the top management team devotes approximately 2 to 4 percent of its time to practical strategic planning. In reality, structured strategic planning isn't something more to do; it's a better way of doing something already being done. Indeed, in the long run, you save time.

But understand, strategic planning can become a time trap. You can become caught in a long slog of planning if you get too mired down in the details. From the outset, you need to establish that the plan is a living document and that it is not written in stone. By doing that, you can avoid strategic planning becoming a time trap.

Why plan in a world that's highly uncertain?

Your efforts in forward planning can become pointless if you fear that the plan may be overwhelmed by unanticipated events and developments. Uncertainty is, indeed, a major problem in forward planning. However, the greater the uncertainty, the greater the need for good strategic planning because you want to try to be ready for the unknown.

How can we be confident that our planning will be successful?

Even in the presence of a structured strategic planning process, it's quite possible to formulate unsound, inappropriate strategies and/or to fail at implementation. But this book helps you avoid these many pitfalls. Strategic planning is worth the effort because it helps you run your organization better. You can be confident that the information and best practices outlined in this book result in a successful strategic planning process. I promise!

What is strategic thinking?

Strategic thinking means asking yourself, "Are we doing the right thing?" It requires three major components:

- Purpose or end vision
- Understanding the environment, particularly of the competition affecting and/or blocking achievement of these ends
- Creativity in developing effective responses to the competitive forces

The Strategic Plan's Key Elements

A company's strategic plan is the game plan that management uses for positioning the company in its chosen market arena, competing successfully, satisfying customers, and achieving good business performance. Most business owners and executives have countless excuses for not having a formal strategic plan. I've heard everything from "We're too new," to "We're not big enough," to "We've never had one; why start now?"

If these excuses sound familiar, check this out: Studies indicate that roughly 90 percent of all businesses lack a strategic plan. Of those that have a plan, only 10 percent actually implement it. So, if you're part of the 90 percent, ask yourself these questions:

- ✔ Can your company be more focused?
- ✔ Can you be more effective?
- ✔ Can your employees be more efficient?
- ✔ Can your company be more successful?

I'm guessing that the majority of you answered *yes* to all the above. And that's okay, so in the following sections, I help you understand how each part of a strategic plan can change how you answer the above questions.

Vision: Bringing things into focus

You get what you focus on. Everyone knows this, but most companies are busy tending to the urgent problems of the day and not focusing on key long-term issues. Unless your staff can focus on a common vision, the company can go nowhere. A strategic plan helps direct energy and guide staff toward a shared goal in an ever-changing world.

Orit Gadiesh, chairman of Bain & Co., says, "In the current environment, companies can't afford *not* to have a set of guiding principles — a vision that communicates *true north* to the entire organization." Can your company be more focused? Yes, and to help find your true north check out Chapter 6.

Mission, goals, and objectives: Empowering employees

The mission statement, goals, and objectives are the roadmap in a strategic plan to empower your employees to be more effective (and you too, for that matter). Don't let these elements be just a paragraph on the break room wall or bullet points in a memo; let them shine as primary guidelines for leading the organization to higher levels of performance. They provide the framework for independent decisions and actions initiated by departments, managers, and employees into a coordinated, company-wide game plan. Head to Chapter 6 for more info on developing your mission and Chapter 12 for developing your roadmap.

Strategy: Explaining the how

After the mission, goals, and objectives are clear, (see previous section) establish how you're going to achieve those items. A strategy provides the vehicle and answers the question "How are we going to get there with the resources we have?" A good strategy focuses on efficiency through:

- ✔ Achieving performance targets
- ✔ Out-performing your competition
- ✔ Achieving sustainable competitive advantage
- ✔ Growing your revenue and maintaining or shrinking your expenses
- ✔ Satisfying customers
- ✔ Respond to changing market conditions

Basically, strategies keep your whole company acting together while strengthening the company's long-term competitive position in the marketplace. See Chapter 14 for more info on helping your employees be more efficient.

Execution and evaluation: Ensuring success

A strategic plan is a living, dynamic document. It drives your business and must be integrated into every fiber of your organization, so every employee is helping to move the company in the same direction.

All the best missions and strategies in the world are a waste of time if they aren't implemented. To be truly successful, the plan can't gather dust on the bookshelf. You know what shelf I'm talking about. If you ran the white glove over the shelf, you'd find layer upon layer of dust. You really should clean more often.

No, strategic planning success isn't about cleaning, it's about keeping the plan active so that it doesn't gather that proverbial dust. Know what your end result looks like and where your milestones should be. Plan your near term actions and evaluate your progress each quarter. Are you where you thought you'd be if you had been on target? Or, if you're off target, how far are you off? The course correction to put you back on track becomes your next action plan.

When your company has a clear plan and acts accordingly to the plan, you're going to go from where you are, to where you want to go, therefore ensuring your success! Check out Chapter 14 for more on this topic.

Tips for Better Strategic Planning

Before you get too far into your strategic planning process, check out the tips below — your quick guide to getting the most out of your strategic planning process:

- ✓ **Pull together a diverse, yet appropriate, group of people to make up your planning team.** Diversity leads to a better strategy. Bring together a small core team — between six and ten people — of leaders and managers who represent every area of the company.

- ✓ **Allow time for big picture, strategic thinking.** We tend to try to squeeze strategic planning discussions in between putting out fires and going on a much needed vacation. But to create a strategic plan, your team needs time to think big. Do whatever it takes to allow that time for big-picture thinking (including taking your team off-site).

- ✓ **Get full commitment from key people in your organization.** You can't do it alone. If your team doesn't buy into the planning process and the resulting strategic plan, you're dead in the water.

- ✓ **Allow for open and free discussion regardless of each person's position within the organization.** (This tip includes you — the CEO.) Don't lead the planning sessions. Hire an outside facilitator, someone who doesn't have any stake in your success. When you do, people wonder whether you're trying to lead them down the path you wanted all along. Encourage active participation, but don't let any one person dominate the session.

- ✓ **Think about execution before you start.** It doesn't matter how good the plan is if it isn't executed. See Chapter 14 for more on this topic.

- ✓ **Use a facilitator, if your budget allows.** Hire a trained professional who has no emotional investment in the outcome of the plan. An impartial third party can concentrate on the process instead of the end result and can ask the tough questions that others may fear to ask.

✔ **Make your plan actionable.** To have any chance at implementation, the plan must clearly articulate goals, action steps, responsibilities, account-abilities, and specific deadlines. And everyone must understand the plan and their role in it.

✔ **Don't write your plan in stone.** Good strategic plans are fluid, not rigid and unbending. They allow you to adapt to changes in the marketplace. Don't be afraid to change your plan as necessary.

✔ **Clearly articulate next steps after every session.** Before closing the strategic planning session, clearly explain what comes next and who's responsible for what. When you walk out of the room, everyone must fully understand what they're responsible for and when to meet deadlines.

✔ **Make strategy a habit, not just a retreat.** Review the strategic plan for performance achievement no less than quarterly and as often as monthly or weekly. Focus on accountability for results and have clear and compelling consequences for unapproved missed deadlines.

Warning Signs That You Need This Book

Planning for the future is important but very few businesses actually do it. Instead of listing the benefits of business planning and strategic planning (see Chapter 2 for those), the following list of warning signs can tell you that you need a new strategy for your strategic planning process:

✔ Someone asks where your business will be in one year, and you don't have an answer. You ask your partners or management team the same question, and you hear wildly different answers.

✔ You have some idea where you want to go in the next year, but you don't have any idea what you're going to do to make next year a reality.

✔ Your company won't hit its revenue goals this year. Although there can be many reasons for the shortfall, you're not sure how to grow the top line.

✔ There are inconsistencies in your brochure, Web site, sales collateral, and so on. You can't understand the content. More importantly, neither can anyone else. You find that when you explain your business to a potential client, you tell different stories about how you provide value.

✔ You're ignoring your competition. You don't know who your number one competitor is and what they're doing, who their clients are, what prod-ucts they offer, their pricing, or key message points. When your cus-tomers ask you to explain why your company is different, you don't have a good response.

✔ Everything on your to-do list is a priority. You don't know where your time is best spent.

✔ Friends and colleagues can't refer you because they aren't sure exactly what value your business provides and to whom. They often ask, "What is it you do again?"

✔ You're presented with a business opportunity, and you are unsure how to evaluate whether it's something your company should pursue. In fact, you normally pursue all opportunities for fear you may miss the big one.

✔ You enjoy what you do, but you aren't passionate about your business. You'd quit everything and follow that passion tomorrow if you could.

✔ Your business development consists largely of attending networking events, but you spend most of your time talking to people you know. You rely solely on word-of-mouth for new customers.

✔ You don't know why your customers buy from you. The majority continues to do business with your company, but you're not sure what keeps them coming back. You've never really asked.

✔ You find your clients contracting with other companies for services you provide. When asked, they say they didn't know you offered those services.

✔ You ask your employees what success looks like, and they don't have a consistent answer. And your incentive plan doesn't synch up with performance expectations.

✔ You complain when your customers call because you just don't have time to talk to them. And you notice your staff complaining too.

✔ You don't do market research or solicit customer feedback because you (think you) know your market. You've been in the industry for years and you know customers' need and wants.

✔ You determine your pricing by looking at your competitor's prices and discounting slightly. All your prices are based on your competitors' offerings.

✔ You can't articulate what your company does best, but it's a good point of discussion at a cocktail party.

✔ You're asked why you're in business, and your only response is *profit*.

Do any of these statements sound familiar? If so, it's time to get serious about your business and get focused. Having a strategic plan and a succinct strategy brings clarity and focus to your organization. It ensures that your time, resources, and actions aren't wasted. If every part of your organization isn't pointed in the same direction, you can end up going in circles and frustrating yourself and your employees. Why not get strategic now and make it your most successful year ever?

Chapter 2

Why Strategic Planning Impacts Your Growth

Success isn't a matter of chance but rather a matter of choice. This concept really encapsulates why it's important to have a clear strategic direction and strategic plan. Business success isn't going to happen by accident. You must look into the future and create a plan for wherever it is you're trying to go. Forget about failure rates and all that garbage. If you aren't intentional about the direction of your business or department, you aren't likely to get there.

This chapter gives you many reasons why you should care about strategic planning. If you or your boss need convincing, the statistics as well as the intangibles are covered in the sections that follow. A peek at what high-growth organizations are doing can show you how planning impacts your growth.

Reason #1: Strategic Planning Is the Leading Management Tool

Over the past dozen years, you may have witnessed an explosion in the use of management tools and techniques — everything from Six Sigma to benchmarking. Keeping up with the latest and greatest, as well as deciding which tools to put to work, is a key part of every leader's job. But it's tough to pick the winners from the losers. As new tools appear every year, others seem to drop off the radar screen. Unfortunately there's no Consumer Reports for management tools, so choosing and using tools can become a risky and potentially expensive gamble, leaving many leaders stymied.

In 1993, Bain & Co., a leading management consulting company, launched a multi-year research project to get the facts about management tools and trends. The objective of the study was to provide managers with information to identify and integrate tools that improve bottom-line results as well as understand their strategic challenges and priorities.

Bain has assembled a database that now includes 7,283 businesses from more than 70 countries in North America, Europe, Asia, Africa, the Middle East, and Latin America. The *Bain & Company's 2005 Management Tools* survey received surveys from a broad range of international executives. To qualify for inclusion in the study, a tool had to be relevant to senior management, topical as evidenced by coverage in the business press, and measurable.

The results? Out of all the tools used, 79 percent of respondents use strategic planning. In fact, strategic planning is a long-time favorite tool, having been used by more than half of companies in every survey since Bain started this project. Not surprisingly, the most popular tools are the ones that create the highest satisfaction ratings. Respondents were most satisfied with strategic planning out of all 25 tools. See Figure 2-1 for details.

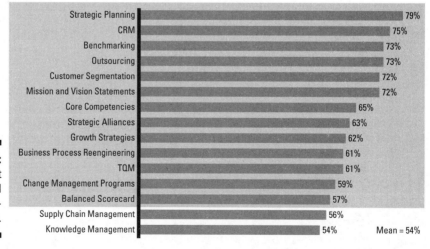

Figure 2-1:
Most widely used management tools.

Tool	Percentage
Strategic Planning	79%
CRM	75%
Benchmarking	73%
Outsourcing	73%
Customer Segmentation	72%
Mission and Vision Statements	72%
Core Competencies	65%
Strategic Alliances	63%
Growth Strategies	62%
Business Process Reengineering	61%
TQM	61%
Change Management Programs	59%
Balanced Scorecard	57%
Supply Chain Management	56%
Knowledge Management	54%

Mean = 54%

So what does this study tell us? That year after year, strategic planning is used by companies worldwide with very high satisfaction rates. Strategic planning isn't just a management fad likely to blow away. For more information on this study, check out the following Web site: `www.bain.com/ management_tools/home.asp`.

Reason #2: Failing to Plan Is Planning to Fail

If organizations fail to anticipate or prepare for fundamental changes, they may lose valuable lead time and momentum to combat them. These fundamental elements of business are customer expectations, employee morale, regulatory requirements, competitive pressures, and economic changes, and they're always in flux. Many times businesses achieve a level of success and then stall. Strategic planning helps you to avoid the stall and get off the plateau you find yourself on. Accidental success is dangerous. Succeeding without a plan is possible, and plenty of examples exist of businesses that have achieved financial success without a plan. If you're one of them, consider yourself lucky, but ask yourself this question: Could you have grown and become even more successful if you'd organized a little bit better? I'm willing to bet your answer is yes.

Another danger is that the lack of a strategic plan negatively impacts the attitude of an organization's team. Employees who see aimlessness within an organization have no sense of a greater purpose. People need a reason to come to work everyday (besides the paycheck). Lack of direction results in morale problems because, as far as your employees are concerned, the future is uncertain, unpredictable, and out of control. These depressing conclusions can only be seen as a threat to employment, which negatively impact productivity.

To avoid these dangers, you need to get rid of the naysayers (including possibly yourself). Questioning the value of strategic planning is normal because planning can be intense and costly, but if the attitude that planning isn't necessary becomes part of your corporate culture, it can prove deadly. So look out for the warning signs of indifference:

- ✔ Short-term thinking
- ✔ Leadership indifference
- ✔ Deeply entrenched traditional perspectives

> ✔ Complacency of stakeholders
>
> ✔ Confusion among the employees
>
> ✔ Lack of unity

In the rest of the chapter, you discover why strategic planning can help you navigate troubled waters. If you don't have the problems listed above in your organization but need more proof or ammunition to get those around you to see the benefits of planning, you also find the backup you need in the next sections.

Reason #3: The Best of the Best Do It

High-performance organizations have fundamental differences that set them apart from other organizations. Anecdotally, these companies are better than their competitors at everything they do. They work more diligently and incessantly to improve faster than their competitors.

There are tons of studies out there that dig into the hows and whys of companies that are ahead of the pack. But instead of getting lost in the details and differences of these studies, take a look at the basics.

At the end of the day, high-performance organizations accomplish extraordinary results, and they do it with ordinary people. If you keep waiting for extraordinary people to come along and make things happen, you're going to wait a long time. Instead, your goal should be to transform your organization in such a way that your people are capable of delivering high performance every minute and every hour of every day.

What makes great companies great

Becoming the best at something is often achieved by modeling the behaviors of winners and putting those behaviors into practice. Here are the characteristics of a high-performance company:

> ✔ Has a purpose that focuses the energy of all its members (typically, that purpose is to be the best there is or ever was)
>
> ✔ Simultaneously and continuously maximizes the self-interests of all its stakeholders
>
> ✔ Outperforms all others (by any measure) not because of what propels it, but in spite of any and all obstacles that impede it

> ✔ Makes it possible for ordinary people to perform in an extraordinary fashion
>
> ✔ Transforms its people into owners of the organization's destiny
>
> ✔ Is a healthy organization committed to being great, no matter what it takes
>
> ✔ Knows that the execution is more important than the strategy

Whereas a strategic plan is the means, growth and high-performance are the end to those means.

An example of a high-performance company is a mid-sized graphics and print shop in Georgia. The owner attributes the company's success, which was recognized as one of the best in the industry, to the employees' dedication to the mission. Its mission includes total focus on customer solutions. According to the owner, the employees practice the mission, not just preach it. To support that action, the company enables all employees to be responsible and accountable for serving its customers. Not to mention that the employees are proud of their work and take rightful ownership of their accomplishments. To that point, they perform extraordinary work.

What are successful CEOs spending their time on?

Have you ever wondered what the guy next door is doing all day? Or, more interestingly, what are growing organizations' CEOs spending their time on? If you could just be a fly on the wall in the offices of some of the Inc. 500 CEOs, I bet you'd discover quite a bit about what it takes to grow an organization.

The Inc. 500, produced by Inc. magazine annually, comprises the top CEOs of the business world. To be eligible for Inc. 500, companies have to be independent and privately held, have grown from at least $200,000 in net sales in Year One to $2 million by Year Five. In summary, they're the fastest growing privately-held organizations in the United States today. The majority of the Inc. 500 CEOs spend an average of 60 hours a week a building their business. (This should be a relief to you if you're putting in such long hours and often think you're all alone.)

Although these CEOs are characterized as hard-working, they're not workaholics because they set goals first and take action second. Most importantly, they take the time to reward themselves and others based on the achievement of the goals and action. Workaholics, on the other hand, usually take action first, set goals second, and don't necessarily celebrate successes. If you're one of those workaholics out there, consider the strategic planning process as a way to help you to set goals and focus on actions you can celebrate.

The Inc. 500 CEOs regularly spend 50 to 90 percent of their time on strategy and business development. Obviously an organization isn't going to be a high-growth organization if time isn't spent on both active strategy and business development. Granted, 50 to 90 percent is quite a large margin, but it gives you an idea of how these 500 CEOs spend their time. Take a look at how you're spending your time each day, and figure out what it really takes to be part of a high-growth company.

Reason #4: You Get Better Results (1 Promise)

Everyone wants better results, right? Those results can be to earn more money, to use resources better, to create a more effective and efficient team, to improve your work/life balance, and so on. And strategic planning helps. The benefits to strategic planning are both intangible and show hard bottom-line ROI.

The day-to-day impact

Every day your work impacts aspects of your business. In the next sections, you discover the true day-to-day impact of having a strategic plan in place.

Spend more time on high impact, high-growth activities

High impact, high growth activities are where you want to spend as much time as possible. With these maneuvers, you spend less time spinning your wheels. Think back on the past month. Were there any projects or activities you were part of directly or indirectly that didn't actually move the organization forward because they were dead end opportunities? I bet there were. Get rid of this dead weight as fast as possible!

Identify true opportunities versus false starts

If you know what you're best at and where you want to go, you can more quickly identify true opportunities versus false starts. You want to pursue true opportunities and quickly throw out false starts. Strategic planning helps you to put the boundaries on your business. When you ignore extraneous distractions, you use your resources more effectively and more quickly to grow your organization.

Adapt quickly

The ability to adapt quickly is the name of the game in today's business climate. When everyone on your team is on the same page and is pulling in the same direction, you can easily absorb shifts, make changes, and innovate on the fly. If there's no clear direction in your strategic plan, your team may not know how and what to adapt to.

Be proactive instead of reactive

Being in a reactionary mode all of the time puts you one (or more) steps behind your competition. Make sure that your strategic plan maps out proactive choices to propel your company forward.

A complaint that I hear from a lot of clients is that they feel like they're always trying to catch up. If you're out of breath, stop running and get ahead of the change curve. If you have a strategic plan in place and you're working on key strategic activities, you have a little bit more time to think about how to take advantage of market movement instead of always reacting to what's going on your environment.

Achieve your vision for success

You started your organization for a reason. You likely have a vision for your business. You want to achieve your vision for success. You have to specifically figure out how you're going to get there. Having a strategic plan makes success intentional.

Increase employee commitment

Strategic planning increases employee commitment — especially in this tight labor market, helping your employees see the vision that you have for success and growth helps you work toward that goal.

The bottom line impact

As business owners, you care about what falls to the bottom line. I do too. A major reason my company focuses on strategic planning is because it does make a financial difference. To verify this, in 2004, we conducted a research study of strategic planning and strategy execution of 280 firms in the United States. The bulleted list below provides the results of that study and explains what you can expect to achieve as well. (Note: To the reader who needs talking points to convince his or her management that strategic planning is profitable, this section is for you.)

✔ **Impact on sales volume:**

- Of those firms whose top management had a high commitment to execute strategic planning, 80 percent reported that their sales volume increased during that year.

- Of the firms whose top management had a lower commitment (average or below) to execute strategic planning, only 59 percent reported that their sales volume had increased during the year.

- From another perspective, firms whose top management had a high commitment reported 12 percent greater increase in sales volume than did those with a lower commitment.

✔ **Impact on net income:**

- Of the firms whose top management had a high commitment to execute strategic planning, 33 percent reported that their net income had increased during the year.

- Of those whose top management had a lower commitment (average or below) to execute strategic planning, only 19 percent reported that their net income had increased during the year.

- From another perspective, firms whose top management had a high commitment reported 11 percent better net income than did those with a lower commitment.

✔ **The role of being proactive:**

- Of the organizations whose top management was proactive, 78 percent reported that their sales volume had increased during the year.

- By contrast of those who were more reactive, only 60 percent reported that their sales volume had increased during the year.

If you compare these stats to the Inc. 500 growth organizations (covered in "What are successful CEOs spending their time on?"), you notice that these figures aren't actually that high. Many of the Inc. 500 companies realized 100 to 200 percent growth over five years. However, the percentage increases listed above are *in addition to* the growth you're already projecting. Therefore, strategic planning helps you either make up part of your growth expectations or it's an addition to your projections.

Your new bottom line

To get you excited about strategic planning before you start, why not calculate your new bottom line? With the quick formula taken from the results of the research above, you can see the potential impact you can expect.

Figure 2-2 and Figure 2-3 provide you with a worksheet to calculate how profitable strategic planning can be to your business. Figure 2-2 looks at sales volume or revenue, and Figure 2-3 deals with net income. Note that these calculations can't be added together because they're mutually exclusive. Adding them together is like double counting. If you're a not-for-profit, this information applies to how much greater utilization of your resources you can expect.

		Your Company	ABC Company
Figure 2-2: Calculating the impact of strategic planning on your sales volume or revenue.	a.) This Year's Sales/Revenue **X**		$1,000,000
	b.) Next Year's Anticipated Growth Rate **X**		**X** 10% = $1,100,000
	c.) Strategic Planning Growth Rate =		**X** 12% = $1,232,000
	d.) Next Year's Projected Sales/Revenue		$1,232,000
	e.) Impact of Strategic Planning (d–b)		$132,000

ABC Company is provided as an example in these figures. Use your own sales volume, anticipated growth rate, and net income to determine the impact of strategic planning on your organization.

		Your Company	ABC Company
Figure 2-3: Calculating the impact of strategic planning on your net income.	a.) This Year's Net Income **X**		$300,000
	b.) Next Year's Anticipated Growth Rate **X**		**X** 10% = $330,000
	c.) Strategic Planning Growth Rate =		**X** 11% = $369,600
	d.) Next Year's Projected Net Income		$369,600
	e.) Impact of Strategic Planning (d–b)		$39,600

Putting Planning into Action Today

Successful strategic planning is as much about picking the right time as it is about developing the right strategy. Not ready to embark on a strategic plan quite yet? I understand. How about sticking your toe in the waters of strategic planning instead of diving in head first?

One way to start slowly is to forget about all the detailed strategies, goals, objectives, and so on necessary to put a plan together. Instead, pick one activity that's essential to moving the company strategically forward and put it into action. In the next sections, I've provided activities to get your plan going. Pick one and implement it.

Drive the organization with big vision

Growth requires thinking big and then executing like crazy. Success is ten percent inspiration and 90 percent persistence. But that ten percent is critical, otherwise the 90 percent is lost, aimless, and unproductive. Don't lose sight of the big ticket items while you're focusing on the small goals. That way, you head in the right direction to meet your goals. Chapter 6 provides tons of examples of big visions and helps you to develop yours.

Establish big goals

Every organization sets goals, but sometimes they aren't big, and sometimes they're not written down! A big vision is achieved through accomplishing big objectives and goals. That's all execution really is – your organization's ability to achieve goals. An example of a big goal is to be the best, number one, or leader in your industry. A small goal is to sell a set dollar volume in goods and services. Here a few best practices to help you establish big goals that get results:

1. **Objectives and goals must be understood.**

   Everyone needs to understand how the people contribute to and impact the goals.

2. **The goals must be measurable and actionable by appointing someone responsible and having a due date.**

   Review regularly and hold people accountable.

3. **Create a culture that makes people feel responsible for not missing a deadline.**

   That's all there is to it — it doesn't have to be complicated, confusing, or time consuming.

Celebrate wins

Publicly share big accomplishments, milestones, project completions, and revenue goals. This sharing drives growth in two ways:

- ✔ It motivates the people driving those accomplishments to press on.
- ✔ Success and profit sharing breeds confidence, fueling enthusiasm for further growth.

Everyone wants to be appreciated, and you may fall into the routine of dwelling on what you've failed to achieve instead of celebrating the small wins. By rejoicing in the achievements of your employees and the achievements of your plan, you create an atmosphere with a feeling that you're in this together.

Seek out new ideas

Invite left and right-brained people into your organization to create a complete brain trust of skills and competencies. Your left-brained folks bring the analytical perspective to the table. They think of things like analyzing data for discoveries and exploring parallel industries for new methods. The right-brained people focus a bit more on creativity and can invent creative solutions, challenge the status quo, find hidden connections, and see new models.

The sharing of ideas can have a huge impact on your business. Take these instances for example:

- ✔ Henry Ford couldn't have grown faster than everyone else had he not borrowed the division of labor manufacturing line concept from a meat packing plant.
- ✔ Walgreens couldn't have grown as fast as they did had they not changed their approach to increased convenience instead of big store, big ticket items.
- ✔ Southwest couldn't have grown had they not reinvented airline service by putting its employees first, which drastically improved customer service.

Challenge conventional wisdom to solve your customers' issues and pains with non-traditional approaches.

Ignore distractions

In tandem with new ideas, you must focus! Focusing is a never-ending struggle for entrepreneurs — too many ideas, too few resources. But you must ignore distractions, so you won't derail your plan.

In an increasingly competitive environment, growth comes from being great at one thing at a time. Succeed at one thing that you know customers need. That takes focus on the customer and focus on what you choose to do better than anybody. Use your vision as a filter to keep out distractions. If the activity isn't in line with your big goals, even if it's a good idea, table it and move on.

Empower through ownership

Taking ownership is similar to accountability. Entrepreneurs like to build and own their work. They are achievement-oriented and take pride in results.

Empower your people by assigning ownership. Recognition is the number one motivator. You can unleash powerful output by clearly defining roles and responsibilities. Give ownership of key business metrics. Then give that individual or team the autonomy and authority to drive that revenue past the forecast!

Neutralize negativity

If you want your company to be successful, you have to squash the negative attitudes throughout the entire employee network. Have the attitude that there's no such thing as trying, only doing. That attitude can bring sustainable growth to your company.

Hang signs around your office that say, "What do we need to make it?" not "Are we going to make it?" Have answers ready for how you can make it. Remember to be realistic because most growth companies don't grow quickly without sustaining some damage. Consider how to avoid road blocks and road bumps along the way.

Be passionate

If you're motivated and excited about what you're doing, people will follow and your organization will grow because positive attitudes and energy are contagious. Having and showing passion about your work may be the most important elements because there's true spirit behind growth.

Chapter 3

Getting Set Up for Successful Planning

*S*trategic planning can seem just as confusing as accounting, where debits and credits are exactly the opposite of their definitions. (Forgive me if you're a CPA.) Strategic planning doesn't need to be counterintuitive. What makes it less confusing is understanding how all the parts of a plan work together.

Planning doesn't have a set rule book, so no common language exists. People refer to objectives as goals and to goals as objectives. Mission gets confused with vision and no one seems to know where strategies actually fit in. Then you have indicators, measures, metrics, targets . . .

This chapter (or book for that matter) won't stop the debate between semantic differences. But in this chapter, you do look at the elements of a strategic plan, understand the planning process itself, assess if you're ready to begin, and discover how to spot the pitfalls inherent in the process.

The Elements of a Strategic Plan

Not to oversimplify the planning process, but by placing all the parts of a plan into three areas, you can clearly see how the pieces fit together. The three pieces of the puzzle are

- ✔ Where are we now?
- ✔ Where are we going?
- ✔ How will we get there?

Each part has certain elements to show you how and where things fit it. For a visual on this discussion, see Figure 3-1.

How are we going to get there?	
Strategic Objectives	Strategies
Goals	Scorecard
Priorities	Execution
Action Items	

Where are we now?		Where are we going?
Strategic Review		Vision
Mission		Competitive Advantage
Values		

Figure 3-1: The elements of a strategic plan.

Here's an outline of a typical strategic plan:

- ✔ **Mission statement:** To define the organization's core purpose. Why do we exist?

- ✔ **Vision statement:** To explain where you are headed, your future state. To formulate a picture of what your organization's future makeup will be and where the organization is headed. What will our organization look like in 5 to 10 years from now?

- ✔ **Values statement or guiding principals:** To clarify what you stand for and believe in.

✔ **SWOT:** To assess the particular strengths, weaknesses, opportunities, and threats that are strategically important to your organization. (You may or may not choose to include your SWOT in your strategic plan but as supporting documentation.)

✔ **Competitive advantage:** To define what you are best at. What can your organization potentially do better than any other organization?

✔ **Strategic objectives:** To connect your mission to your vision. Strategic objectives are long-term, continuous strategic areas that get you moving from your mission to achieving your vision. What are the key activities that you need to perform in order to achieve your vision?

✔ **Strategies:** To establish a guide that matches your organization's strengths with market opportunities to position your organization in the mind of the customer. Does your strategy match your strengths with how you will provide value and be perceived by your customers?

✔ **Short-term goals/priorities/initiatives:** To set goals that converts the strategic objectives into specific performance targets. Effective goals clearly state what, when, how, who and are specifically measurable. What are the 1- to 3-year goals you are trying to achieve to get to your strategic objectives?

✔ **Action items/plans:** To set specific actions plans that lead to implementing your goals. Are your action items comprehensive enough to achieve your goals?

✔ **Scorecard:** To measure and manage your strategic plan. What are the key performance measures you can track in order to monitor if you are achieving your goals?

✔ **Financial assessment:** To determine if your strategic plan makes financial sense. Do the estimated revenue projections exceed your estimated expenses?

But what matters most is having a strategy and therefore a strategic plan that is effective. An effective plan and execution require several elements:

✔ **Purpose-driven:** A plan based on a mission and a real, true competitive advantage is key. Without it, what is the point of the plan or the organization?

✔ **Integrated:** Each element supports the next. No objectives that are disconnected from goals and no strategies that sit all alone.

✔ **Systematic:** Don't think of the plan as one big document. Instead, give it life by breaking into executable parts.

✔ **Dynamic:** Not a static document, but a living document.

✔ **Holistic:** All areas of organization are included. Don't plan based on departments first because you risk limiting your thinking. Plan by thinking about the organization as a whole entity and then implement on a department by department basis.

✔ **Understandable:** Everyone gets it. If anyone, from the top of the organization to the bottom, does not understand the plan or how they fit in, it won't work.

✔ **Realistic:** You can implement it. Don't over-plan. Make sure you have the resources to support the goals you decide to focus on.

Where are we now?

As you think about where your organization is now, you want to look at your foundational elements (mission and value) to make sure there has not been a change. More than likely, you will not revise these two areas very often. Then you want to look at your current position or your strategic position, which is where you look at what is happening internally and externally to determine how you need to shift and change Here are your foundational elements:

✔ **Mission statement:** The mission describes your organization's purpose — the purpose for which you were founded and why you exist. Some mission statements include the business of the organization. Others explain what products or services they produce or customers they serve.

Does your mission statement say what you do? Why does your organization exist? See Chapter 6 for more information about creating your mission.

✔ **Values and/or guiding principles:** This clarifies what you stand for and believe in. Values guide the organization in its daily business.

What are the core values and beliefs of your company? What values and beliefs guide your daily interactions? What are you and your people really committed to? See Chapter 6 for a detailed discussion of values and principles.

✔ **SWOT:** SWOT is an acronym that stand for strengths, weaknesses, opportunities, and threats. These elements are crucial in assessing your strategic position with your organization. You want to build on your company's strengths; shore up the weaknesses; capitalize on the opportunities; and recognize the threats. See Chapters 7 through 10 for more info on SWOT.

Where are we going?

The elements of the question *Where are we going?* help you answer other questions, such as, What will my organization look like in the future? Where are we headed? What is the future I want to create for my company? Because the future is hard to predict, you can have fun imagining what it may look like. The following elements help you define the future for your business:

- ✔ **Sustainable competitive advantage:** Sustainable competitive advantage explains what you are best at compared to your competitors. Each company strives to create an advantage that continues to be competitive over the time. What can you be best at? What is your uniqueness? What can your organization potentially do better than any other organization? See Chapter 5 for more on advantages.

- ✔ **Vision statement:** Your vision is formulating a picture of what your organization's future makeup will be and where the organization is headed. What will your organization look like 5 to 10 years from now? See Chapter 6 for info on refining your vision.

How will we get there?

Knowing how you'll reach your vision is the meat of your strategic plan, but it's also the most time consuming. The reason it takes so much time to develop is because there are a number of routes from your current position to your vision. Picking the right one determines how quickly or slowly you get to your final destination.

The parts of your plan that lay out your roadmap are as follows:

- ✔ **Strategic objectives:** Strategic objectives are long-term, continuous strategic areas that help you connect your mission to your vision. Holistic objectives encompass four areas: financial, customer, operational, and people. What are the key activities that you need to perform in order to achieve your vision? See Chapter 12 for more info.

- ✔ **Strategy:** Strategy establishes a way to match your organization's strengths with market opportunities so that your organization comes to mind when your customer has a need. This section explains *how* you travel to your final destination. Does your strategy match your strengths in a way that provides value to your customers? Does it build an organizational reputation and recognizable industry position? See Chapter 10 for info on different strategies.

✔ **Short-term goals/priorities/initiatives:** Short-term goals convert your the strategic objectives into specific performance targets. You can use goals, priorities, or initiatives interchangeably. In this book, I use goals to define short-term action. Effective goals clearly state what you want to accomplish, when you want to accomplish it, how you're going to do it, and who's going to be responsible. Each goal should be specific and measurable. What are the one- to three-year-goals you're trying to achieve to reach your vision? What are your specific, measurable, and realistic targets of accomplishment? See Chapter 12 for info on goal setting.

✔ **Action items:** Action items are plans that set specific actions that lead to implementing your goals. They include start and end dates and appointing a person responsible. Are your action items comprehensive enough to achieve your goals? Head to Chapter 13 for a discussion on action items.

✔ **Scorecard:** A scorecard measures and manages your strategic plan. What are the key performance indicators you need to track to monitor whether you're achieving your mission? Pick five to ten goal related measures you can use to track the progress of your plan and plug them into your scorecard. For help with scorecards, head to Chapter 14.

✔ **Execution:** In executing the plan, identify issues that surround who manages and monitors the plan and how the plan is communicated and supported. How committed are you to implementing the plan to move your organization forward? Will you commit money, resources, and time to support the plan? See Chapter 14 to put your plan to work.

Before You Start, Are You Ready?

If you're embarking on this strategic planning journey for the first time, it's wise to assess if you're ready before you start. Successful strategic planning and implementation require a keen understanding of how well your organization can adapt to this new process. Introducing it at the right time is key to successful adoption.

Assessing your readiness

This is the point in your planning where it is critical to be brutally honest with yourself. Companies that jump into planning because they assume they are ready will likely fail somewhere mid-plan and derail the whole process. You can avoid this completely by honestly answering the questions in Figure 3-2. These are the key areas for you to assess your readiness.

Yes	No	Questions
		We have complete commitment and support from top leadership, especially the CEO, key management, and the board.
		We have a commitment to clarify roles and expectations for all participants in the planning process, including who will contribute to the plan and who will be the decision maker.
		We are open to learning about and responding to the organization's internal and external to collecting information through outside research so we don't plan in a vacuum.
		We have a team comprised of big picture thinkers, subject matter experts, and a strategic plan manager.
		Top-level manager is willing to be inclusive and encourage broad participation so that everyone feels ownership of the plan and energized by the process.
		We believe we have committed adequate organizational resources to complete the planning process as designed, for example, staff time, board time, dollars spent on the process and implementation.
		Everyone understands the purpose of planning because we realize what it is and is not. We have consensus about the desired outcomes of the planning process.
		We have a culture that is open to looking beyond the status quo to find new ways of doing things; a willingness to ask the hard questions, face difficult choices, and make decisions that are best for our clients.
		We want to grow our organization.

Figure 3-2: Assessing your readiness.

Ideally, you want to answer all the questions with a "yes." But that may not be possible. In my opinion, one of the most important questions is, do you want to grow? If your organization doesn't want to grow, strategic planning isn't going to be very effective. At the end of the assessment, decide whether strategic planning is a go or no go. If your decision is a no go, make a quick action plan to solve the problem where you determined your company is not ready. If your decision is a go, you should feel confident that your organization can move through the planning process, barring any unforeseen circumstances that might pop up.

Knowing the right climate for planning

Strategic planning is doomed to failure when certain circumstances aren't in place. If you're aware of what you need to make the process work well, you're more likely to be successful. If you're in the middle of a planning process, review the list below to make sure you have a climate for planning. Go down the list and check off any of the items that are true for your group. When you can check all of them off, you know you have a climate that is right for planning.

- ✔ No high-impact decisions in the next six months (mergers, management changes, and so on)
- ✔ No serious conflict between key players
- ✔ Top-level commitment to process
- ✔ Staff understands the purpose of planning
- ✔ Adequate resources (staff time and money)
- ✔ Organization has been around for at least a few years
- ✔ Commitment to implement key strategies
- ✔ Successful outcome of the process identified
- ✔ An organizational climate that inspires forward thinking and rewards creativity
- ✔ Agree on common language and timeframe

The Step-by-Step Strategic Planning Process and Timeframe

To put a plan together, you need a system in place to help you achieve the end result. In a disciplined mode, the process requires a focus and pattern to stay on track and be productive. Planners take a critical, unbiased look at what has worked before and what hasn't. Gather info from any past planning experiences and use this section to help you run a smooth planning process.

No two companies are alike, and no two strategic planning processes will be the same. In this section, you find the steps to create your strategic plan. You may move through these steps in one day or over the course of a year. No matter how it works for your company, remember that the process is continuous, not linear. Figure 3-3 illustrates the how planning is a continuous process.

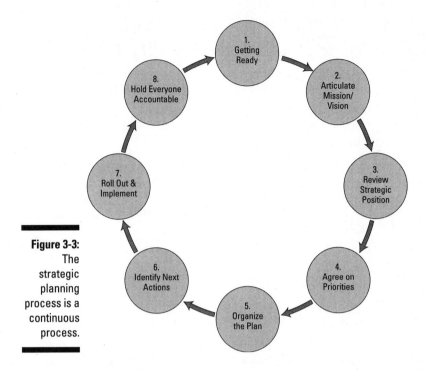

Figure 3-3:
The strategic planning process is a continuous process.

Establishing your strategic planning process

You will also want to develop a strategic planning process for your company that is continuous and cyclical. The speed and frequency at which you move through the process is up to you. Some organizations do it quickly and regularly, others on an annual or bi-annual basis.

Here's an overview of the strategic planning process to get you started:

1. **Get ready.**

   Identify specific issues and choices the process needs to address; clarify roles, create a planning committee, develop an organization profile, and identify the information that must be collected to help make sound decisions. For tips on these processes, see "Before You Start, Are You Ready?" in this chapter.

2. **Articulate the mission and vision.**

Reach a consensus on why the organization exists; determine its primary business, identify your values, and create an image of what success looks like. For tips on these processes, see Chapter 6.

3. **Review your strategic position.**

   Gather up-to-date information on internal strengths and weaknesses and external opportunities and threats so you can develop an understanding of critical issues. Use the SWOT tool to organize your information (see SWOT info in Chapters 7, 8, and 9).

4. **Agree on priorities.**

   Identify the broad approaches (strategies) for addressing critical issues and the results to be sought (long-term and short-term objectives and goals). See Chapter 12 for info on these approaches. Then you and your team can agree on key priorities.

5. **Organize the plan.**

   Put the pieces together into one coherent document that is practical, can be implemented, and easily managed and monitored. (See Chapters 13 and 14.)

6. **Identify your next actions.**

   After the plan is together in one cohesive document (Step 5), determine what actions to take next for each team, individual, and department. (Flip to Chapter 14.)

7. **Roll-out the plan.**

   Communicate the plan across the organization so everyone knows the game plan. For tips on getting the word out, see Chapter 14.

8. **Hold everyone accountable.**

   Monitor your plan by reporting performance metrics at monthly or quarterly strategy staff meetings. Keep track of all measures by regularly updating the organization's scorecard (scorecards are covered in Chapter 14). Hold people accountable for making sure organizational activities are happening. Link these processes to incentive compensation if possible. Evaluate performance and what is happening. Make corrections based on key measurements. Manage activities to drive future results. Some of these ideas are covered in the next section, "Making strategy a habit, not an event."

Use Figure 3-4 to guide your strategic planning process. It's a checklist to help as you develop your plan.

1. **Get ready and organized**: Identify specific issues and choices the process should address.
    - ☐ Determine organizational readiness
    - ☐ Create the planning committee
    - ☐ Identify the information which must be collected to help make sound decisions.

2. **Articulate the mission and vision**: Owners/managers clarify why the organization exists and what the end game is.
    - ☐ Determine its primary business and organizational purpose
    - ☐ Identify the corporate values
    - ☐ Create an image of what success would look like

3. **Review strategic position**: Gather up to date information to develop an understanding of the critical issues. Information should include:
    - ☐ Internal strengths and weaknesses
    - ☐ External opportunities and threats through a competitive analysis
    - ☐ Market opportunities through customer surveys
    - ☐ Synthesize into a SWOT

4. **Agree on Priorities**: Identify the broad approaches for addressing critical issues
    - ☐ Solidifying the organization's competitive advantage
    - ☐ Determine long-term goals/objective
    - ☐ Select strategies for customer segments
    - ☐ Establish SMART short-term goals/objectives and the results to achieved
    - ☐ Draft this year's action items

5. **Organize the plan**: Put the pieces together into one coherent document with the following reports:
    - ☐ Complete Strategic Plan – for reference
    - ☐ One-Page Strategic Plan – for communicating

6. **Roll out the plan**: Communicate the plan across the organization:
    - ☐ Everyone in the organization has received a copy of the plan in some form (printed, emailed, posted on a wall in the break room)
    - ☐ Identify the strategic plan leader
    - ☐ Provide budgetary and resource support

7. **Identify next actions**: Make the plan tangible to each member of the team by clearly identifying what he/she is responsible for:
    - ☐ Scorecard – for measuring
    - ☐ Action Sheets – for executing

8. **Hold everyone accountable**: Monitor your plan by reporting performance metrics on a monthly or quarterly basis.
    - ☐ Identify the source of each metric associated with measurable goals
    - ☐ Set up systematic process for monthly or quarterly reporting
    - ☐ Communicate to each responsible person when and how to report on their goals
    - ☐ Hold monthly or quarterly strategy meetings
    - ☐ Regularly monitor, evaluate, and adapt

Figure 3-4:
Your
strategic
planning
process
checklist.

Making strategy a habit, not an event

The purpose of strategic planning is to help organizations make good decisions. If the planning process only happens once a year, planning then becomes a barrier to good decision making instead of a catalyst. The point is to stop thinking of strategic planning as an annual event. Instead, consider embedding the strategic planning process into the culture and day-to-day activities of your company.

Holding meetings helps focus your goals on accomplishing the organization's top priorities and accelerating the growth of the organization. Although the meeting rhythm structure is relatively simple, it requires a high degree of discipline.

Each of the meetings listed in the following sections correspond with Figure 3-5, which helps explain what part of the strategic planning process you're involved in.

Annual strategic planning retreat

The meeting rhythm should begin with an annual strategic planning session of at least two days in length. Ideally, you should hold this retreat at an offsite location. Although this isn't necessary, it does help shut out distractions.

During this session, the team reviews how well they're executing their business strategies and achieving the targets they set. The review process goes as follows:

1. **Start with a review of the mission, vision, and values.**

   Make sure that these statements are current and still relevant to your organization.

2. **Assess the long-term business assumptions and conduct a traditional SWOT (strengths, weaknesses, opportunities, and threats) analysis.**

   This step provides a current understanding of the marketplace and the true capabilities of your organization. (SWOT analyses are covered in Chapters 7, 8, and 9.)

3. **Identify the long-term strategic objectives.**

   Quite often these stay the same for several years, with just a few modifications. Your strategic objectives are the big mileposts on the way to your vision.

4. **Set short-term goals and action items if possible.**

Normally the team does not spend time in the details; instead, assign a goal to a team member who can then flesh out how it will get accomplished.

5. **As the manager of the strategic plan, collect all of the work completed in this session and compile it into a final document.**

   Distribute copies of the compiled document, so everyone knows what they're responsible for achieving.

This annual session takes you through the entire strategic planning process explained in Figure 3-4 from Steps 1 to 7.

Quarterly planning update

At these standalone meetings, which last anywhere from two hours to half a work day, the team assesses these issues and items:

- ✔ Any changes in their operating environment
- ✔ How well they accomplished their goals to date
- ✔ A scorecard report
- ✔ What modifications may need to be made to goals

The primary question at these sessions is, "Based on what we know today, what are the most important and impactful items that the organization needs to accomplish in the next quarter to achieve its annual priorities and targets and move closer to attaining its envisioned future?"

The strategic plan manager should update the strategic plan and distribute the revised plan accordingly.

The quarterly sessions take your team quickly through Step 3 of the strategic planning process, but the majority of the time is spent on Steps 4 through 8 of the process in Figure 3-4.

Monthly strategy meetings

During these meetings, which should last from 30 to 60 minutes, key team members report on the progress they have made towards goals they are responsible for, including reporting on metrics in the scorecard they have been assigned. The agenda should include 10 to 15 minutes to work on one specific topic, or on one of the quarter's priorities where decisions need to be made. Once defined, the topic should be carried to conclusion. Do not waste time debating several different topics that cannot be brought to conclusion. See Chapter 14 for a guide on how to run these meetings.

Monthly strategy meetings focus on Steps 6 and 8 of the process. If modifications to the plan need to be made, the plan manager can revisit Steps 5 and 7.

Making your process go smoothly

Strategic planning is a process that you want to flow smoothly, but I've had to face the facts: When I plan for a smooth ride, it never goes that way. Something always throws a wrench in the plan: It's an unpredictable process. Fresh ideas at an afternoon meeting may change decisions made earlier in the day.

But I don't want you to get frustrated, so I've included a few tips to help your process move along with less uncertainty:

- ✔ **Think about execution before you start planning.** A strategic plan that sits on the shelf is a colossal waste of time and energy (of which no one has extra to give away!). Outline your ideas on how you see the plan being implemented. Even better, talk to your key employees and get everyone's buy-in on executing the plan before you actually put the plan together. Consider reading Chapter 14, which focuses on execution.

- ✔ **Determine if you want a top-down or bottom-up planning process.**

  - A *top-down approach* involves the board and executive team setting the vision and long-term goals and the staff developing the short-term goals and actions.

  - A *bottom-up approach* works with the staff developing the whole plan and submitting it to the board and executives for approval.

  Normally, organizations end up somewhere between these two extremes. What is important is deciding who takes the first pass at developing the vision and long-term goals because these are the guidelines for the rest of the plan.

- ✔ **Commit to a schedule.** Set a very specific deadline for when the plan needs to be completed. Additionally, set the schedule for ongoing strategy meetings and reporting.

  Use a large desk calendar to map out the whole year as you embark on the planning process.

- ✔ **Make everyone feel included.** Everyone probably won't have a seat at your strategic table, so openly communicate who's involved in what step of the process and why. Explain how everyone's input is being solicited and how it's being used.

- ✔ **Celebrate success.** No matter what you do or where you are in your strategic planning agenda, end your planning days on a high note. Do something fun such as play a quick game, run through a fun exercise, or go out to dinner.

I can't say this enough because there never seems to be enough time to have fun. Never let your strategic planning sessions end on a low note where everyone is feeling overworked and brain dead.

✔ **Don't over-plan.** One of the biggest mistakes in strategic planning is becoming overly ambitious and overwhelming the company with the amount of work that needs to get done. When you're done putting your plan together, put it away and come back to it a week later. Make sure it still makes sense and you haven't planned the company into oblivion.

Selecting Your Planning Team

The values and vision of your organization are embedded in the strategic framework. As a result, involving the whole organization in at least part of the planning process is vital. Although everyone can't be involved in every part of the process, they do all play a role. In the following sections, I give you some guidelines for the different people in your organization and who should be involved when.

Getting everyone involved

Yes, you want everyone involved (at certain times). The next few sections show you how do it in a way that isn't a recipe for a disaster.

The role of the CEO

The CEO naturally assumes a prominent role on the planning team, setting the vision, driving that vision, and enforcing results. If strategic planning isn't the CEO's passion, it will never happen. Only the CEO has the force to drastically change the company's alignment. However, during the strategy development part of the planning process, the CEO should remain in the background so that other members' ideas can emerge.

The visibility of the CEO in the strategic planning process can't be overemphasized. The CEO should attend as many planning sessions as possible — the annual, quarterly, and monthly meetings.

The planning team members

The planning team's ideal size is 9 to 15 members with an outside facilitator and an internal coordinator. Planning team members should represent different segments of the company — not just the top-level employees such as the vice presidents, division and department heads, and other executive level managers who report to the CEO. A team consisting of operating, marketing, and sales personnel brings balance when it comes to considering internal and external needs.

Search out key players from your employees, board members, and top management who can help you strategize. Figure out how to get them involved. If some can't take part in person, share early drafts of the plan with them and get their feedback as the process continues. Make sure you tap your big picture thinkers as well as get a diverse set of perspectives.

Everyone else, regardless of position

Employees who have a chance to contribute feel they're making a difference. It's exciting to be part of the strategic planning process, so make sure that everyone has this opportunity. Employees always have different perceptions from top management on how the business is run. I promise that you'll be amazed at the outstanding ideas that come from your employees. To help ensure planning success, the team must solicit their opinions in a confidential, risk-free atmosphere.

Try out these ideas to gather employee information:

- ✔ **Small group meetings.** If you have an open and honest company culture, small groups are a good way to get input from your staff. The benefit to bringing groups together is synergy that results from the discussion and brainstorms.

- ✔ **Anonymous surveys.** Online anonymous surveys allow every employee to voice his or her own opinion, without being influenced by others.

- ✔ **Assessments.** There are numerous staff assessments available that evaluate everything from satisfaction to specific actions and strategies. See Chapters 7, 8, and 9 for more on these tools.

Nonemployees

Also consider the input of people who don't work for your company. These folks include customers and suppliers; they frequently have unique insights into your business. Customers can identify problems the plan should address and may have ideas about how to improve overall effectiveness. Suppliers can offer alternatives to operational problems that hinder delivery of products or services to customers.

The Strategic Plan Manager

The CEO must appoint a respected member of the staff to champion the strategic plan. The Strategic Plan Manager's responsibility is to keep the process moving forward, monitor progress, and alert decision makers if the company strays off strategy or off performance.

Although this position may add responsibility to a current staff member, managing the strategic plan is critical to the organization's success. Appoint someone who's seeking additional responsibility and is looking to move up in the organization. It's a fabulous leadership development opportunity.

Determining who's involved when

The question often arises, Who should be involved at what stage in the planning process? Running a strategic planning process democratically is not the best way to go. Set expectations before you jump into the process so no one feels blind-sided or left out.

Figure 3-5 maps the different stages of the planning process to the different groups of people who should be involved. Note: This chart should be used as a guide to develop your own planning team.

As you can see in Figure 3-5, the CEO and Strategic Plan Manager are involved in just about every step of the process. Other groups take part where needed.

Going It Alone or Hiring a Facilitator

In an age of facilitators, organizational leaders, and planners for everything under the sun, hiring a helper doesn't come cheap. You need to consider three costs to your company for strategic planning:

- ✔ First, you have the value of your participants' time — more precious than ever in this time-starved world.

- ✔ Second, you have the cost of any facility rental, AV equipment, travel, food, and lodging.

- ✔ Finally, you have the opportunity cost if, following your meeting, plans and decisions aren't carried out or your team's behavior doesn't change for the better.

Strategic Planning Process Phase	Who Should Be Involved?
1. Getting ready	CEO/Owner Strategic plan manager
2. Articulate the mission and vision	CEO/Owner Strategic plan manager Board Key executive staff/management/dept. heads
3. Review strategic position	CEO/Owner Strategic plan manager Key executive staff/management/dept. heads Planning team Everyone else (through surveys and assessment) Customers and suppliers
4. Agree on strategic priorities	CEO/Owner Strategic plan manager Key executive staff/management/dept. heads Planning team
5. Organize the plan	Strategic plan manager
6. Roll-out the plan	CEO/Owner Key executive staff/management/dept. heads
7. Identify next actions	Key executive staff/management/dept. heads Everyone else (by department)
8. Hold everyone accountable	CEO/Owner Strategic plan manager Key executive staff/management/dept. heads

Figure 3-5:
Your
strategic
planning
team.

Add these actual and figural costs up, and it's easy to see how strategic planning represents a real investment. One way to maximize your investment is to engage the services of a professional facilitator. Obviously, not every meeting calls for a facilitator, but your annual retreat probably could use one.

In the following sections, you look at how to run planning sessions yourself as well as how and when to hire a facilitator.

Running the planning sessions yourself

For any planning sessions that you choose to run yourself, there are some best practices that you should follow — having a clear agenda, requiring participants to come prepared, starting and ending on time, and managing the conversation in the room.

To run strategic planning sessions, you probably want to gather a set of facilitation techniques for different parts of the process. There are a number of different facilitation exercises and methods available to you. Some of my favorite include the following sources:

✔ ***Best Practices for Facilitation:*** This source is the second in The Grove's Facilitation Guide Series and is a user-friendly manual of 176 field-tested group practices. The resource should prove invaluable to facilitators, managers, team leaders, and consultants looking for facilitation alternatives such as virtual team work, graphic templates, agenda design, and group decision making. You can purchase the book at `www.grove.com/store/mf_books.html`.

✔ `www.iaf-world.org`: This Web site from The International Association of Facilitators (IAF) is the recognized source for credible and valuable professional help for practicing facilitators. On this site, you find tons of resources related to the facilitation of best practices.

✔ `www.postit.com`: The 3M Post-It Note Web site provides immediate access to sticky notes of all sizes. A strategic planning meeting without sticky notes is like an ice cream sundae without the cherry. You can do it, but it might be boring (and not taste as good — the cherry, not the post-its)! In all seriousness, the use of sticky notes can help you gain consensus quickly, keep important ideas and topics posted on posterboard sized notes, and allow for quick brainstorming.

Using a facilitator

A facilitator brings a fresh perspective to the process. He/she keeps the discussion on track and encourages all team members to act as equals. An outside facilitator levels the playing field between CEO and team members. In an atmosphere of informality, team members can address any issue within the organization without fear of unjust reprisal. The CEO should be involved when appropriate for his/her leadership, knowledge, and guidance.

Finding a good one

Facilitation is different from public speaking or training. It's not about having solid content, good platform skills, or an understanding of adult learning principles. Instead, facilitation involves working with groups of people in the moment. The job requires being tuned in at all times to what's happening and being able to suspend or change the process accordingly.

When selecting a professional to guide your session, look for the following characteristics:

- An understanding of organizational issues (industry knowledge isn't necessary).
- Superb communications skills.
- Can offer insight and empathy while conducting themselves with authority and credibility.
- Experience in running strategic planning processes.
- Conflict management skills and confidence about handling conflict.
- Able to help you clarify your outcomes and a commitment to helping you reach your desired outcomes.
- Honesty and fairness. (Don't look for total objectivity. Anyone worth using has opinions; you just want him or her to make a clear distinction between opinions and facts.)
- Understanding of group process theory — A good facilitator is able to apply concepts such as leadership, group norms, team development, systems theory, dialogue, and experiential learning to the design and facilitation of your meeting.
- Logic, self-discipline, and the ability to operate systematically.
- A style that suits your organization.

By using an experienced facilitator in the right situations, you almost certainly accomplish more in your meetings, delve deeper into critical issues, and then resolve them. Equally important, participants leave with positive feelings, stronger cohesiveness, a sense of accomplishment, and a renewed belief in the team.

Deciding whether a facilitator is a good idea

So just when should you use a facilitator? Check out the following important instances to enlist a facilitator:

- **When you want to participate yourself:** Most of the time, it's not possible to facilitate and participate at the same time. Some people can do it effectively, but most can't. If you're the boss, forget it. You can't effectively facilitate because people still react to you as their superior.

- **When you need to address sensitive issues, including conflict:** An outsider's perspective can diffuse heated exchanges and channel intense emotions into constructive problem solving. Consider solving the conflict just with the involved parties and bringing the rest of the team together after the problem has been resolved.

✔ **When your team is stuck:** A skilled facilitator uses sensitivity to raise to the group issues that are being avoided and to point out dysfunctional behaviors that are being denied. The aid of the helper in this scenario gets the team moving to a new level of functioning.

✔ **When your group must deal with complex issues and a variety of viewpoints:** A seasoned facilitator brings a wealth of group processes and activities to scope issues, generate options, make decisions and build consensus.

Futurecasting: Visualizing the Future

In order to make the most of your planning effort, you need to put your strategic thinking hat on and envision the future. Companies spend a lot of time predicting what sales will be like in the future, but little time actually thinking about the factors that impact that future. These factors include

✔ Underlying dynamics

✔ The sweeping trajectory of new competition

✔ The way customers evolve

✔ The collision course one industry may be on with another

Consider starting off your annual strategic planning retreat by *futurecasting* — the practice of trying to envision your company's future. Really push your team to think about what will be happening in five or ten years.

A strategic plan is as much about the *planning* as it is about the *strategizing*. Futurecasting helps you really push your big picture thinking to develop a strategic plan that's truly, well, strategic.

Getting into the right frame of mind for futurecasting

Unfortunately, most people can't just jump mentally from now to the future. A mind-bending exercise can help your team get their creative juices flowing.

Ask your team the following questions in a group setting. Read the answers after everyone has responded in an open setting. (Note: Some may have heard this before, so ask those already wise-ones to stay quiet.)

✔ **How do you put a giraffe into a refrigerator?** The correct answer: Open the refrigerator, put the giraffe in, and close the door. This question tests whether you tend to do simple things in an overly complicated way.

✔ **How do you put an elephant into a refrigerator?** Wrong answer: Open the refrigerator, put in the elephant, and close the refrigerator. Correct answer: Open the refrigerator, take out the giraffe, put in the elephant, and close the door. This tests your ability to think through the repercussions of your actions.

✔ **The Lion King is hosting an animal conference. All the animals attend except one. Which animal doesn't attend?** Correct answer: The elephant. The elephant is in the refrigerator, remember? This tests your memory.

✔ **There is a river you must cross. But it's inhabited by crocodiles. How do you manage it?** Correct answer: You swim across. Why? All the crocodiles are attending the animal conference. This tests whether you learn quickly from your mistakes.

According to Accenture Consulting, around 90 percent of the professionals they tested got all questions wrong. But many preschoolers got several correct answers. Accenture Consulting says this conclusively disproves the theory that most professionals have the brains of a four-year-old.

Leaving your assumptions at the door

You're dead in the water if you let your assumptions take over strategic thinking. Ask your team to think about how they solved the brainteaser in the previous section. Relating to that problem, how would they answer these questions:

✔ What assumptions have you made?

✔ What rules have you assumed?

✔ How do your own perceptions influence the world you inhabit?

✔ How do you see the world and how is your view different from that of other people? What advantages and disadvantages are there of each way of thinking?

With those thoughts in mind, how can you and your team think differently? How would your team answer these questions when imagining the problem from someone else's angle? Have your team think about the following ideas as they relate to a different viewpoint:

✔ What happens in other countries/cultures/companies?

✔ How can you change the situation to make a solution work?

✔ Visit or read about other people's lives and try to understand why they think in the way they do. (Maybe not the animal kingdom!)

Working a strategic thinking exercise

It's time to apply strategic thinking to your business. Have your team try to answer the following scenario:

> What will your company look like and how will they compete in the year 2015? What trends do you need to consider in your planning?

Ask your team to come up with a list of ideas, statements, or activities to describe how the world looks in these five areas:

✔ Economically

✔ Socially

✔ Politically

✔ Technologically

✔ Ecologically

With these lists on the wall, consider which trends apply to your business. Use this information as you're developing goals and objectives for your strategic plan:

✔ How can this trend influence our current customers?

✔ How can it influence our current core business?

✔ How can it create new customers?

✔ Who are the potential customers?

✔ What are our competitors doing about this trend?

✔ How fast is this trend developing? What accelerates it or slows it down?

✔ What are the risks of committing to this trend? What are the rewards?

Part II
Looking Backward to Move Forward

The 5th Wave   By Rich Tennant

"Isn't that our bookkeeper?"

In this part . . .

A great strategic plan is based on your organization's core, which encompasses your purpose, mission, values, and competitive advantage. You may have developed your core during your years (or months) of operation, but in this part, you take what you already know about your company, customers, market, and competitors and develop stage one of your strategic plan. You review the last year to determine what went well and what could've gone better, and then you develop or revise your mission, vision, and values. You also examine your competitive advantage to establish what your organization does that's unique and better than the rest.

Chapter 4

Taking Lessons from the Past

. . . .

. . . .

*D*idn't you always hate it when your mom (or grandma) would say, "Back in my day. . . ." Yeah, yeah, I know. You walked everyday to school uphill both ways in a perpetual snowstorm. God bless her for trying to share her past, but it always seemed so trying. The future's much more exciting than the past. The future is where the action is. It's moving. It's shaking. It's sexy and bright. The past just slows us down. It's like getting stuck in molasses or running underwater. Or is it?

Learning from your past can save hours and hundreds of dollars spent on fruitless activities. Ignoring your past can be very costly because you aren't adding to your knowledge base. Instead, you're just continually trying new things. By taking a good look at your past performance, you can move faster into the future by avoiding roadblocks and pitfalls you've already encountered.

In this chapter, you look at your past performance. You don't have to spend too much time wandering down memory lane, but taking a few hours by yourself or with your team to work through the exercises in this chapter may pay high rewards in the future. With a better understanding of what happened last year and the years before that, you're able to catapult your company's growth by developing a strategic plan based on your operating history.

Reviewing What Happened Last Year

Because you're not a new organization, you've accumulated invaluable information about your past activities, customers, employees, and financials that can help prevent do-overs. Tap into that invaluable resource to review last year's performance.

As a first step in your strategic planning process, use the questions in the following section to guide your review of last year. Conduct the review either individually, by requesting that employees respond to the set of questions from the list below, or facilitate the discussion in a regularly scheduled staff meeting. You can add this information to your SWOT, which is covered in Chapter 9, or use it simply as a standalone exercise.

When you have identified your successes and failures, look at what goals and objectives continue into this planning year. Create a notes page labeled "Goals and Objectives" and start a list of potential items you want to include in this year's plan based on your lessons from the past.

Recognizing what you achieved

Everyone wants to feel successful and recognized for a job well done, but it's human nature to brush by achievements. By listing what you achieved last year as an organization, you help motivate and inspire your team to work smarter and harder in the coming year. Additionally, why not try to replicate what did work well last year? Here are some questions to get the conversation started:

- ✔ What goals did we achieve? Why?

- ✔ What hurdles or challenges did we overcome? How?

- ✔ What new customers did we acquire? How?

- ✔ Who joined our team?

- ✔ What were the bottom-line results we achieved? (Also see the end of this chapter for more discussion of this area.)

- ✔ What projects were successful? Why?

List your successes on a white board or big sticky note and leave them posted for a few weeks. Ask your employees to add to them as they see fit. This lets your team know that last year's achievements were important. Dig into the hows and whys of your actions to make the list as specific as possible. When you have your list, use it to guide your planning efforts in the coming year. You can add the achievements to your list of strengths in your SWOT (see Chapter 7).

Understanding why you failed

Success and failure are like peanut butter and jelly. It seems like you can't have one without the other. More than likely, you didn't achieve everything you expected to last year. Even more to the point, you may have a goal or a project that rolls over from one year to the next. You've identified it as important, but you can't seem to move the ball down the field. Now is the time to figure out why.

As with your successes (previous section), use the following questions to identify last year's failures and determine what you need to do this year to prevent a repeat performance.

- ✔ What lessons did we learn last year?
- ✔ What decisions would we have changed in the past year?
- ✔ What goals or projects did we not accomplish? Why?
- ✔ What roadblocks or hurdles do we keep stumbling into? Why?
- ✔ What challenges did we fail to meet over the past few years? Why?

Use the responses to these questions to fill out the weaknesses section of your SWOT (see Chapter 7).

Eliminating pesky problems

If you've identified a problem or a roadblock that just won't go away, it's time to do something about it. Every organization experiences two types of problems: *gremlins,* or small annoyances; and *monsters,* which are big, scary, strategic issues. Tackling gremlins is easy because they're quick to exterminate. They're identifiable and solvable. Monsters, on the other hand, are often so big that it's easier to ignore than confront them. If monsters aren't dealt with, they can eventually be the undoing of an organization.

If you have either gremlins or monsters, here's a quick problem solving process:

1. **Define the problem.**

   This part is both the most obvious and hardest of this exercise. Resist reacting to what you and your team *think* the problem is. Instead, work to understand *what* the problem is. Write down a clear problem statement.

2. **Determine the causes of the problem.**

   Dig into the *why* of the problem. Get input from your team to help identify the causes. Write the cause of the problem by answering who, what, why, when, and where.

3. **Identify alternative solutions to the problem.**

   Brainstorm for solutions to the problem. List everything that's suggested or comes to mind.

4. **Select the best solution.**

   Which solution is the most likely to solve the problem for the long term? Do you have the time and money to execute the solution?

5. **Put an action plan together.**

   Develop a quick action plan to implement the best solution. What needs to happen in the next 30, 60, and 90 days? Remember a solution that someone is "just going to try harder" isn't going to solve the problem.

6. **Verify if the problem has been eliminated.**

   Check back after the action plan has been completed. Is the problem resolved? Take away lessons for the future. What changes can be made to avoid this type of problem in the future?

The above procedure can be done as part of your strategic planning process or on an as-needed basis.

Evaluating Your Products and Services

By looking at the financial performance of your products and services over the past several years and matching it up with market attractiveness, you can identify which products and services to use to grow. Every organization has a portfolio of products or services that it offers to its customers. That portfolio needs to be managed just like your personal investment portfolio. In the financial world, you buy and sell stocks and bonds to yield the highest return. When an investment is no longer generating a positive return, you ask your investment advisor to sell it and find something else that's performing with a better return.

Managing your product/service portfolio is no different. Although you probably don't have as many products or services as you do stocks or bonds and you're likely to move slower between deciding when to buy or sell, the principle is the same. You want to invest in products and services that are doing well and divest the ones that aren't.

Without a doubt, every company has one or more products or services that are losing money. (Although you may be an exception to the rule, this tends to happen more often than not.) The big issue is that most businesses don't know which of their products and services are winners and which ones are losers.

The primary reason for not being able to figure out the difference is that the monthly financial reports are consolidated. They don't shed light on how each product in your portfolio is performing. You want to be sure that you're selling a product or service for less than it costs to produce it, which is called your gross profit. To get to beyond your gross profit, you have to dig deeper into your numbers.

Picking the winners

Determine the period of time before you start. You may choose to look at last year's performance, but that may not provide you with enough history. If possible, look at how each product and service has performed over the past three years.

Before you start on this exercise, remember that some products or services may still need to prove themselves and others may be integral to another item in your portfolio. And some clients generate enough revenue that they help even out work flow. So while you assess the profitability of each product or service, pay attention to how it interacts with the rest of your portfolio. In some instances, it may be enough for the product just to contribute to overhead costs.

Open up a new Excel spreadsheet and determine your winners and losers by following these steps:

1. **Create a column for every primary product or service (or client) you provide across the top of the spreadsheet.**

   Start with Column B.

2. **In Column A, down the left side of the spreadsheet, label the first line *Sales,* and then list all the expenses directly related to producing the product or service (also called *cost of goods sold*), and then label the next line *Gross Profit.***

Then in the expenses, you can include all the components of selling and marketing each of your products or services such as advertising, marketing, commissions, royalties, and so on.

3. **Fill in each line on the schedule for each product or service.**

This may take some digging as some numbers may not be readily available. If you can't find the number, make an educated guess. Make sure that when you add up the columns, you end up with numbers that agree with your income statement.

4. **Add up all the expense lines and subtract this sum from your sales line to determine the gross profit for each product you sell.**

You might be shocked to find a lot more of your products, services, or clients have a negative or smaller gross profit than you thought.

5. **Repeat this process for each of the past three years.**

Add the gross profit lines for each product and year together. Use a separate spreadsheet for each year.

6. **Identify which products, services, and clients are winners and which are losers.**

The larger the gross profit, the bigger a winner it is.

Service companies may want to evaluate your service lines, as well as your clients. Which of your larger clients are profitable or winners and which are losers? Follow the same steps above to make this determination.

Dumping the losers

Consider eliminating those products or services that are losing money or firing clients that are losers (not losers themselves, but those who aren't making you money). Take a look at how much money you could immediately put to the bottom line by not engaging in activities that are losing money.

Don't forget that some products may experience seasonality issues and some may be complementary products/services. Evaluate your findings with your specific business issues in mind.

Another option is considering raising the prices of products, charging higher service fees, or increasing rates to your clients. Alternatively, you can run through the problem solving activity in the previous section to determine if there's a way to make the losers profitable. The key isn't to get caught up in trying to save something just because you or your staff like it or because you think you should be able to make money. Know when to cut your losses.

Putting Your Portfolio Together (In the Matrix)

After you've determined which products or services make money and which ones take money (see previous section), evaluate which ones to invest in by looking at how attractive the market is.

A widely used tool for conducting a portfolio analysis is the General Electric Matrix, developed by the consulting company McKinsey and Company. (Don't worry, Keanu Reeves and Laurence Fishburne aren't are going to make you swallow any colored pills.) The GE Matrix provides a framework that works with your products and services as listed in the previous section. The framework looks at your portfolio based on the strengths of each product/service and its market attractiveness. Check out Figure 4-1 to see the framework.

Market Attractiveness

	High	Medium	Low
High	1	1	2
Medium	1	2	3
Low	2	3	3

Business Strength

Figure 4-1: Use the GE Framework Matrix to determine your product portfolio in relation to market attractiveness and business strengths.

Evaluating market attractiveness and business strength

The purpose of using the GE Matrix is to fit your products/services in one of the nine boxes (as shown in Figure 4-1).

Determining what factors make a market attractive and what are product and/or service strengths can be difficult to pin down. A healthy dose of intuition is also helpful when determining where to place your products and services in the matrix. Based on where these items fall, you can use the recommendations listed below to help guide your planning efforts.

Factors that affect market attractiveness

Although any assessment of market attractiveness is necessarily subjective, there are several factors that can help determine attractiveness. Use your knowledge and best judgment to determine market attractiveness. Here are some key factors that may help:

✓ Market size

✓ Market growth

✓ Pricing trends

✓ Intensity of the competition

✓ Overall risk in the industry

✓ Opportunity to differentiate products and services

The more attractive the item, the higher up you place it on the vertical axis of the GE Matrix. The less attractive, the lower it's plotted.

Factors that affect business strength

A key business strength is product/service profitability. Start with the analysis from the sections on sorting out the winners from the losers. The more profitable, the stronger the product or service. But profitability isn't everything. Here are some other factors to consider as you plot your products and services on the GE Matrix:

✓ Product or service uniqueness

✓ Brand recognition

✓ Market share

✓ Customer loyalty

✓ Relative cost position (cost structure compared with competitors)

✔ Production capacity

✔ Distribution strength

✔ Record of innovations

Determine the business strength of each product or service. The stronger it is, the further to the left you place it on the horizontal axis. The weaker it is, the further to the right it's plotted.

Creating your own matrix

After looking at business strength and market attractiveness (see "Evaluating market attractiveness and business strength" earlier in the chapter), you can put together your own matrix similar to Figure 4-1 and arrange every primary product or service somewhere in the nine boxes. Based on where each product or service falls, the guidelines below help develop goals for your strategic plan.

Here are the options that relate to each of the numbered boxes:

✔ **Grow and invest**

- Focus your resources and efforts on maintaining and growing products/services in this box.

- Work on improving some of your weaknesses and strengthen your strengths.

✔ **Selective investment**

- Products/services in these boxes are either in a highly attractive market or capitalize on a business strength.

- Modify your activities to eliminate weaknesses.

- Keep these products/services and concentrate any investments in promising areas with limited risks.

- Build on the competitive position you've managed to secure.

- Invest in areas that build on this advantage and that help you move products/services in this box to Box #1.

✔ **Harvest and divest**

- Focus on maximizing your profits while reducing costs.

- Limit your investment in products/services in this box.

- You may want to divest any products/services in this box.

- Cut costs and don't invest.

List the goals you develop from this exercise on the note page labeled *Goals and Objectives.*

Looking at Your Financial Performance

The financial health of your organization is critical to your corporate growth. Therefore, evaluating your financial situation is part of your strategic planning process. Want to know how your business is *really* doing? Evaluate your financial performance by looking beyond the numbers on your balance sheet and income statement. By themselves, these statements are informative, but not nearly as informative as the relationships between the numbers.

Understanding the financial dynamics of your business

Instead of evaluating your past financial statements, analyze the financial ratios. Financial ratios are derived from pulling two numbers from your financial statements and dividing one by another. By doing this, you create a ratio that eliminates any problems of comparing one company to another. With ratios, you take out any size difference so you can compare apples to apples. Additionally, you can compare your ratios to your industry averages to determine if you're doing well.

Dealing with financials statements and numbers can be daunting. But don't worry. You don't need to track and monitor everything, just key numbers that help you understand the financial dynamics of your business. When tracked and measured regularly, these key financial ratios allow you to

✔ Get a more accurate understanding of your company's financial performance

✔ Compare performance against the prior year, current budget, and your industry as a whole

✔ Establish benchmarks to see where you're going and how you're doing

To make interpretation and management of these ratios easy, I have grouped them into four categories: liquidity, risk, profitability, and productivity. In the next four sections, a fictional company, Wacky Widgets, is used to illustrate the ratios. Don't worry if your numbers aren't as large as Wacky Widget's are. It's not the size of the numbers, but the ratios, that count.

Checking your liquidity

Of primary importance to all organizations is the ability to pay their bills on time every month. The difference between your current assets (those you intend to convert to cash within a year) and your current liabilities (the obligations you have to pay within a year) is your liquidity. Your liquidity is the safety net that protects you from a financial crisis. Here are ratios you need to look at:

- ✔ **Current ratio:** The current ratio looks out over a 12-month time horizon and measures the cash available to meet current liabilities. The current ratio is determined by looking at your balance sheet and dividing current assets by current liabilities.

  With $300,230 in current assets and $200,100 in current liabilities, Wacky Widgets' current ratio is 1.5, which means that for every dollar of obligation due in the next 12 months, the company expects to have $1.50 to meet those obligations. You should shoot for a ratio of about 2.0.

- ✔ **Quick ratio:** The quick ratio is a tighter test of your ability to pay your bills. It uses assets that convert to cash within 60 to 90 days rather than 12 months, typically involving only cash and current receivables.

  Wacky Widgets has $271,000 in cash and receivables. Dividing by $200,100 (current liabilities) yields a quick ratio of 1.35. For every dollar in obligations, the company has $1.35 in quick cash to meet them. You want your quick ratio to be above a 1.0.

For Wacky, the current ratio may raise a little concern because it's less than 2.0, but with a quick current ratio exceeding 1.0, they have a reasonable cash position.

Gauging your risk levels

The mix of your debt and equity indicates your risk level. Although there are other ratios that fall into this group, your debt-to-equity is the key to figuring your risk of how leveraged you are or aren't.

Debt-to-equity ratio says a lot about the general financial structure of your company. This ratio measures the relationship of liabilities, or other people's money, in the business to the owners' or shareholders' money in the business. Often, banks are the largest component of other people's money and watch this ratio very closely, hoping to see plenty of equity to support the debt. To calculate debt-to-equity, you divide total liabilities by owner equity.

Wacky Widgets has $110,000 in total liabilities and $389,000 in owner equity, for a debt-to-equity ratio of .28. In other words, for every dollar Wacky Widget owners have put into their business, other people have put in 28 cents. "Other people" would feel fairly safe with a cushion as comfortable as this, meaning the company isn't over leveraged. Companies should be concerned when liabilities outweigh equity. That said, every industry has a debt-to-equity ratio that's considered acceptable because some businesses require higher capital investment than others.

Monitoring your profitability

Profitability ratios tell you how well you measure up when it comes to creating financial value for your company. Although net profit is your bottom line, profitability is what you're aiming for year after year. In the previous section, you looked at gross profit by product or service. Here you look at the profitability of your company as a whole, which includes net profit margin and return on equity (ROE):

- **Net profit margin:** Net profit margin is calculated by dividing gross sales into net profit. If your net profit margin is low compared to your industry, that means your prices are lower and your costs are too high. You aren't efficient. Lower margins are acceptable if they lead to greater sales, more market share, or investing in the future. But make sure they don't go too low. High margins are typically never a bad thing. Watch this ratio each year and use your industry average as a gauge to monitor your performance.

- **Return on equity (ROE):** ROE measures how much profit comes back to the owners for their investment. This ratio is calculated by dividing net profit by the owner's equity investment.

Wacky Widgets has a net profit of $65,000 and gross sales of $778,000 for a pre-tax profit margin of 8.3 percent. In other words, the company is making 8.3 cents on every dollar. The owners of Wacky Widgets have an equity investment of $294,000 in the company, so with a net profit of $65,000, their ROE is 22 percent. This means that the owners make almost 22 cents on every dollar invested in the company as equity. A 20 percent ROE is a reasonable return for risking $294,000.

Measuring your productivity

The ratios in this section give you a good picture of how productive your company is in using its assets to generate profit. Ratios in this group should be benchmarked against your industry to determine how well you're performing and where you might find areas of improvement.

Check out these ratios:

- ✔ **Sales-to-assets:** Sales to assets measures how productive your assets are. Look at what you've invested in to generate sales and how productive those investments are. This ratio is calculated by dividing gross sales by total assets.

  Our fictional toy company has gross sales of $778,000 and total assets of $1,120,000, for a sales-to-assets ratio of .69. This means that for every dollar the company invests in assets, it generates 69 cents in sales. This might be considered a rather inefficient use of assets. The management of Wacky should launch an investigation: possible reasons include too much production capacity or old assets. Outsource production and sell assets.

- ✔ **Return on assets (ROA):** ROA is another measure of how profitable the company assets are, and you calculate ROA by dividing net profit by total assets.

  With a net profit of $65,000 and total assets of $1,120,000, Wacky Widgets' ROA is 5.8 percent. This means the company makes almost six cents of net profit for every dollar invested in assets. This ratio should be interpreted in light of the overall risk, and in this instance, the owners of Wacky might consider putting the money in a CD and collecting the interest instead of assuming risk with so little return.

- ✔ **Inventory turnover:** Inventory turnover measures how many times you sell what's on your shelves and/or in your warehouse (in the case of a service company, inventory is time). Turnover is calculated by dividing cost of goods sold by the cost of the inventory.

  Wacky Widgets has a $423,000 cost of goods sold and $115,000 of inventory, for an inventory turnover ratio of 3.67. Dividing 365 days by 3.67 indicates it takes 99 days for Wacky Widgets to sell everything in the warehouse. The faster inventory turns, the less it costs and the more efficient operations are. A smart business owner strives to keep inventory turning faster than his/her industry peers.

- ✔ **Receivable turnover:** This is the ratio of the number of times that accounts receivable amount is collected throughout the year. A high accounts receivable turnover ratio indicates a tight credit policy. A low or declining accounts receivable turnover ratio indicates a collection problem, part of which may be due to bad debts. To determine the collection time on accounts receivable, divide total sales by accounts receivable.

  Wacky Widgets has gross sales of $778,000 and $178,000 in receivables, for a ratio of 4.3 times a year. After dividing this into 365 days, it takes Wacky Widgets 84 days to collect its receivables. This number should be closer to 45 to 60 days.

✔ **Accounts payable turnover**: This ratio shows how many times in one accounting period the company turns over (repays) its accounts payable to creditors. A higher number indicates either that the business has decided to hold on to its money longer or that it is having greater difficulty paying creditors. A lower number indicates the company is paying is creditors quickly. To calculate the accounts payable ratio, divide the cost of goods sold by accounts payable.

Accounts payable (A/P) turnover for Wacky Widgets are $49,000, with cost of goods sold totaling $423,000, for an A/P ratio of 8.6 times a year. So Wacky Widgets pays its vendors, suppliers, and others about once every six weeks. This isn't bad, but wouldn't you want to be paid in 30 days? Thirty days is what you should be shooting for. So Wacky should strive to pay its vendors promptly.

Sorting out three-year trends

Armed with information about how to calculate financial ratios (see "Looking at Your Financial Performance" earlier in this chapter), you want to set up a spreadsheet that shows financial trends ideally for the past few years. If you don't have complete financial data, put together ratios for the years that you do have information on. Follow these steps to get started:

1. **Set up a spreadsheet that lists financial ratios down the left-hand side and the three years across the top.**

2. **Calculate each ratio for each year based on the formulas provided in the previous sections.**

3. **Label the furthest column to the right (the one after the most current year) "Benchmark."**

4. **Enter the benchmark number based on the few recommended levels provided above, your desired targets, or industry benchmarks.**

5. **Identify which ratios are performing above or below the benchmark.**

6. **Determine possible corrective action and list your ideas on the note page entitled "Goals and Objectives."**

Trailing your numbers over 12 months

You need a dynamic way to look at your performance month after month because you'd like to see if your growing or shrinking. The Trailing 12 Months (T12M) chart, developed by Kraig Kramers — founder of CEO Tools — can help you track your annual total each month. T12M charts graphically tell you whether you're improving or slipping.

Take a look at both Figure 4-2 and Figure 4-3. Figure 4-2 is an ordinary monthly chart. This type of chart is often misleading and shows little other than seasonality. On the other hand, Figure 4-3 (a T12M) shows a true trendline on sales, gross profits, or whatever key data you use these charts to track.

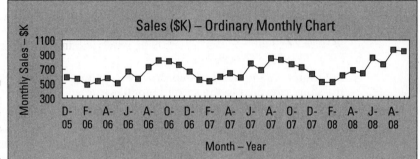

Figure 4-2: An ordinary monthly sales chart.

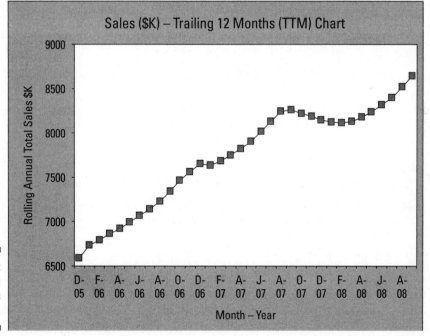

Figure 4-3: A trailing 12 months chart.

Here's how to create your T12M:

1. **Open a new spreadsheet in Excel.**

   Label Column A *Month/Year*; Column B *Monthly Sales*; and Column C *TTM Sales*.

2. **In Column A, list the months in chronological order, starting with the oldest date first.**

   Label January 2005 as J-05, February 2005 as F-05, and so on.

3. **In Column B, enter the monthly sales for each corresponding month.**

   In the J-05 column, enter your January sales. In the F-05 column, enter your February sales, and so on.

4. **In Column C, add the first month's sales to the second month's sales in the same row next to the second month's sales.**

   Move down one row, add the sum above it (the first two month) to the sales in month 3. This is a simple 12-month sum that moves forward one month (and down one row) at a time. You're adding the current month to the running total in the row above.

5. **In Excel, select Insert⇨Chart from the drop-down menu.**

   Use the line chart to graph Column C. You should see a trendline going up or down similar to that in Figure 4-3.

6. **Evaluate your T12M chart.**

   If it's going up month to month, that indicates positive performance. If it's going down, that means you're performing worse than in previous months.

For additional information on the tool, check out Kraig Kramers' Web site www.ceotools.com, where you can print out a version with a full explanation. (Click *New Tools Catalog*, scroll down to *Trailing 12-Month Chart*, and click the PDF symbol to bring it up on your screen and print it out.)

By watching your T12M month to month, you can immediately see if and when you need to take corrective action. If your trendline is moving upward, that means keep on doing what you're doing — growing!

Evaluating your numbers

Evaluating your ratios against those in your industry provides an objective look at how you're performing. It helps you to determine how other companies similar to yours are doing. When you have industry numbers to compare your company to, you can see if you are performing better than or worse than other companies similar to yours. With that information, you can take corrective action or keep on doing what you are doing.

For access to industry benchmark sources, try out these sources:

- ✔ BizStats.com (`http://bizstats.com`) is a free online resource that provides industry averages for numerous different ratios.

- ✔ BizMiner.com (`www.bizminer.com`) provides reports of financial ratios by industry. Use the coupon provided in this book to purchase reports at a discount.

- ✔ Dun & Bradstreet publishes a report called *Industry Norms and Key Business Ratios*. For more information, visit Dun & Bradstreet online at `www.dnb.com/us/dbproducts/risk_management/assess_risk/inkbr/index.html`.

- ✔ Financial-data services:

  - Standard and Poors: `www2.standardandpoors.com`

  - Value-Line: `www.valueline.com`

  - Moody's: `www.moodys.com`

Chapter 5

Focusing on What You Do Best

. . . .

. . . .

*B*usinesspeople and laymen alike throw around the term *competitive advantage* like it's the most common word in the English language. Not only is it widely overused, but also it's widely misunderstood. You aren't alone if you've ever wondered what a competitive advantage really is and what you do with it. Your competitive advantage is what you, your company, or your department does better than anyone else. It's what makes you unique, and it's *why* you're in business, and more importantly, why your business continues to prosper over time.

Think of your competitive advantage as your organization's DNA — a collection of genes and attributes that makes you unique. When you are capitalizing on your uniqueness, you are healthy, fit, and successful. When you aren't, you feel uncomfortable, slow, and are exerting more effort than you should.

Not only do I strive in this chapter to clear up any confusion you may feel, but I also help you uncover your competitive advantage and show you how to use the advantage in your planning process and business growth.

Knowing Your Competitive Advantage

What's the number-one attribute Warren Buffet, arguably one of the most successful investors in the world, looks for in a company? "Sustainable competitive advantage," he told an interviewer. If one of the most successful businessmen of today puts this at the top of his list, you should too. So what is it exactly?

Your competitive advantage is what you, your company, or your department does better than anyone else. It is what makes you unique. The sustainable part refers to your ability to continue to do those activities over a long period of time. And yes, you can have more than one advantage and you can develop advantages as well. You don't have to possess them all at this moment.

I can't emphasize the importance of understanding your competitive advantage enough. When you really have it nailed down, it helps you and your staff recognize the following:

- Which opportunities to pursue and which to pass by
- Where to allocate resources and where to cut back
- How to do what you already do well, better
- Know the difference between an opportunity and a distraction
- When to outsource (to another department or externally) and when to keep it in house

Your competitive advantage(s) is the foundation, the cornerstone of your strategic plan. Throughout your planning process, you evaluate every part of your plan to determine whether it supports or detracts from your competitive advantage. In the process, you discover what draws customers to buy the product or service from you instead of the competition.

Knowing how to define your competitive advantage is the first step toward applying it to your organization. Ninety-five percent of all companies don't know their competitive advantages, let alone how to use them to communicate a compelling reason to choose their product or service. If Buffet examined your company, would he find what he's looking for? You find out in the sections to come.

The 30-second competitive advantage challenge

Here's a 30-second test to determine if you know your competitive advantage. A test already? I know; you feel like you're in school again, don't you? Don't worry — it won't hurt. Ready?

I meet you at a local networking event and you introduce yourself.

"Hi, I'm Bob Jones with ABC Company."

"Hi Bob. Nice to meet you. Tell me a little about your company. What is your company best at?"

. . . 29, 30. Time's up!

Could you answer my question in less than 30 seconds, succinctly and with clarity? If yes, go ahead and skip to Chapter 6. If not, don't worry, you're in good company. Honestly, this question is hard to answer; a majority of businesses are also trying to figure out what they do best. Try to narrow your focus more than you're comfortable with. By the end of this chapter (if you read the whole thing), you should be able to share your competitive advantage with confidence and shout it from the rooftops.

What competitive advantage isn't

Often starting with what something isn't is easiest. So your competitive advantage isn't a list of your strengths. (Not to down play strengths because they're important too — especially in Chapter 7.) But if your competitive advantage list only comprises strengths, it's not very *competitive* now, is it? You have to be better than your competitors in order to have a competitive advantage.

A management team from a mid-sized financial services group reported that its competitive advantages included the following:

- ✔ Good reputation in the community
- ✔ Skilled staff
- ✔ Outstanding team and well-respected leader
- ✔ Knowledgeable
- ✔ Strong client list and loyalty
- ✔ Flexible and responsive

Blah, blah, blah. You've heard all this before and so have I. Couldn't you say this about almost any professional service firm? This list shows you why bulleting your strengths isn't what comprises your competitive advantage. This is a list of strengths.

What competitive advantage is

A competitive advantage is something you do that is unique. To compete, you must have a *unique* advantage. If you peek at the list in the previous section, you notice that it's not a list of unique qualities — basically anyone in business today needs to achieve that level of competency just to be in the game.

Specifically, a competitive advantage comes from leveraging a company's unique skills and resources to implement a strategy that competitors cannot implement as effectively or copy.

When the financial services firm went through the exercises that are described in the next section, "Uncovering Your Advantages," they uncovered their competitive advantages. Here is what they came up with:

✔ Ranked in top 10 percent of money managers who beat Standard & Poor's nationally

✔ Fastest-growing American Funds money manager in '00, '01, '02

✔ Only firm ever featured by American Funds in its advisory newsletter

That's more like it! Wow! Doesn't that say a lot more about the competitive advantage than a good reputation and a skilled staff? This transition is the one you need to make when explaining the competitive advantage of your organization or department.

Here are a few more examples from businesspeople who answered the question, "What is my company best at?":

✔ Sandy, owner of an interior design firm, determined she was best at increasing developers' sales ratio by 35 percent and was the only design team chosen by the top 10 luxury developers in the state.

✔ A clothing manufacturer named Joe said he was the best at wearable clothing because "our clothes fly off the racks."

✔ The emergency service division of a county in Washington is the best at providing disaster management and response and recovery efforts for all agencies within its service territory because of its skilled people and emergency response equipment.

The remaining sections of the chapter focus on helping you identify and articulate your competitive advantage.

Why having a competitive advantage is so important

Although you can put together a strategic plan without a clear understanding of your competitive advantage, you'd be missing the boat. Your goals, strategic objectives, and action plans tend to change and shift over time. Your competitive advantages, after you've identified them, endure and grow stronger. Other elements of your plan tend to morph. But what makes your company unique is that your competitive advantages stay constant.

Founding your strategic plan on the basis of your competitive advantages is the most important thing you can do as a leader of your business or department. The leading organizations in this world have a razor sharp understanding of their competitive advantage. Everything they do builds and nurtures their DNA. You don't have to be a Fortune 100 company to be that effective.

Uncovering Your Advantages

No company or department can be all things to all people. Some businesses try and quickly realize that they are spending time and resources on activities that are not profitable.

What are the sources of your success? What makes your company or department unique? Is your success tied to your ability to innovate new products or services? Or to your ability to respond quickly? Or to your brand and community reputation? Or to the creative power of your marketing and sales department? It is likely there are many sources that can contribute to your success.

Ultimately, *you* know what makes your company unique. You live it day in and day out. However, for your uniqueness to be useful in strategic planning, you need to state what you know to be absolutely true about your company. Your list of competitive advantages should make someone say, "Wow, I want to do business with you." To get your list of wows, you need to look at your business from different perspectives.

Be brutally honest — your insights can be instrumental in moving your company to the next level. Think about this process of uncovering your uniqueness like an exercise in genetic exploration. You know there are unique genes in your department or company. So go find them.

What's your distinct purpose?

Your organization exists for a very specific reason, and most likely its purpose is different than any other company out there. Companies are founded for reasons as varied as something to do during retirement to making the world a better place. Unfortunately, sometimes business owners lose sight of why they started their business. If that's you, here are a few questions to consider in determining your purpose:

✔ Why did I start my business?

✔ What business am I really in?

✔ Why does my business exist?

To jump-start your thinking, here are some examples of distinct purposes from organizations large and small:

✔ To solve the growing diabetes crisis

✔ To capitalize on a real estate growth trend

✔ To work for myself

✔ To provide quality window and door products better than anyone else

✔ To make fitness a way of life for everyone by making it fun, easy, and accessible

✔ To make my community a better place to live, work, and recreate through publicly accessible open space

✔ To provide people with a great place to work

✔ To be the perfect clown

An excellent way to uncover the purpose of your business from a different perspective is to talk with your employees. What do they think the distinct purpose of your organization is? Use the questionnaire in Figure 5-1 to obtain feedback from all your key staff members. Use your staff members' responses to uncover your competitive advantage. You may be amazed at the insightful comments you receive back from your team. Consider filling out the questionnaire yourself because that might also surprise you!

How do you make money?

If I asked you how you make money, more than likely you'd reply by explaining the types and number of products or services you sell. Although your answer is technically correct, I want you to look at your revenue generation from a different perspective. For the moment, resist looking at your income statement. Hey, I said resist! Put that paper down! No peeking.

WHAT IS THE PURPOSE OF OUR BUSINESS QUESTIONNAIRE for Employees
1. What is the mission or purpose of our company?
2. What do you think our company does best?
3. What doesn't our company do well?
4. What does our company do differently than our competitors?
5. Why are our customers our customers?

Figure 5-1: Capturing your staff members' impressions of your business' purpose.

Instead of looking at the old income statements, you're going to gain new insight into what really drives your profit. Think about your revenue in terms of profit per X. Here are some examples:

- ✔ Profit per customer or client
- ✔ Profit per customer visit
- ✔ Profit per employee
- ✔ Profit per household
- ✔ Profit per product or service
- ✔ Profit per product or service line
- ✔ Profit per region
- ✔ Profit per billable hour

You may be tempted to look at the above list and decide that several of these are your profit engines. The challenge, however, is to determine which one is actually the *best* revenue driver for your business. That is to say, they may all bring money into the business, but one will have the biggest impact. Looking at your revenue generation from this perspective is just like panning for gold. You do not need to change your activities, but you might need to look at your pan from a different angle to see the nugget.

Your profit engine is unique to your business. Below is a list of attributes that make up a good profit engine. Use this list as well as the examples above to identify yours.

- ✔ **Broad measure:** A good profit engine is broader than a typical financial metric such as number of products sold or number of customers per day.

- ✔ **Customer focused:** It should add to the customer experience and increase your customer focus. For example, by looking at your services from your customers' eyes, you may realize that instead of profit per product or service, your profit engine is profit per customer.

- ✔ **Improves resource sharing:** You only have so much time, money, and resources. If you can share your resources, you're increasing their use and your company's output. For example, a consultant only has so many hours in the day. Instead of looking at profit per hour, she could look at profit per client. Even further, if this consultant has a special methodology she uses in her consulting, her profit engine may be profit per number of uses (books, speaking, training other consultants, licensing, and so on).

How does this relate to uncovering your competitive advantages? The following sidebar, "Pegging profitability" provides an example.

Evaluating your business, consider what one measure drives your revenue. Use Figure 5-2 to develop your top three possible profit engines and evaluate them against the criteria provided. Select the profit engine that best meets all three of the criteria.

FINDING YOUR PROFIT ENGINE		
List your top three possible profit engines. Use the three criteria to determine your best profit engine.		
Profit per ____	☐ Broad Measure ☐ Customer Focused	☐ Improves Resource Sharing
Profit per ____	☐ Broad Measure ☐ Customer Focused	☐ Improves Resource Sharing
Profit per ____	☐ Broad Measure ☐ Customer Focused	☐ Improves Resource Sharing

Figure 5-2: Revving up your profit engine.

Pegging profitability

Sam, the owner of a chain of regional retail auto parts stores, thought his focus should be on profit per store. Although the profitability of a particular location is crucial, it's not the only variable that counts. As a result of understanding what makes a good profit engine (as explained in the section "How do you make money?"), he discovered that looking at the profit per customer is an even better measure of profitability. Now instead of stores competing, they collaborate.

Sam now provides a far superior customer experience than his competitors because stores are not fighting for customers. Customers get appointments quicker and their cars are repaired faster. Also, Sam can share assets, such as people and parts, between all the stores. Sam's improved customer experience is a new-found competitive advantage. His scope of services is not matched by any of his competitors.

Strategic planning is often about doing what you're already doing but tweaking it slightly. In this case, you can see how looking at profitability by customer instead of store can be a competitive advantage. The retail store now makes decisions that support the customer being the profit center instead of the store. Having a single focus on profitability can help hone your attention when trying to identify your key areas of uniqueness.

Why do customers buy from you?

Nothing in business ever happens if money doesn't exchange hands. More than likely, your organization has been around for several years because it provides a product or service that people want or need. Ideally, you're performing some market research and asking your current customers why they use your services. But I bet you have a general sense of what it is that drives people to buy from you. Here are some questions to ask yourself to determine what is bringing customers through your door:

- ✔ How do you help your customers? What need do you meet?

- ✔ Are your clients referring your business? Why or why not?

- ✔ If you are being referred, what part of your business do your customers talk about?

- ✔ What area of your business is growing? What product or service line sees the most action in terms of sales?

Even better than answering these questions yourself is asking your customers to answer the questions, if you both have time. Pick your top ten accounts and ask them to respond to the questionnaire in Figure 5-3. Anonymous responses yield the best results, so ask a colleague or an intern to make the calls on your behalf.

Similar responses from different customers to the questions on the form in Figure 5-3 guide the development of your competitive advantage in Figure 5-4 later in this chapter.

Pinpointing Your Competitive Advantage

Now that you have asked everyone who is important to your business to define your competitive advantage, it is time to summarize the findings and pinpoint your areas of uniqueness. Look at the responses to the questionnaires from both your employees and customers as well as your own answers to the questions from the previous three sections.

In your strategy notebook, capture the common themes or ideas from your customers, employees, and yourself. Use a separate page for each one of these perspectives. Collect these thoughts from Figures 5-1 and 5-3.

WHAT IS THE PURPOSE OF OUR BUSINESS QUESTIONNAIRE for Customers
1. If you were to describe <Your Company Name> in one sentence or one word, what would it be or how would you describe us?
2. What are we doing that you like? How do we help meet your needs?
3. What are we doing that you don't like? Or in what areas could we improve?
4. Is there anything that we are not currently providing that you need?
5. When your friends are looking for <Your type of product>, do you refer our company? Why or why not?

Figure 5-3:
Gather
feedback
from your
customers.

Perusing a few examples

Learning from others can be helpful in identifying your own competitive advantage. Check out the following two examples to see how these organizations define their uniqueness.

Pershing General Hospital is a 125 bed, primary-care facility located in a rural area with no other hospitals within 50 miles. Because the organization operates with almost zero competition, it doesn't need to focus on how to beat out other hospitals. However, it does need to decide what services to offer with its limited governmental funding. By offering services that are based on its competitive advantages, it can maximize the funding it does receive. Here is what Pershing's employees and customers said the hospital does the best:

✔ Provides the one-and-only, high-quality emergency, primary care, and retail pharmacy within its service area

✔ Staffs the hospital with personnel that have superior knowledge to support efficient operations

✔ Offers the best care possible by maintaining its full staff of highly-experienced nurses

Surfrider Foundation is a grassroots, non-profit, environmental organization that works to protect the oceans, waves, and beaches. With 60 chapters and 40,000 members nationwide, the foundation achieves its purpose through membership dues and grant funding. As with the proceeding example, the Foundation must focus on its *competitive advantages* to maintain its funding and be effective. Here are the themes from the employee and customer questionnaires:

✔ Defined focus on environmental issues that relate to the ocean and only the ocean

✔ Committed people who are extremely passionate about protecting the ocean

✔ Dedicated to maintaining a bipartisanship view to foster broad-based support

Stating your competitive advantage succinctly

Go back to the fictitious networking event in this chapter in the section "The 30-second competitive advantage challenge." You needed to be able to answer what your company was best at in 30 seconds. Here's a second chance. Look at Figure 5-4 where your findings are summarized; use the formula from that figure to put your list of unique activities into a succinct statement or bulleted points.

FORMULA FOR A COMPETITIVE ADVANTAGE		
A statement that explains what your company is best at.		
Your business name	**+ What you are best at**	**+ Why**
Honda	is best at developing precision engines and power trains	because its products are the leaders in reliability and technological advancement
Bikram Yoga	is best at productizing the yoga experience and practice	because it is packaged for franchising
Google	is best at optimizing searches for any type of information	because it continues to innovate and push technology past what was thought possible
Now it's your turn...		

Figure 5-4: Drafting your competitive advantage.

Putting your advantage to the test

It isn't enough just to have an advantage over your competitors. For your business to be great, it needs to be sustainable and able to endure the test of time. You have to be able to combat today's fierce market forces and uncertainty. Do you want to know why? I'll tell you.

Think about the graveyard of businesses from the dot-com era. Many of these companies didn't pass the sustainability test. You don't want your company to be a distant memory. In fact, you probably want it to live on past your time. And if you're a department manager, you probably want to see your department continue on instead of being restructured.

Here are the cold hard facts:

- Roughly 70 percent of all new products/services can be duplicated within one year

- 60 to 90 percent of process improvements (learning) eventually diffuses to competitors.

You need to make sure that your competitive advantage is something that's long-lasting and not easy to duplicate. So how do you know *when* you've developed a sustainable competitive advantage? You need criteria to help you gauge your success. Take a look at the measures below to see if you're on the right track:

- **Consistent difference:** Customers must see a consistent difference between your product/service and those of your competitors. This difference needs to be obvious to your customers and it must influence their purchasing decision.

- **Difficult to imitate:** Your competitive advantage must be difficult to imitate. You want to have an advantage that your competition can't easily duplicate or don't understand how to copy. Often this comes in the form of people, proprietary knowledge within your organization, or business processes that are behind the scenes.

- **Constantly improved:** The first two bulleted items in this list must create activities that can be constantly improved, nurtured, and worked at to maintain an edge over your competition. The comparison of Wal-Mart over Kmart is a great example of how one continued to improve its supply chain management and purchasing whereas the other didn't. Unfortunately for Kmart, it lost its edge because it didn't constantly improve. Wal-Mart invests in ever-refining its product selection and processes.

Use the form in Figure 5-5 to quickly evaluate if your advantage withstands the test of time. The more responses to the right-hand side of the form, the better, but don't worry if you don't pass each one. Think about how you can add to your competitive advantage to make it even more sustainable. When you develop goals in Chapter 12, take action to shore up any areas that may concern you.

TESTING YOUR COMPETITIVE ADVANTAGE

Will your customers see a consistent, superior difference between your product/service and those of your competitors?

No difference ------------------------------- Huge difference

How difficult will it be for competitors to imitate your advantages?

Not difficult ------------------------------- Very difficult

Can your company constantly improve?

Little improvement ------------------------------- Extensive improvement

Figure 5-5:
Putting your
advantage
to the test.

Breaking away from the pack

Developing competitive advantages isn't always easy or straightforward. For many, a competitive advantage is developed by nurturing a strength over time. This process turns the activity or intangible asset into something that's difficult to copy. If you have a strength where you can break away from your competition, it's worth spending your energy and resources to develop it further. Here are some great ways to break away from the pack:

✔ **Consistency:** One of the hardest and one of the best advantages is the ability to deliver the same product or service time after time after time. To do so, a company must have rock solid processes that deliver consistency no matter what.

Think about Starbucks. Everyone says you can get the same cup of coffee in San Francisco as you can in Chang Mai, Thailand, and it's true (I had to find out)! Starbucks delivers high-quality service with consistency time after time, which is an amazing core competency. In the product world, this tends to be easier, but in the service world, people are involved every step of the way. And by our nature, businesses are inconsistent. Putting consistency into your delivery can be a solid core competency.

✔ **Brand development:** Growing and developing your brand over time can be a core competency worth more than all the past years' marketing budgets combined. Developing your brand happens by reinforcing your image in the marketplace through everything you do.

Think Kleenex. You don't say "Hand me a soft facial tissue"; you say, "Hand me a Kleenex" even if the brand is something else. Coke is similar. Many people refer to all soda products as Coke. Those brands have become the product type they represent.

✔ **Depth of knowledge:** Consider how much knowledge you gain in your business year after year. I like to call it *tribal knowledge.* The longer you're in business, the more that tribal knowledge grows. But it only feeds on itself if you capture your experiences in a systematic way. Just as employees can be a key strength, they can also be a key weakness if they move on without leaving the knowledge with the tribe.

✔ **Continued innovation and improvement:** Some organizations excel at innovation whereas others struggle. Innovation is the ability to develop products and services that your market wants better and faster than your competitors.

Intuit, with its Quicken and QuickBooks products, is a company that fosters continuous improvement based on customer feedback. Improvement for improvement's sake is a black hole. Quicken product sales show how this core competency can be worth the time it takes to develop it.

✔ **Longevity:** The pure staying power of a company over time can be a testament to its strength. It's hard to nurture longevity, but it's something that can be leveraged if you have it. Family businesses are great examples of firms that can use their market history as a core competency.

Using Your Advantages Now

Focusing on your competitive advantages can have a tremendous impact on your business. If you only have time to work on one part of the planning process, I recommend spending time to formulate your competitive advantage. By knowing what you're best at, you can focus on what matters for success and profitability.

You don't have to wait until your strategic plan is complete to put your competitive advantages to work for you. Because your list of advantages are probably things you're already doing, you can start doing them better or even start talking about them to raise the level of awareness in and outside of your company.

Implementing your advantages

Here are some quick uses of your advantages that you can implement today:

- ✔ **Use your competitive advantages in your marketing material.** Turn it into a tagline. Use it in a press release. Add it to your corporate About Us page on your Web site.

- ✔ **Communicate the advantage daily.** Include your competitive advantage in your signature line on your e-mail. Add a line in your voicemail message or your automated voice attendant.

- ✔ **Tell your employees.** Post it in common area. Add it to your internal blog.

- ✔ **Refine it by obtaining feedback from your customers.** Ask a few of your best clients if they agree with your list of advantages. Improve or add to it based on their responses.

- ✔ **Make it better.** Develop a handful of 30-day actions that you and your staff can start working on to make your competitive advantages even stronger.

Measuring your advantages

Now that you've got it, why not try to find a way to quantify your most important competitive advantage and promote that quality about your company? Do you have the metrics that matter and support monitoring your uniqueness? Find a way to support your claim through numbers that you can use to answer, "Why us?" Establishing a measurement based on a core element of your business elevates the importance in your organization and helps you monitor whether you're sustaining the advantage or letting it slip.

Industry data can be helpful in identifying how to quantify your competitive advantage. Referral statistics and retention rates offer other opportunities. Here are other places to look:

- ✔ Inventory turns
- ✔ Delivery times
- ✔ Return rates
- ✔ Satisfaction rates
- ✔ Guarantees
- ✔ Terms
- ✔ Referral rates

AOL's advantage: Make it personal

Remember back in the early 1990's, when Internet Service Providers (ISPs) were springing up everywhere? If you bought a computer from a major manufacturer in those early days of Windows, odds were that you also got up to three separate trial ISP accounts preloaded on your computer at the factory. I got CompuServe, Prodigy, and America Online preloaded in 1993.

Years later, America Online is now the biggest ISP. Prodigy and Compuserve are virtually unheard of anymore. How did America Online win the war? The folks at AOL understood two key things customers valued at that time:

✔ **Personalization of accounts:** A person could get an e-mail address like `joesmith@aol.com` from AOL, whereas Prodigy assigned him the e-mail address `JS12345@prodigy.com`, and CompuServe assigned `56789@compuserve.com`. As a customer, I want my name if I can get it, or something else that is personally meaningful to me, like a personalized license plate. If you could get a personalized plate from the DMV at *no extra charge*, would you do it? Most people would.

✔ **Fewer rules:** AOL has fewer rules governing the virtual community of chat rooms and bulletin boards. People could pretty much talk about whatever they wanted to in cyberspace within AOL, whereas CompuServe and Prodigy had more restrictions on that kind of activity. Naturally the virtual community growth was viral, multiplying their user base tenfold.

Over time, most people picked AOL over the competition. AOL went for customization and personalization against the bigger, more well-funded competition. That's using competitive advantage to dominate your space, to grow, and to become successful!

Putting your advantages in your plan

Your strategic plan needs to include a section that states your competitive advantage. But you can also include it in full or parts of it in other areas of your plan. Here are a few ideas:

✔ Include the intent of your competitive advantage in your mission statement. (Check out Chapter 6 for mission statements.)

✔ Use the information you collected from your customers and employees to start the list of your strengths and weaknesses (Chapter 7).

✔ Develop long-term goals that make your competitive advantage sustainable (Chapter 13).

✔ Include measures to monitor your competitive advantage.

Most importantly, you use your competitive advantages as a yardstick for every part of your strategic plan. Chapter 14 asks you to evaluate your strategic plan based on how well each section supports your competitive advantages.

Thinking about what you do best helps you build the strongest foundation possible for your business. When you're looking at your list of competitive advantages, be careful that your strategies do nothing to weaken your company's competitive advantage or take away from the key capabilities that got you where you are. Remember, now that you've identified your DNA, everything should grow from these cells.

Chapter 6

Refining Your Mission, Vision, and Values

*W*hile on vacation, a businessman bought fish from an old fisherman every day. One day he arrived to find the fisherman docking his boat at noon. "Is something wrong?" he asked. A smile wrinkled the seller's leathery face. "By no means. All is well." "Then why are you docking your boat so early?" asked the businessman.

"So I can go to my house, sit on my porch, and sip tea with my wife," the fisherman replied. The man of commerce objected. "But the day is still young. You can still fish." "No need to," the fisherman said. "I've made enough money for today."

"Enough? Absurd. You should keep working." The spry old man stopped and stared at his well-dressed visitor. "And why should I keep working?"

"To sell more fish."

"And why sell more fish?"

"Because the more fish you sell, the more money you make. The more money you make, the richer you are. The richer you are, the more boats you can buy. The more boats you buy, the more fisherman sell your fish, and the richer you become. And when you have enough, you can stop working, sell your boats, stay home, and sit on the porch with your wife and drink tea."

The fisherman smiled. "I can do that today. I guess I have enough."

This story, which you've probably heard in a variety of versions, quickly explains the importance of having a clear mission, vision, and set of corporate values. Knowing why you're doing what your doing (your mission), where you're trying to go (your vision), and how you're going to go about it (your values), are the glue that hold an organization together. You preserve these elements, while your strategies and goals change and flex with the market. You may modify your mission, vision, or values, but the intent stays unchanged. So just like the fisherman, you too will have complete clarity when making critical business decisions that impact your future.

Your mission, vision, and values can sound abstract, esoteric, and downright fluffy to a lot of people, especially those who are burning to move forward with a real-world project. These people don't want to hang back conceptualizing about people's wishes and dreams. Don't let being pragmatic get in the way of this important stage of building a strong foundation of consensus for your organization. If you don't take the time to articulate mission, values, and vision on the front end, you may pay for it later when you're trying to write goals and objectives without a crystal clear strategic direction.

In this chapter, you develop and revise your mission, vision, and values statements. Take a look at your strategic foundation by using the framework in Table 6-1:

Table 6-1	Your Strategic Foundation
Your Core	*Your Future*
DNA: What you do best (competitive advantage from Chapter 5)	Future vision: Where you're headed (vision statement)
Core purpose: Why you exist (mission statement)	Future description: What does it look like (vivid description)
Core values: What you stand for (values statement)	

Assessing Your Mission

A *mission statement* is a statement of the company's purpose or its fundamental reason for existing. The statement spotlights what business a company is presently in and the customer needs it's presently striving to meet. To build a solid foundation for a successful business, it's essential to have a written, clear, concise, and consistent mission statement. This statement should simply explain who you are and why you exist.

The mission statement of Olsen & Associates Public Relations is "Dedicated to improving and optimizing public perceptions on behalf of our clients." If the company doesn't live up to this mission, it has no reason to exist.

Elements of an effective mission statement

Your mission statement serves as a guide for day-to-day operations and as the foundation for future decision-making. Make sure that your statement includes the following criteria:

- ✔ **Focuses on satisfying customer needs:** Focus the business on satisfying customer needs instead of spotlighting your product or service.

- ✔ **Based on your core competencies:** Base your mission on a competitively superior internal strength or resource that your company performs well in comparison to your competitors.

  McDonald's core competency is providing low-cost food and fast service to large groups of customers.

- ✔ **Motivates and inspires employee commitment:** Your mission statement should be motivating. Don't base it on making more sales or profits but on employees' significant work and how the mission contributes to people's lives.

- ✔ **Realistic and clear:** Avoid making the mission too narrow or too broad. A mission needs to contain a purpose that's realistic to avoid "mission creep." Many organizations can go off on tangents that aren't core to their purpose and are unrealistic because their mission isn't clearly defined.

- ✔ **Specific, short, sharply focused, and memorable:** Write a precise statement of purpose that describes the essence of the business in words your employees and customers can remember you by.

When thinking of a length for your mission, make sure that it can fit on a T-shirt. The International Red Cross's mission is "To serve the most vulnerable."

✔ **Clear and easily understood:** Develop and write your mission statement so that you can quickly and briefly tell people you meet at a party or on airplanes why your company exists. If you keep that concept in mind, your statement can automatically be short and comprehensible. Make sure to give your company team a profoundly simple focus for everything it does as a business.

✔ **Says what the company wants to be remembered for:** In the end, a mission statement leaves a lasting impression. How do you want the world to think of you? Your statement can provide simple insight into why you do business.

Evaluating your current mission statement

Many mission statements are works in progress. Others have been handed down over the years to the point that they've lost their relevance. If you have a mission statement, it may be time to dust it off or give it a polishing for updates or total overhauls. Generally, if five years have gone by and you haven't even touched your mission statement, it's definitely time for reviewing, fine-tuning, or even rewriting your mission statement.

Sit down with your senior staff or management team and evaluate your current mission by using Figure 6-1. Collect everyone's thoughts and suggestions, but the final decision on how to change the mission is the CEOs. If you do decide to change it, leave the wordsmithing to one person.

The worst thing for your planning effort is to have a mission statement that is meaningless to your staff and other stakeholders. Use Figure 6-1 to evaluate the effectiveness of your existing mission statement.

Writing a new mission statement

You've determined the need for a new mission statement. It's okay; I'm here to help you start from scratch or even revise the one you currently have. The three components in the list below can help you craft your mission statement.

Examples of world-class mission statements

Mission statements are as varied as organizations. Some meet all the effective criteria listed above and others deviate completely. Here are a handful of mission statements to get your creative juices flowing.

- **3M:** To solve unsolved problems innovatively.

- **The Elephant Sanctuary:** A natural-habitat refuge where sick, old, and needy elephants can once again walk the earth in peace and dignity.

- **Fannie Mae:** To strengthen the social fabric by democratizing home ownership.

- **Google:** To organize the world's information and make it universally accessible and useful.

- **LCJ Marketing Source:** To make your company stand out in the crowd.

- **Marine Stewardship Council:** To safeguard the world's seafood supply by promoting the best environmental choices.

- **Marriott Hotel:** To make people who are away from home feel they are among friends and really wanted.

- **Merck:** To provide society with superior products and services by developing innovations and solutions that improve the quality of life and satisfy customer needs, and to provide employees with meaningful work and advancement opportunities, and investors with a superior rate of return.

- **New Jersey Section of the American Water Works Association (NJAWWA):** Dedicated to the promotion of public health and welfare in the provision of drinking water of unquestionable quality and sufficient quantity. NJAWWA must be proactive and effective in advancing the technology, science, management, and government policies relative to the stewardship of water.

- **Rotary International:** To support its member clubs in fulfilling the Object of Rotary by: Fostering unity among member clubs; Strengthening and expanding Rotary around the world; Communicating worldwide the work of Rotary; and Providing a system of international administration.

- **Small Business Technology Solutions:** To provide small businesses the functionality of big business, within a small business budget.

- **Sony:** To experience the sheer joy of advancing and applying technology for the benefit of the public.

- **Southwest Airlines:** To provide the highest quality of customer service delivered with a sense of warmth, friendliness, individual pride, and company spirit.

- **Sun Microsystems:** To solve complex network computing problems for governments, enterprises, and service providers.

- **University of Phoenix:** To educate working adults to develop the knowledge and skills that enable them to achieve their professional goals, improve the productivity of their organizations, and provide leadership and service to their communities.

Mission Statement Evaluation	Yes	No
The mission statement is a statement of our company's purpose.		
The mission statement fits the current market environment.		
The mission statement is based on our core competencies. (A core competency is a unique strength.)		
The mission statement is motivating and inspires employee commitment.		
The mission statement is realistic.		
The mission statement is specific, short, sharply focused, and memorable.		
The mission statement is clear and easily understood.		
The mission statement says what the company wants to be remembered for.		

Figure 6-1:
Evaluating your mission statement.

Consider answering these questions from your customers' perspective and you'll instantly see an improvement in your responses.

- What is the purpose of our business?
- What activity are we going to do to accomplish our purpose?
- What do we intend to accomplish on behalf of our customers? Or who benefits from our work?

Follow these steps below to create your mission statement:

1. **Collect ideas and opinions (either through a group meeting or an individual survey) of your senior staff and key employees about the organization's mission.**

   Ask for responses and input specifically on the three questions listed above. If you hold a meeting, just brainstorm and allow everyone's ideas to be collected.

2. **Collate and synthesize the responses, looking for similar themes. Develop several different versions of a draft mission statement.**

   Consider using present tense language so the statement reflects what you are and not what you aspire to become.

3. **Evaluate the different drafts against the checklist in Figure 6-1.**

Keep the ones that meet the guidelines in the figure and throw out the others.

4. **Circulate the draft statements and ask for feedback.**

   Have the staff vote on their favorite version.

5. **Select the best one and make sure every employee receives a copy.**

   If you're developing the mission statement as part of your strategic plan, consider waiting to communicate the new mission statement until the plan is finished.

The organization's purpose and its final mission statement shouldn't be developed by a committee. Use the process above to solicit ideas and input, but ultimately senior management and leaders set the strategic foundation for an organization. It's really not a democratic process.

Don't get stuck on this part of your process. If need be, develop a mission statement or a revised statement that's dubbed as a work in progress or a draft. Many organizations get caught up in developing the most perfect statement possible. This thought process misses the reason for a mission statement in the first place. While you can use your statement in your marketing collateral or with customers (so you may want to spell- and grammar-check it), the mission statement's primary usage is to clearly state the purpose of your organization to your employees and other stakeholders. Sometimes it takes years to perfect the statement for public usage. In the meantime, you have a team that understands why they come to work everyday.

Evaluating Your Organizational Values

Values are enduring, passionate, and distinctive core beliefs. They're guiding principles that never change. Values are why you do what you do and what you stand for. Values are deeply held convictions, priorities, and underlying assumptions that influence your attitudes and behaviors. They have intrinsic value and importance to those inside the organization. Your core values are part of your strategic foundation.

More and more companies are articulating the core beliefs and values underlying their business activities. Strong values account for why some companies gain a reputation for such strategic traits as leadership, product innovation, dedication to superior craftsmanship, being a good company to work for, and total customer satisfaction. A company's values can dominate the kind of strategic moves it considers or rejects. When values and beliefs are deeply ingrained and widely shared by managers and employees, they become a way of life within the company, and they mold company strategy. They're also called *guiding principles*.

On the beaches of Normandy

Although World War II historians often point out that the superior Air Forces of the Allies were instrumental in securing Allied victory during the D-Day invasion, many often miss the importance of the philosophical and operational differences between the Allied and Axis forces and commands. The German Army was the finest fighting army on the planet. They knew an attack was coming. They were prepared. Their veteran troops were up against mostly green Allied troops that had never seen combat. Why did the Allies prevail?

One of the most overwhelming factors of Allied victory during the Normandy invasion was that every Allied soldier knew his mission and was empowered to act in support of that mission, no matter what happened. So even when troops landed on the wrong portion of a beach, or air dropped in the wrong landing zone, Allied forces re-organized themselves spontaneously. They led themselves, under the most extreme conditions, often with no contact with higher command or local leadership to direct their efforts.

The German High Command was rigid, where initiative was punished. On the other hand, the Allied High Command was flexible, where initiative was encouraged.

The Allied Commanders pushed the mission to the lowest possible levels within the organization, to ensure that there was alignment and integration of the efforts of the differing divisions of personnel. From the highest ranking officer to the lowest ranking soldier, everyone knew the big picture and their part in it.

Conversely, the German commanders communicated through key channels and key leaders. When things didn't go as planned, often the Axis troops hesitated and waited for orders from higher command. With communications disrupted and leaders absent or arguing with each other about the proper response to the invasion, the Axis powers were paralyzed. The Allied foothold on the continent prevailed and grew.

Obviously, the stakes aren't as high in the business world as they are in war time. However, the extreme conditions of warfare often illustrate the best examples of successful organizational philosophies and operational processes. Modern businesses follow many practices first perfected within the military. The entire concept of an organizational mission statement has its roots in military history. CEOs, COOs, and company presidents often take the time to craft an organizational mission statement, often with the help and input of their direct reports. However, having a mission statement and having it understood by and mean something to the rank and file are two separate things. How integrated and understood is *your* company's mission statement to the people that matter the most?

Herb Kelleher, former CEO of Southwest Airlines, speaks about core values: "We always felt that people should be treated right as a matter of morality. Then, incidentally, that turned out to be good business, too. But it didn't really start as a strategy. It began with us thinking about what is the right thing to do in a business context. We said we want to really take care of these people, we want to honor them, and we love them as individuals. Now that induces the kind of reciprocal trust and diligent effort that made us successful. But the motivation wasn't strategy, it was core values."

Elements of effective organizational values

Developing core values can be tricky because you're transferring something that's very personal into a group and business setting. As you're working toward developing a values statement for your organization, beware of the personal and emotional connection most of your team members have with creating the values statement.

Here are some guidelines:

- **One word isn't enough to convey the real meaning of a value.** Create phrases, but not paragraphs.

- **Make these values specific, not generic.** More than one word is needed to define specificity.

- **Some values-driven language may be part of your mission statement.** That's fine, but consider not repeating what you've covered elsewhere.

- **Values need to be shared.** While you don't need consensus from everyone in your organization, you do need agreement from senior management.

- **Keep the list of values to between five and seven.** They need to be memorable to your staff, so having a few statements is better than having so many that nobody remembers any.

To illustrate these guidelines in action, look at Herman Miller, an innovative furniture company.

- Rather than using the word *excellence*, Herman Miller chose the word *performance*, and explained what that means this way: "It isn't a choice, it's about everyone performing at his or her own best; we measure it; it enriches our lives and brings value."

- Rather than using the word *teamwork*, Herman Miller uses the word *inclusiveness*, and describes it this way: "To succeed as a company, we must include all the expressions of human talent and potential . . . when we are truly inclusive, we go beyond toleration to understanding all the qualities that make people who they are, that make us unique, and most important, that unite us."

Developing or updating your organizational values

You don't set or establish core values. You discover them. The exercise in this section helps you focus on discovering shared values within your organization by starting with individual's values and moving up to the organization.

You can use this exercise to update your current values statement or develop a new one. Focus this exercise on answering three questions:

- ✔ What are the core values and beliefs of our company?
- ✔ What values and beliefs guide our daily interactions?
- ✔ What are we really committed to?

Evaluate your values using Figure 6-2. Because your values are a key foundational element to your company and strategic plan, you want to be doubly sure they're the right ones.

Identifying Authentic Core Values	Yes	No
If you were to start a new company, would this core value be part of its foundation?		
Will you continue to stand by and hold this value no matter what happens in the competitive environment?		
Are you willing to stand by this value no matter what the cost – for example, lost clients or lost revenue?		
Do you believe that employees who do not share this value should continue to be part of your company?		
Do you demonstrate this core value in your leadership?		
Would you sell your company before giving up this core value?		
Do you apply this core value in your personal activities?		
If you could do anything in the world, would you continue to apply this core value to your productive activities?		

Figure 6-2: Evaluating your values statement.

Here are the steps to developing your organizational values statement:

1. **Solicit a list of five to seven core values from each of your key staff members and senior management team.**

Ask each person to provide the list of values to you individually through a survey or e-mail by answering the questions above. Unlike with the mission and vision exercises, values are best solicited individually instead of in a group to begin with. Request that they explain each value they provide.

2. **Merge the lists provided by combining values that are listed more than once.**

The purpose here is to develop a draft list of values. You may have more than five to seven at this time.

3. **Bring the group together to discuss the list of values.**

Ask people to comment on what is listed. Revise and modify until you have generated a final values statement.

4. **After you have your list of organizational values, use Figure 6-2 to evaluate each value for effectiveness.**

You can do this as a group or individually.

5. **Put the finishing touches on the values statement and communicate across the company.**

See the next section for ideas on how to use your values statement today.

Need some ideas to get started on discovering your organizational values? See Figure 6-3 for a bunch of words that you can use to stimulate those gray cells. Give a copy to your values team to help them generate their individual list.

Acting on your organizational values

Developing a set of values is one thing, living by them is something completely different. Having a values statement that's all talk and no commitment undermines your leadership and the management team's credibility. Here are some ways to bring your organizational values to life:

- ✔ **Communication:** Send a letter to every employee; develop a brochure; visit every office to personally explain the values; post the values in a public area.

- ✔ **Training:** Develop short training sessions about the different value topics. If that sounds like a lot of work, consider holding a brown bag lunch focused on one of the values. Allow an open discussion about what it means to act on and live by each value.

- ✔ **Reinforcement:** Engrain your values through performance reviews, in your goal statements, and in your everyday language.

✔ **Rewards/Recognition:** Host contests to give employees a fun reason to discover and integrate the values.

✔ **Hiring:** Use your values statement as a guide in your hiring process. Structure interview questions around each one of your values to ensure that you're bringing people into your company who align with your corporate culture.

✔ **Alignment:** Look at your values and figure out specific ways to align daily activities with the values. For example, if one of your values is innovation, then install a system to reward innovation. If customer satisfaction is a value, then set a policy of 100 percent money back guarantee.

dedicated	customer care	positive
consistent	strategic	trustworthy
outstanding	training	genuine
value	support	real
helpful	principles	excellent
customer service	beliefs	sensitive
image	competent	knowledgeable
service	sincerity	synergy
relationships	self-confident	maximum value
dependable	relationships	stand behind our work/people
guarantee	efficient	long-term relationships
100% effort	opportunity	do the right thing
dedication	honesty	referrals and customer goodwill
commitment	productivity	high expectations of
adaptable	performance	family
security	ability	no hype
trust	professionalism	friendly
people	retaining	energetic
personal growth	development	loyal
company growth	responsive/ness	teamwork
respect	integrity	creativity
community responsibility	passion	pride
continuous improvement	collaboration	entrepreneurial spirit
quality	customer expectations	innovation
embracing change	rewarding work	high performance
environmental responsibility	excellence	leadership
energy	enthusiasm	fairness
personal responsibility	dedication	independence
advocacy	expertise	customer satisfaction
openness	employee participation	reliability

Figure 6-3:
Ideas, words, and phrases for your values statement.

Visioning: Focusing in on Your North Star

Forming a strategic vision should provide long-term direction, delineate what kind of enterprise the company is trying to become, and infuse the organization with a sense of purposeful action. Vision serves as a unifying focal point for everyone in the organization — like a North star. In fact, your vision statement needs to be something you can achieve at some point in the future. Visions are also referred to as big, hairy, audacious goals or BHAGs.

A vision statement can be as far reaching as 100 years or as short as five years. Some people think if you aren't planning for 20 years in the future, you're being too short-sighted. Others say that the world is changing too quickly to plan more than a few years out. Either way, your vision statement needs to work for your company and the industry you operate in. I recommend developing a vision statement that's far reaching but attainable. If you attain it in a shorter amount of time, congratulations! But if you don't push your thinking out far enough, you find yourself being too tactical in your strategic planning.

Your vision should include

- ✔ **A vision statement:** A short, concise statement of your organization's future state.
- ✔ **A vivid description:** A long list of words and phrases that describe what that future state is like.

Because the items in the above bulleted list go hand-in-hand, you can develop them simultaneously.

Here are two examples of visions or BHAGs that were very lofty at the time they were established:

- ✔ We will put a man on the moon before the end of the decade and bring him back (President John F. Kennedy).
- ✔ A computer on every desk and in every home using great software as an empowering tool (Microsoft).

These two statements don't sound so crazy now, do they?

Elements of an effective vision statement

Your vision statement needs to incorporate many elements. The following list contains elements that you can include in an effective vision statement (you don't have to use *every* one, but keep them in mind when you're writing or evaluating):

- ✔ **Audacious:** Represents a dream that's beyond what you think is possible. It represents the mountaintop your company is striving to reach. Visioning takes you out beyond your present reality.

- ✔ **Capitalizes on core competencies:** Builds on your company's core competencies. It builds on what you've already established: company history, customer base, strengths, and unique capabilities, resources, and assets.

- ✔ **Futurecasting:** Provides a picture of what your business looks like in the future.

- ✔ **Inspiring:** Engaging language that inspires. It creates a vivid image in people's heads that provokes emotion and excitement. It creates enthusiasm and poses a challenge.

- ✔ **Motivating:** Clarifies the direction in which your organization needs to move and keeps everyone pushing forward to reach it.

- ✔ **Purpose-driven:** Gives employees a larger sense of purpose, so they see themselves as building a cathedral instead of laying stones.

Imagining your future — vividly

The vivid description in your vision needs to be just that: vivid. You should include a list of ideas, phrases, adjectives, and so forth that thoroughly explain what it's like to achieve the vision statement. Try to imagine your organization when you reach your vision. Your vivid description explains what it feels like. Your description should be vibrant and engaging and should translate the vision from words into pictures that people can carry around in their heads.

Here are some helpful questions to develop a vivid description of your vision:

- ✔ What does your company look like? How many employees do you have? Where are you located? How many offices are at this location? What is the office environment like?

- ✔ Who is on the staff? What are their skills, degrees, and areas of expertise? How does everyone work together? What is the culture like?

- ✔ Who are your clients? How many customers do you have?

Examples of big, hairy, audacious vision statements

Because it's always fun (and educational) to see what other organizations are aiming for, here is a variety of vision statements:

✔ **BearingPoint:** To be the world's most influential and respected business advisor and systems integrator.

✔ **Chemtura:** To be the world's best specialty chemicals company.

✔ **DuPont:** To be the world's most dynamic science company, creating sustainable solutions essential to a better, safer, and healthier life for people everywhere.

✔ **Health Care for All:** All people in our state will have access to quality healthcare, regardless of ability to pay.

✔ **Heinz:** To be the world's premier food company, offering nutritious, superior tasting foods to people everywhere.

✔ **M3 Planning:** To start a strategy revolution.

✔ **McDonald's:** To dominate the global food-service industry.

✔ **Novo Nordisk:** To be the world's leading diabetes care company.

✔ **Pershing General Hospital:** To be the provider of first choice for our community and a leader in rural healthcare for Nevada.

✔ **Recording for the Blind and Dyslexic:** For all people to have equal access to the printed word.

✔ **Visa:** A world in which buyers and sellers can conduct commerce anywhere, anytime, and in any way they choose.

✔ What type of projects are you working on? How many products or services are you selling?

✔ What is your industry, business community, or media saying about your company? What are the headlines? What publications or TV stations are you featured on? What awards have you won?

Updating your vision statement and vivid description

Updating or creating a new vision statement can be one of the most exciting parts of strategic planning. Creating your vision statement can be achieved in a fashion similar to that of creating your mission and values statements.

Follow these steps to create your vision:

1. **Gather your senior staff and key employees together for a one- to two-hour meeting.**

   Visioning is best done in a group setting. If your group is bigger than five people, break up into small groups of three to five to allow everyone to have a voice in the process.

2. **Generate a list of ideas and phrases based on the responses to these three questions:**

   • What will our organization look like five to ten years from now?

   • What does success look like?

   • What are we aspiring to achieve?

   Allow the group to brainstorm, even if some of the ideas are totally wacky.

3. **Ask the group to pair up ideas that have similar themes.**

   Identify the ideas that most closely resemble the vision for the organization.

4. **Ask one or two people to develop a draft vision statement based on the condensed list of ideas.**

   The vision statement should be short and use verbs phrases that are forward-looking such as *to be*.

5. **Ask another one or two people to generate the vivid description based on all of the themes identified.**

   When developing the vivid description, use the future tense, such as "We will . . ."

6. **Bring the vision statement and vivid description back to the group.**

   Revise until you have something everyone agrees on.

7. **Evaluate the vision statement against the mission and values statements.**

   Make sure they all connect.

Envisioning your personal future

Because your personal life and your business life are intertwined, you should have a BHAG that runs in tandem with your corporate vision statement. This statement is called the *Owner's Vision Statement* and isn't necessarily shared with your employees but is developed specifically to develop a single focus point for all equity shareholders.

Many small businesses don't have owner's visions because their founders haven't looked at life outside of business ownership. An owner's vision, even though it may seem far out, is imperative for anyone who's founded or purchased a business.

An owner's vision answers the question "What is my endgame?" In other words, where do you see yourself in the business three, five, or ten years from now? If you're looking to sell the business, turn to Chapter 17 for the discussion about business valuation and exit strategies.

Take out a note page and label it *Owner's Vision Statement.* List your ideas about your end game. Consider when you plan on exiting, how to exit, how much return you want to see and so on. Add a note to revise this list after reading Chapter 17 on exit strategies.

Finalizing Your Strategic Foundation

All the elements of your strategic foundation — competitive advantage, mission, values, vision, and vivid description — should work together. Remember these are the elements of your organization that don't change, or at least they don't change significantly. Your strategies, goals, objectives, and actions change based on market conditions, but they're always built on your strategic foundation.

Bring all of these elements together in a strategic foundation sheet like the examples shown in Figure 6-4 and Figure 6-5. This sheet is an excellent document to include in a new employee packet, post in the break room, hand out to every employee, and use in strategy meetings. It's exciting! It gives everyone a bigger sense of purpose and an understanding of what your organization is all about.

SpeakShop

Competitive Advantages – Our DNA *What we do best*	Vision Statement – Our Future *Where we are headed*
• Operational effectiveness through an open marketplace and operational cost efficiency • Specialization in foreign language services • Supplier and consumer loyalty • Early entry and network effect • Latin America and online education domain expertise	Revolutionize language education and establish a new model for business based on loyal yet independent sellers and customers who improve their communities and geopolitical understanding by developing friendships and partnerships worldwide.
Mission Statement – Our Core Purpose *Why we exist*	Vision Description *What it looks like*
To change lives by: • Providing exceptional Spanish language education to people of all abilities through one-on-one tutoring via online video conferencing. • Creating sustainable, entrepreneurial opportunities for skilled Spanish tutors in developing countries by bridging the digital divide.	Make foreign language learning available to anyone anywhere, thereby providing previously unattainable access to education, employment, and inter-cultural exchange to a wide range of learners. Inspire other companies to link profits and social impact and make them co-dependent. Create a business that is as close to human as possible. We will make it clear that we are created by people, for people. Constantly innovate effective, practical, and fun ways to make a positive impact on people, widening our circle of impact broadly along the way. Help millions of people communicate in other languages and become inspired by their own progress. Show them that they are not so different for each other. Help them understand the reasons for their differences.
Values Statement – Our Core Values *What we stand for*	
High performance should be rewarding (fair competition) We are in this together (community & compassion) Individuals can change their lives (determinism) Liberty and justice for all (freedom & equality)	

Figure 6-4:
An example
of strategic
foundations.

Transition Dynamics Enterprises, Inc.

Competitive Advantages – Our DNA *What we do best*	**Vision Statement – Our Future** *Where we are headed*
Providing clear, organized, in-depth training and ongoing support to all professional coaches.	Having a network of certified professionals using the Transition Dynamics program with clients in career and life transitions in U.S. and English-speaking countries.
Mission Statement – Our Core Purpose *Why we exist*	**Vision Description** *What it looks like*
To help people use difficult life transitions as a springboard to create better, more fulfilling lives.	We will have an extensive network of certified professionals in the U.S. and other English speaking countries around the world. We will have a virtual organization that functions smoothly and effectively to support the professionals and their clients. We will continue to develop and provide innovative transition programs that provide end users with hope, insight, and a sense of direction. We will support professionals in building thriving business by providing marketing, sales and business strategy training, materials and community support.
Values Statement – Our Core Values *What we stand for*	
Generous with time, knowledge, and materials. Sharing what we've learned so new business don't have to recreate the wheel. Responsive to requests, problems, and inquiries Thorough, efficient, streamlined programs Committed to the success of the team.	

Figure 6-5:
Another example of strategic foundations.

Part III
Sizing Up Your Current Situation

The 5th Wave   By Rich Tennant

"I ran an evaluation of our last pie chart.
Apparently it's boysenberry."

In this part . . .

Strategic planning is as much about planning and execution as it is about decision making. Good decision making comes from collecting the right data on which to base your decisions. In this part, you figure out what internal and external information to collect and analyze to assess your business and its capabilities. You also take a peek at your company through the eyes of your customers.

Chapter 7

Assessing Your Business and Its Capabilities

In This Chapter

▶ Summarizing your strengths and weaknesses

▶ Evaluating how to hire, develop, and retain your best and brightest employees

▶ Checking out your capabilities and resources and linking them together

▶ Assessing your profit margins

*I*magine you're setting out on a road trip. You hop on MapQuest or open up the AAA roadmap to select the quickest route from your home to your destination. With your trip plan in mind, you consult your friend because he traveled that road before. After you're feeling good about your route, you check your resources against your trip plan to make sure that you have enough time and gas to get there. Then, you assess your VW bus to ensure that it's in working condition and that your CD carrier (or iPod) is full of great music. You pack your bags and invite two friends because they're fun to have around.

Sound familiar? This situation may sound too methodical, but more than likely, you went through all those steps before you headed out on the road (even if you were driving a beater bus!). Mapping a strategic plan is just the same: Your company needs a roadmap or plan to make the strategic plan work. This chapter focuses on your bus. More specifically, this chapter takes a look at the following points:

▸ **How does being on your bus feel?** How it feels on the "bus" is your company culture — teamwork, leadership, climate for action.

▸ **Are the right people on your bus and in the right seats? Are you keeping them there?** The bus passengers are your employees who represent their skills and capabilities, too.

> ✔ **What type of bus are you driving?** The type of "bus" you drive indicates your operations — lean and mean or clunky and slow.

> ✔ **Does your bus run with the right amount so there is something left-over for your shareholders?** This is your profit margin, which indicates how well you used your resources to get to where you wanted to go.

Using the road trip analogy helps explain the unexplainable in strategic planning. Understanding how your company's resources, capabilities, and processes are used to grow the organization is critical to successfully executing your strategy and growing your company. Often, pinpointing all the things that need to come together to move a company forward is difficult.

This chapter focuses on assessing your company's strengths and weaknesses that define where you stand today. Later, you use this information to guide the goals and objectives in your strategic plan.

Identifying Your Strengths and Weaknesses

To move from where you are today to where you want to go, you have to determine your *strategic position*, where you stand today. It's kind of like taking your bus into a mechanic for the annual tune-up. You get an assessment of what's working, what's not, the things you need to fix, and the things that can wait.

In this chapter and Chapters 8 and 9, you perform an annual tune-up of your business with the help of a trusted business planning tool: the SWOT. SWOT stands for **S**trengths, **W**eaknesses, **O**pportunities, and **T**hreats. The four quadrants in Figure 7-1 help you focus on the key factors that define your strategic position.

Your focus in this chapter is on your company's strengths and weaknesses; Chapter 8 looks at your strengths and weakness too, but through the eyes of your customers. In Chapter 9, you focus on identifying your opportunities and threats. You see the SWOT again in Chapter 12 when you develop your company's goals and objectives based on this information.

By breaking down your internal environment into capabilities, resources, and processes, you have a place to start assessing your company. Without these categories, the task can seem a little daunting. This format ensures that you're looking at your strengths and weaknesses holistically, instead of approaching them haphazardly. (To complete the full SWOT analysis, turn to Chapter 9.)

Internal   **External**

Strengths

Capabilities:
- ☐ Human capital
- ☐ Organizational capital
- ☐ Knowledge capital

Resources:
- ☐ Financial resources

Processes:
- ☐ Operational processes
- ☐ Customer management processes
- ☐ Relationship management processes
- ☐ Innovation processes

Weaknesses

Other Process Areas:
- ☐ Technology management
- ☐ Communication
- ☐ Productivity

Current Customers (Chpt 8):
- ☐ Customer mix
- ☐ Satisfaction
- ☐ Loyalty
- ☐ Strength of your value chain
- ☐ Strength of your value prop

Opportunities

Operating Environments:
- ☐ Political/legal
- ☐ Environment
- ☐ Social
- ☐ Technologies

Industry:
- ☐ New competitors
- ☐ Substitute products
- ☐ Power of suppliers
- ☐ Power of buyers
- ☐ Competitive rivalry

Market:
- ☐ Growing, shrinking
- ☐ Size of markets
- ☐ New markets

Threats

Competitors:
- ☐ Who they are
- ☐ Strengths, weaknesses
- ☐ Strategies
- ☐ Objectives

Figure 7-1:
SWOT Analysis. Determining your strategic position by evaluating your internal strengths and weaknesses.

Your organization's strengths encompass everything your company does well, including capabilities, skills, and resources you can leverage and draw on to execute plans and actions in your company. Weaknesses, conversely, encompass everything that's holding your company back from achieving your goals or serving your customers. Check out the questionnaires in Figure 7-2 and Figure 7-3 for a quick survey of your company's strengths and weaknesses.

Now it's time to dig a little deeper to get more specific about each area. Each section of this chapter is likely to give you insights and ideas about your strengths and weaknesses. To capture all your thoughts and keep them in order, draw a horizontal line across the middle of a sheet of notebook paper. Label the top section *Strengths* and the bottom section *Weaknesses*. For instance, jot down thoughts about your effective customer relationship processes under *Strengths* and problems with employee retention under *Weaknesses*.

As you answer the questionnaires and track your ideas throughout this chapter, you have a good starting point to summarize and add to your key strengths and weaknesses. (Remember, these ideas can become the basis for goals in your strategic plan.) You can then translate those thoughts into a grid like Figure 7-1. After you read through this chapter, you should have enough thoughts to fill in the two left-side quadrants on the grid. Consider this a running list of thoughts about your strategic position as you move through the rest of Part III. You complete your full SWOT at the end of Chapter 9.

	Strengths		Weaknesses		Critical to your growth this year
How good is your company at... ?	**Excellent**	**Good**	**Fair**	**Poor**	
Hiring qualified employees					Yes No
Developing and training employees					
Retaining current employees					
Building employee satisfaction					
Managing the flow of information					
Communicating the vision and strategy of the company					
Managing and completing the key projects deemed critical					
Working together as a team					
Capturing the institutional knowledge					
Sharing and leveraging institutional knowledge					

Figure 7-2: Fill out the questionnaire to get a snapshot of the strengths and weaknesses of your company's intangible assets.

Assessing Your Capabilities

The first phase of identifying your strengths and weaknesses is looking at your capabilities or intangible assets (*intangible* means incapable of being realized or defined). These assets point to why organizations are good or not good at identifying and leveraging people, culture, and knowledge.

By breaking down your capabilities into certain areas, you can start to define your strengths and weaknesses. After they're defined, align them with the strategic direction you want to go. You need people with the skills and knowledge who are motivated and resourceful to make your strategic plan a reality. Otherwise, you just have a bunch of good ideas on a piece of paper.

Human capital: Having the right people in the right seats

How many times have you heard "Our employees are our most important asset"? And how often do you feel like your company (or any company for that matter) backs up that statement? The time has come where big and small businesses alike no longer pay lip service to this statement. The trend is to spend more time and money on recruiting absolutely the best people. No matter how busy you are, it's always better to hire no one than to hire the wrong person.

After you have the right people on your bus, making sure that they're in the right seats means they have the skills and abilities to do their jobs. Just hiring them without training and development is like buying a house and doing nothing to maintain or improve it. You're letting your asset go to waste.

After you get the right people in the right seats, you want to keep them there. Nothing is more harmful and costly than losing good people. Harmful because knowledge walks out the door, and costly because you have to train someone else. So, hiring the best people is good, but hiring the best people and making sure that they're developed with the right skills and abilities is better.

In the following list, evaluate how well you do these management tasks:

- ✔ **Hiring:** Only you can answer whether your current hiring process yields good results. Every company has its own unique approach to evaluating potential employees — personality tests, rounds of interviews, special questions. No one way is superior to another. What really matters is getting the right people on board. But a great way to see quick results in your company, if you're having employee problems, is to hire slow and fire fast.

- ✔ **Developing:** How effective is your training and development program? Do your employees have the best tools and work environment to do their jobs? You may have a formalized program, but, again, what really matters is that your employees are doing their best work and achieving their fullest potential. If employees really are your most important asset, you need to develop them to realize the full value of your investment.

Training and development needs to be linked directly to improvement *at work*. Make sure that you're training for the capabilities that your organization needs to move forward. I'm constantly amazed at how many training programs aren't linked to the overall strategy. For example, if you want to improve your productivity, send your employees to a time management workshop instead of a teambuilding ropes course.

- ✔ **Retaining:** The words *employee retention* hit most business owners in the gut. Managing people can be a hard concept for some people, and retention seems to be the perceived outcome of poor management (which isn't necessarily the case because employees leave for numerous reasons unrelated to their jobs). Nevertheless, do you know the number one reason people leave their jobs? Not feeling appreciated by their boss. Employees need to feel appreciated, challenged, and fairly rewarded to stick around.

> How is your retention rate? Because you have invested a significant amount of time and money into your employees, retaining them becomes imperative. Otherwise, you let your most valued asset walk out the door.

Obviously the outcome of not performing these management tasks well is a high turnover rate. However, you don't want to wait until people leave to make improvements. You can evaluate these three areas through employee surveys, exit interviews, bringing in an HR consultant, and also by monitoring overall employee satisfaction.

GoDaddy.com, the number one Internet domain registrar in the world, is known for putting its money where it really matters. No $5,000 office chairs or $10,000 conference tables. Founder Bob Parsons invests in the two assets that contribute to profitability: people and technology. Although he focuses on keeping costs down, Parsons doesn't scrimp on employee incentives. He gives away televisions, trips, motorcycles, a car, and even a year's rent or mortgage. Why? Because as his call centers grow, he wants them to be a fun place to work. When his people are having fun, his customers are happy because they get to talk to happy employees. When his customers are happy, production and sales go up.

Organizational capital: Getting a feeling for your corporate culture

The second phase in the assessment of your company capabilities is reviewing its organizational capital. Now that you have people on your bus and in the right seats, answer the following questions:

- ✔ How does it feel to be on your bus? (How is your work environment?)
- ✔ Do you and your employees like coming to work?
- ✔ Is everyone getting along?
- ✔ Is someone driving the bus? (Who's running the show?)
- ✔ What is your organizational culture like?

Organizations are made up of people, and the people determine what goes on at work. At the end of the day, every person is responsible for how the work gets done and how the organization functions.

Structure, teamwork, management, and leadership dictate how it feels to be working in your business environment. Evaluate your organizational capital by looking at the following areas:

- **Structure:** Structure does serve a purpose — to have an efficient flow of information for action and decision making. Normally, organizational charts look like a bunch of departments cobbled together because businesses grow and morph over time. Is your organization structured to allow everyone to operate effectively?

- **Leadership:** *Leadership* is the art of getting people to do what you want because they want to. Leadership comes in many styles and flavors, but the end result is the same. Leaders are responsible for setting the vision and the strategy. How is your leadership?

- **Management:** Managers are responsible for making sure that the work gets done and that employees are performing at their peak level. In your company, the lines between leaders and managers may be blurred. Your leaders may be managers and your managers may be leaders. Either way, both are just as important in keeping your bus moving down the road. Is your management team successfully getting the work done and helping your employees achieve their fullest potential?

- **Teamwork:** How do you build a great team? Numerous theories exist that can easily fill the rest of this book. But nothing gets done in business, except maybe answering the phone, without teamwork. For your evaluation, ask yourself if the whole is greater than the sum of the parts. Are your people achieving more together than apart?

Each of these areas has industries built around it. If you are looking to dig into improving one or more of them, look to an outside consulting firm or training course that focuses on the discipline specifically.

Patagonia — an environmentally-conscious, highly innovative outdoor clothing company — is notorious for its enviable culture. Under founder Yvon Chouinard's leadership, the company has reached $240 million in annual sales. The business continues to maintain a complete and total commitment to environmentalism as well as blending work and play. At times, profitability takes a lower priority than upholding the corporate values The corporate culture emanates from the top through Chouinard's philosophy and leadership style. His thoughts are consistently supported by managers, teams, employee internship programs, and the company's lack of cubicles. Surfing at lunchtime or taking major customers skiing is part of Patagonia's business and its culture.

Knowledge capital: Knowing what you already know

The third phase in the assessment of your company capabilities is reviewing its knowledge capital. The institutional or tribal knowledge, as I like to call it, is one of those management fads that come and go. But regardless of what may be hip in the business traditions of today, creating and maintaining an efficient knowledge management system to share information companywide seems like common sense.

Most companies don't maintain and retain knowledge very well because, by some estimates, up to 70 percent of what employees do is nothing more than reinventing what their organization had discovered previously. And why do you want your people wasting time figuring out what someone else in the company has already discovered? Information is an intangible asset that can be a significant competitive advantage if you can harness it.

At its simplest form, managing your tribal knowledge is figuring out a way to capture everything your organization knows and then creating an easy way for everyone in the company to access and share that knowledge. Here's an easy process to make improvements in the area of knowledge capital:

1. **Identify what information is actually knowledge.**

   Information is a lot of data put into context. Knowledge is information that has been processed and identified as continually useful to the organization. Knowledge must contribute to your competitive advantage. Identify what are the key areas of knowledge that make your company run. Think about your core processes, customer service, vendor relationships, client relationships and so on. Think about what would happen if your key employees left. What knowledge do they have that you need to capture?

2. **Capture the knowledge.**

   You want to translate the knowledge from your employee to a place where the information can be stored and "backed up." Capturing knowledge can be achieved through exit interviews, standardizing processes, successfully using customer relationships management (CRM) systems with complete customer profiles, job shadowing, and so on. By capturing the knowledge, you're formally bringing what's in someone's head into your business — permanently.

3. **Share your findings.**

   I know, I know, there is too much information in this world already. I agree! Everyone is on information overload. But your tribal knowledge is the type of information that should make everyone's job easier. Figure out ways to share the knowledge in five-minute debriefings at your staff meeting, a company blog, or a training manual for new hires.

4. Use the knowledge.

Now that you have leverage, make sure that you use it. Put the knowledge into practice by cross training current employees, educating new employees if it is within their functional area, and add to the knowledge base continually. If you've done the other three steps correctly, you should see an improvement in overall productivity.

Identify one or two ways to tackle knowledge management this year. Develop a one-year and a three-year goal for your strategic plan. Knowledge disappearance has been a problem throughout time, and what makes the situation more severe today is that the knowledge that's being lost is more complex, abstract, and difficult to create than ever before. More than likely, knowledge management is an area that can use some improvement in your company. You want to protect the information that your company thrives on.

But don't just listen to me. Listen to one of the most successful entrepreneurs: Bill Gates. "The most meaningful way to differentiate your company from your competition, the best way to put distance between yourself and the crowd, is to do an outstanding job with information. How you gather, manage, and use information determines whether you win or lose."

Examining Your Resources

After your capabilities are sufficiently understood, the next step in the SWOT process is looking at your resources. (Refer to Figure 7-1 if needed.) *Resources* are defined as any physical or quantifiable asset that your organization uses to bring revenue into your business. These assets are defined as tangible. Some assets, such as your brand, are intangible but still have a quantifiable value to your company, just like your long-standing customer relationships.

From a strategic perspective, you need to look at what tangible assets you have versus what you need to achieve your strategic plan. You may need to come back to this section after you've developed more of your plan. But taking stock of where you are now can be helpful in your planning process. Specifically, you need to look at

✔ What tangible assets you have in your company right now that allow you to produce your product or service

✔ What tangible assets you need to continue to provide and exceed your current service levels

Create a page entitled Resources. List the assets you have (strengths), the assets you need (weaknesses), and the assets you desire. Consider coming back to this page when you're further along in your plan development.

To help identify your business resources, group them under the following categories:

✔ **Financial resources:** These resources include all the items available to finance or pay for your strategic decisions. Existing resources include cash balances, lines of credit, other loans, owner's equity, and credit agreements with your vendors.

✔ **Physical resources:** Your physical resources include everything you have and use to deliver your products and services. These resources also include

  • *Production facilities,* which may include buildings, plants, machinery, capacity, investment and maintenance, quality, and organization of your production processes.

  • *Information technology (IT),* which includes systems, computers, and critical software in use in the organization and also encompasses integration with customers and suppliers.

✔ **Intangible resources:** Your intangible resources are everything that you can't touch or feel but that you know has value to your business. These sources include

  • **Goodwill:** The difference between the value of your tangible assets and the actual market value of your business.

  • **Reputation:** Your standing in your community and your industry.

  • **Brands:** Your standing and awareness in the marketplace.

  • **Intellectual property:** When you're managing your knowledge, you actually turn a capability into a resource. This also includes patents, trademarks, and copyrights.

Process: Connecting Your Capabilities and Resources

The next step in the SWOT analysis is looking at the processes (see Figure 7-1). Are you cruising down the road smoothly, or is your bus coughing and sputtering along, barely making it to the next service station? More than likely, your company is somewhere between these two extremes. And you probably go back and forth between states of high and low performance. It's time to open up the hood of your bus and find out what's going on in there. In this section, you're looking at the processes that connect your intangible assets to your tangible assets to produce an outcome, which is a current product or service, a new product, customer service, or development and maintenance of relationships with partners and governmental agencies.

When evaluating your internal processes, they need to pass the efficiency/effectiveness test.

✔ *Efficiency* **is doing things right.** Are your processes producing the end result you desire?

✔ *Effectiveness* **is doing right things.** Are you involved in the processes you should be involved in? If not, this is a potential area for outsourcing.

By reviewing your internal processes, you find some that are operating at full efficiency and others that are barely hanging on. Do you have some processes that continually have problems? Are there others that are working just perfectly? Just like with intangible assets, your processes break down into general business areas. Complete the questionnaire in Figure 7-3 to grasp a better understanding of operational, customer, relationship, and innovation processes. These processes are also described further in the sections below.

How good is your company at... ?	Strengths		Weaknesses		Critical to your growth this year
	Excellent	**Good**	**Fair**	**Poor**	
Developing and sustaining supplier or vendor relationships					Yes No
Efficiently producing products and services					
Effectively delivering your product or service to your customer					
Effectively managing operating risk					
Effectively selecting, acquiring, and retaining your customers					
Growing relationships with your customer					
Effectively managing your alliance relationships					
Managing and completing the key projects deemed critical					
Efficiently innovating and bringing new products and service to market					
Leveraging technology to improve operational efficiency					
Consistently and continually communicating the company's key initiative to everyone on staff					
Enhancing employee productivity					

Figure 7-3: Fill out the questionnaire to get a snapshot of the strengths and weaknesses of your company's processes.

Operational processes

Operations produce and deliver the goods and services to customers. These processes encompass managing your creation of customer value.

Service companies may be tempted to think that processes aren't managed in this area, but consider how your service is delivered. It doesn't happen by magic. You take specific steps to deliver what you do: These are your operational processes. Because strategic planning is about improving the status quo, looking at how to improve operations is the key.

Operations management covers four typical processes:

- ✔ **Developing and sustaining supplier or vendor relationships:** Bringing raw material and goods into your company is a set of processes that feed into how you produce products and services. Do you effectively manage your supplier relationships to ensure that you obtain the total lowest cost of the products and services you buy? Are you efficiently sourcing, moving, storing, and inspecting the raw materials you use?

- ✔ **Producing products and services:** At the heart of your operational processes is the production of your product and service. Are you efficient at production, thereby lowering production costs and increasing your asset utilization? Are you effectively producing your product with minimal scrap, error rates, or returns?

- ✔ **Delivering the product or service to your customer:** Just like with managing your suppliers, you also have processes that manage your distribution. Are you efficiently delivering your products or services to your customers? Are you effective at reaching your customers through your distribution channels?

- ✔ **Managing operating risk:** Not all companies have direct operating risk, but most all are exposed to some kind of risk associated with market fluctuations. Processes in this area deal with effectively and efficiently reducing costs associated with capital costs and taxes.

Erlach Computer Consulting, a small technology service company, improved the one key operational process that nearly doubled the company's revenue in one year. The process? Time tracking. Yes, the process may sound simple, but for Erlach, time is the company's inventory, product, and distribution medium. Starting from the top, management required every employee to track his or her time down to the 15 minute increment. The company was doing this previously, but not with 100 percent compliance. Now that the time is captured, Erlach can account and bill for previously unbilled time. Not only were the employees more conscious of their work day, but clients were also correctly charged for the services they received.

Customer management processes

Customer management processes cut across all your customers — current and new. In evaluating your performance, written or unwritten, your organization goes through the following processes when acquiring and serving your customers:

- ✔ **Selecting customers:** Are you identifying the right customers whose problems you can solve? (Chapter 11 helps you to identify your key customers.)

- ✔ **Acquiring customers:** A quick way to evaluate this process is to look at your customer conversion rate. How many prospects are you turning into customers? How effective is your marketing strategy? Is your message the right one, and does it hit the right people at the right time?

- ✔ **Retaining customers:** Assuming that you've landed the right customers and are able to deliver what you promised, your customers should be sticking with you. While you are acquiring new customers, you still want to take care of the old ones. Word of mouth is also important here. When your customers are highly satisfied, they tell their friends.

- ✔ **Building relationships with your customers:** Are you growing your relationships with your customers or are they stagnant? You can measure this success by seeing if your customers are buying more from you year after year.

Scandinavian Airlines realizes the importance of managing its customers' relationships by breaking down customer relationship management processes to their most basic, uncomplicated level. Jan Carlzon, CEO, says "Last year, each of our 10 million customers came in contact with approximately five SAS employees, and this contact lasted an average of 15 seconds each time. Those 50 million 'moments of truth' are the moments that ultimately determine whether SAS succeeds or fails as a company."

Relationship management processes

Organizations don't operate in an isolated pool with just their employees and their customers. Instead, every company and department has relationships with the communities they operate in, governmental agencies, and partners such as other companies, industry associations, and maybe even competitors. Your company may need to manage relationships with all or a few of these entities because everyone is a piece of the bigger picture.

These relationships breakdown into the following areas and processes:

- ✔ **Environmental stewardship:** If your company impacts the environment, how effective are you at managing your resource consumption, water and air emissions, waste disposal, and overall environmental impact?

- ✔ **Employee well-being and compliance:** How is your employee health and safety performance? Are you efficiently taking care of your employees to minimize any safety accidents or repetitive stress injuries?

- ✔ **Community contributions:** Are you investing in your community through nonprofit organizations or other community programs? Small organizations tend to take a hit-or-miss approach to this, meaning that they don't consistently contribute to an ongoing charity. Consider the time and energy savings with a consistent community outreach program.

- ✔ **Alliance management:** Are you efficiently taking care of the organizations you work with? Do you have a consistent approach to managing these critical relationships? Are you effective with your alliance? In other words, are you working with the right ones?

Maximizing profits is just part of running a big business, according to John Mackey, CEO and cofounder of Whole Foods — the nation's leading natural and organic grocery chain with $4.7 billion in annual sales. He feels there is a larger trend toward businesses having a greater responsibility in society. Employees, customers, and shareholders all want their businesses to be good corporate citizens. Mackey believes that profits and being a good citizen go hand-in-hand. He puts his money where his mouth is, with 5 percent of annual net profits going toward charitable causes as well as numerous community programs.

Innovation processes

The fourth part of reviewing your processes involves taking a look at your creativity. If you're not innovating, you're dead. (At least that seems to be the general consensus of the business community, but I have yet to see anyone keel over!) Without innovation, anyone can imitate what you're offering after a period of time. Also, business gets pretty boring if you have the same old stuff. Busting out of the old mold keeps things exciting and employees engaged. Here are the four procedures necessary to make innovation part of your business:

- ✔ **Identify market opportunities for new products or services.** How effective are you at anticipating customer needs and uncovering new opportunities?

✔ **Manage the ideas in your innovation pipeline.** Are you effectively choosing the right products and services to potentially move into full development?

✔ **Design and develop the new products and services that are worthy and that leverage your capabilities.** Are you efficiently moving products and services through the development stages by reducing time and costs? Or do new products languish until they become stale?

✔ **Bring the new products and services to market.** Are you efficiently getting your new product or service in front of your current customers? Do they know about all the offerings you have?

How do you know if you're efficient and effective at innovating in general? Your *new* products and services sell. That's the metric for all the above processes.

"Pound for pound, the most innovate company in America is W.L. Gore & Associates," according to Fast Company, a well-respected monthly business publication. W.L. Gore is known for its premier brand Gore-Tex, as well as other innovative solutions for the electronics, medical, and fabric industries. How do they do it? They operate on five key philosophies that dictate how the company is run:

✔ **Small teams:** With small groups, the company is able to respond and innovate quickly.

✔ **No rank:** Instead of a rigid chain of command, which can delay decision making, the company eliminated rank. All employees are equal.

✔ **Everyone can lead:** Without rank, it gives every employee the opportunity to be a leader.

✔ **Take the long view.** Great innovations can sometimes take years, not months. By recognizing this, the company does not demand results for quarterly shareholder reports.

✔ **Celebrate failure:** Success requires failure. By celebrating failure, the company encourages employees to test every new idea because you never know which one might be a runaway success.

Other process areas

Other process areas are important and support the previously discussed processes. They neither stand on their own, nor do they exist without a process that tangibly produces results. However, highlighting the following three supporting areas make every organization run a whole lot smoother. Please quickly review Figure 7-1 for perspective on these items.

Technology

Technology in and of itself isn't a strategy. Virtually everyone has access to the same technology, so technology can't give you a competitive advantage. What you do with your technology is a different story. Figure out if it makes you faster or slower. Technology should be a tool to make every other process in your company run smoothly and more efficiently (if selected and implemented correctly). To evaluate your IT, here are two quick questions:

- ✔ Do your IT systems improve the overall operational efficiency of your organization?
- ✔ Does the technology platform let employees take the best care of your customers?

Not to oversimplify systems and decisions, which can be very complicated, but instead of getting caught up in the details, these questions help you look at the big picture. What is the strategic decision you need to make in order to improve either your top or your bottom line? IT should be regarded as any other expense instead of a cost center. Is your IT yielding a return-on-investment (ROI)?

Communication

Another big topic that plagues every organization (and every relationship) is communication. If you could get this right, you could retire tomorrow. That's unlikely to happen, though, so the success of your strategic plan rests on your ability to communicate the plan to your employees. While you're assessing your internal operations, assessing your communication methodology is an important area to review, too. As with the other areas in this section, good communication supports your core processes.

Some of the best corporate leaders in the world can tell you that you can't over-communicate. No one ever complains about being too informed. As with your strategic plan and any other critical initiative in your organization,

- ✔ Make sure that your employees hear and understand your message completely. Having three key points works the best.
- ✔ Communicate the key message points again.
- ✔ Repeat the message over and over again in different settings so everyone knows and is completely clear on your points.

Productivity

Improve productivity happens when you work smarter with the resources that you have or get the same results in less time. Being busy isn't necessarily being productive. Aren't you all busy? Who's not? And you may feel productive, but you're only productive if you're producing results that move the company forward. High-value activities — those that are directly related to getting and servicing your business — are the ones that contribute to bottom-line results. Here are some examples of high-value activities:

- ✔ Making sales calls
- ✔ Writing proposals
- ✔ Producing your product or service
- ✔ Serving your customers
- ✔ Managing your employees who deliver your products and services
- ✔ Communicating with your clients

Think about how much time you deal with e-mails that have nothing to do with customer communication. Like spam. According to Nucleus Research, the average employee receives 13.3 spam messages each day. Spam costs U.S. corporations on average $845 per employee per year. Multiple that by the number of people in your company who have desk jobs. Ouch!

E-mail is a low-value activity. What a great way to waste time feeling productive. If you spend a total of two hours out of an eight-hour workday on e-mail, that's 25 percent of your time. Unless that 25 percent of your time is producing at least 25 percent of your total income, it's a low-value activity. Now granted, e-mail can be a time-saver. But it's only a high-value activity when you're communicating with your customers.

Chris is a sole proprietor who owns Amplitude, an organizational assessment and employee training company. In a day where she isn't doing a full training session, she may write a proposal, go to lunch with a contact from a networking event, make some prospect calls, pay her bills, and organize her files. All these activities are important, yet only writing the proposal and making prospect calls directly brings in business. Chris' productivity improvement comes in making more prospecting calls and spending less time paying bills. In fact, she recently hired an assistant with the extra money she makes from one additional sale.

Checking Your Profit Margins

Are you ready to make more money in your business? Who isn't? Even if you're running a nonprofit or government agency, you're always looking at improving your profit margins. Your margins tell you how much is left over after you've paid your direct expenses. It is how much gas is left in the tank when you arrive at your destination. So what's the secret to making more money? Stop doing things that lose money. Now, before you roll your eyes, don't overlook the simplicity of this statement.

Here's a classic example of losing money: A mid-sized business-to-business software company realized that every dollar of revenue generated from its marketing campaigns cost the business about $1.20. Result: The marketing campaign is costing more than it's worth ($1.00–$1.20). Attributing marketing dollars directly to the sales generated can be a rude awakening.

Ready for some ideas on how to improve your margins? As you read through this list of ideas to follow, keep adding to your list of strengths and weaknesses on that notebook page.

Identifying cash creators

Here are some quick cash creators that yield lasting results in a short time:

- ✔ **Do an expense shakedown.** Take time at least once a year to scrutinize each and every company expense. Remember that old habits die hard. Evaluate your travel expenses, telecommunication expenses, insurance costs, subscriptions, and so on. If the expense doesn't contribute to your company's profitability, eliminate it. You're just about guaranteed to find areas in which costs can be reduced or cut out entirely.

- ✔ **Clip coupons.** Okay, not exactly coupons, but find good deals on business services. Everyone from Costco to Microsoft is catering to the small- to mid-sized business market. Make those companies win your business by comparison shopping. This idea is great when you're talking telephone or cellular phone plans, suppliers, or even interest rates on company credit cards.

- ✔ **Increase your prices.** Not everyone can do this. But if you can back up your price increase by better products, service, and quality, you're likely to keep all your customers. Most people are accustomed to the idea of getting what they pay for. (I have heard the advice of increasing your prices 10 percent per month until you lose 10 percent of your business. Then stop. You might try it again when you improve your products and services. The concept is interesting and it may have some value for your business.)

- ✔ **Be clear about your payment terms.** From the get-go, institute a consistent and firm payment process. Most customers appreciate your professional approach if the way you do business is clear.

You may consider letting your clients make payments over time, but the costs of having customers who pay late is significant, not only on the cash side but also on time spent on collections.

✔ **Ask for more business.** Do your current and past clients know about all the services you offer? Not only should you educate your customers annually about what you offer, but also ask for more business. Chances are, you'll get it. In Chapter 8, you discover more on this subject.

Detecting cash drains

Check out the following ways to detect cash drains and improve your margins:

✔ **Fire "loser" customers.** Remember that you're in business to make money. Customers that are costing you money need to be evaluated. The reality is that some customers aren't worth having, even though you spent time and money getting them. Examples of these type of customers include

- Those who take up too much of your time compared with the profits they generate

- Those who consistently fail to pay on time

- Those who always want more but don't want to pay more

✔ **Market wisely.** No matter what, marketing can be expensive. Whether you're spending money on a TV campaign or paying your employee's salary while she attends a networking event, you need to make sure that your marketing dollars are well spent. With marketing dollars, you need a tangible ROI. If your marketing strategy can't justify the cost, replace the plan with something better or stop what you're doing and save the money until you can figure out a better solution.

✔ **Break even.** Another common cash drain for service firms is inadvertently charging a lower billable rate than your hourly breakeven rate. The *breakeven rate* is the cost per hour to keep your doors open. If you're selling your time, which is your inventory, for less than your cost of overhead, you have a negative profit margin.

✔ **Keep a** "Because we've always done it that way" **list.** Do you ever wonder why you do something a certain way? If the answer is, "Because we've always done it that way," you may have found a time-and-money-waster in your business. If you find yourself saying "Because we've always done it that way," about a process, put the process on the list to be evaluated.

> One of the biggest culprits is producing reports. Check to make sure that the reports you produce are actually being used. Look for other areas where changes can be made or that can be completely eliminated in order to save money.

Benchmarking your place in the pack

Benchmarks are surveys and assessments that help determine how well your company performs compared to other companies in your industry or business size. Below are just a handful of benchmarking tools available:

✔ **BizStats:** Visit www.bizstats.com for instant access to useful financial ratios, business statistics, and benchmarks. BizStats has effective and understandable analysis of businesses and industries. You can benchmark a business in five seconds for free.

✔ **Solution Sage:** An online tool for assessing middle market business strategic and succession readiness. The Family Business Assessment is a simple and inexpensive strategic and succession assessment tool available to family business owners and their professional advisors. Visit www.solutionsage.com for more information.

✔ **DigitalHatch, Inc.:** This company looks at the key areas successful organizations need in order to grow. The activity areas are specifically correlated to profitability so business owners can see the direct link between action and ROI. Industry specific assessments are available. Point your Web browser to www.growthassessment.com.

✔ **The Business Report Card:** This assessment helps companies pinpoint strengths and weaknesses, capitalize on an existing client base, develop invaluable networks and alliances, and increase profitability. To see if you're making the grade, go to The Business Report Card at www.mybusinessreportcard.com.

✔ **B2B Benchmarking Association:** This association brings together a variety of companies for the purpose of process improvement and identification of "Best Practice" companies through benchmarking. Check them out online at http://b2bbenchmarking.com.

Chapter 8

Seeing Your Business Through Your Customers' Eyes

*T*he best thing about your business are your customers. You have a group of people who like what you sell, find your product or service valuable, and give you money in exchange for a bundle of benefits. Seeing your business through your customers' eyes is one of the best ways to uncover the strengths and weaknesses of your organization.

When you neglect your customers, you tend to assume that you know them, what they want, and that they'll continue to buy from you. Businesspeople come up various reasons to neglect their customers (intentionally or not):

- ✔ It takes too much time.
- ✔ It's too expensive to do customer research.
- ✔ You're scared to hear what your customers really think.
- ✔ You don't have time to implement customer recommendations.
- ✔ Your sales are up, so customers must be happy.

In this chapter, you discover some easy ways to get past these excuses to uncover your current customers' needs and wants as well as creating customers for a lifetime. Odds are you could be conducting more business with your existing customers by looking at your operations through their perspectives. Armed with this information, you can make strategic decisions that raise your worth in the eyes of those customers who're most valuable.

Getting to Know Your Most Valuable Customers

Not everything in this world is created equal, and neither are your customers. Most companies lose about 25 percent of their customers every year for a variety of reasons. What is important, is to recognize that you'll lose customers, yet it's common business knowledge that it's substantially cheaper to maintain existing clients instead of acquiring new ones. With this in mind, organizations get trapped in a continuous cycle of trying to fill a leaky customer bucket.

There are two reasons for leaks:

- ✔ Businesses spend a disproportionate amount of money trying to keep all of their customers happy.

- ✔ Businesses try to hold on to every customer, which isn't statistically possible, while constantly seeking new customers and neglecting their best customers.

How can you can stop your customer bucket from leaking? The key is to focus your time and money on the 75 percent of the customers who're likely to stay with you.

Do you need more convincing to keep your current customers happy? Check out these statistics from The Center for Customer Focus that just may persuade you:

- ✔ For every one complaint there are 26 silent or dissatisfied customers.

- ✔ Your buyers aren't complaining; they're just not buying from *you*.

- ✔ Sixty-three percent of silent customers will switch suppliers.

- ✔ Unsatisfied customers will express their dissatisfaction to at least nine other people.

- ✔ Roughly 65 percent of customers are dissatisfied because of the feeling of indifference (everything from a bad attitude to not returning an e-mail) by someone at the company.

- ✔ Your loyal customers will tell three other people about how great you are.

If you take the previous list of statistics into account, you just eliminated 25 percent of your most valued customers. Only 75 percent remain, which could be thousands of customers, depending on the size of your organization. The process of building relationships with all of your constituents and seeing your business from their perspective can be daunting. But don't worry, you can make one more cut before you identify your most valued customers.

The 80/20 customer

Many businesspeople have heard about the 80/20 rule, which states that about 80 percent of company sales come from about 20 percent of its customers. Also known as the *Pareto principle*, this rule was named after the Italian economist Vilfredo Pareto who observed in 1906 that 20 percent of the Italian population owned 80 percent of Italy's wealth. Looking further, he noticed that 20 percent of the pea pods in his garden accounted for 80 percent of his pea crop each year. You can chalk this up to coincidence or sheer luck, but either way, Pareto applied this rule to pretty much everything in his life.

Of course it can be argued that the 80/20 rule is totally hypothetical, but when it comes to business, this simple hypothesis can help you identify who your most profitable customers are.

Here's how to find your 80/20 customer:

1. **Determine your total sales for last year or last quarter.**

2. **Run a report of total sales by each customer or account.**

3. **Identify the individual customers that account for the biggest percentage of your sales by dividing the total customer purchase into total sales for the period.**

These remaining customers are your best few. They're the ones that trust you, enjoy your products and services, and are most likely to buy from you again and again. According the Howard Hyden, founder of The Center for Customer Focus, your existing customer base is five times more likely to buy from you than go to an unknown company. Did you know that these 20 percent who've purchased from you once will buy from you again? What's the catch? You have to ask them! One-fifth of your customer base is just waiting for you to follow-up with them and offer them something new. Talk about leaving money on the table!

These customers aren't only the key to your growth, but also the "lifetime value" of your business.

Determining the lifetime value of your customer

Just how valuable are your customers? A calculation called "The Lifetime Value of a Customer" translates value into hard dollars. The outcome of this calculation represents a relatively accurate estimate of your customer's value to your company over the lifetime of that customer's business.

The following calculation doesn't determine profit, but instead the overall customer value that could eventually be realized in the best-case scenario that a customer stays with you forever.

Find out for yourself just how much money each of your customers is worth to you. Use Figure 8-1 along with the following instructions to calculate your customers' merit:

1. **What is the average sale or amount of money a customer spends per month?**

   Add up your total dollar sales for a year and divide that by the total number of sales transactions you completed. I recommend using the average sales of your 80/20 customer.

2. **How many times a year does an average customer buy from you?**

   Estimate the frequency of purchase of a normal customer. A typical grocery store customer probably shops 52 times per year. A consulting company may only do one project per year for an average client.

3. **What is the expected number of years a customer will use your services or buy your products?**

   The expected number of years is very unique to each company. Think about how long you anticipate maintaining relationships with the majority of your customers. This configuration will give you a good number to work with.

4. **How many people per year does your average customer tell about your company?**

   You may have to make a guess here. It's probably between 3 and 12. Generally, the better your customer service, the higher this number will be.

5. **What percentage of these people actually become customers?**

   The average is usually between 20 and 70 percent. This is a pretty large range, so pick a percentage that you feel comfortable with given your industry.

6. What is the lifetime value of your average customer?

Use the formula listed in Figure 8-1 to calculate the lifetime value of your customers with and without the impact of referrals.

Calculating the Lifetime Value of a Customer to Your Business	
Category	*Your Estimate*
1. Average sale per customer	
2. Number of sales per year per customer	
3. Number of years customer buys from you	
4. Number of referrals from customers	
5. % of referrals that become customers	
6. Lifetime value before referrals Calculation: Gross sales per year per customer (1x2) X number of years customers buy from you (3) =	
7. Lifetime value of referrals = Calculation: Referrals who became customers (4x5) X lifetime value before referrals (6) =	
Total Lifetime Value of a Customer (6+7)	

Figure 8-1: Determining the lifetime value of your customers.

Take a look at how Strategic Essentials, a personal coaching business, applies this calculation: If each coaching session is $150 and the average customer has two sessions a month, gross sales per customer is $3,600 per year. Estimating that a customer stays with a personal coach on an average of five years, the lifetime value of this customer, before referrals, is $18,000. Customers that see results from personal coaching will more than likely tell their friends. The power of positive word-of-mouth magnifies the value of each customer. Conservatively estimating that each customer tells four people, and 50 percent of those referrals, or two people, become customers, the gross sales from referrals is $36,000. Therefore, the total lifetime value of a customer is $54,000 (the gross sales per customer plus gross sales from referrals). Wow! Doesn't that change the importance of a $150 per hour client?

Whether your lifetime value figure is three figures, six figures, or more, producing a concrete dollar figure gives you a tangible point around which to design customer strategies. Starting today, build the following ideas into your strategic plan and into your daily activities:

Other departments are your customers too

As a department manager, you rely on other departments and groups to get your job done. Thinking about those other departments as customers can help if you need to move from single department thinking to cross-departmental thinking. Besides, departments are always resource constrained. If you grease the skids of your relationships with other departments by thinking about how you provide value to them, you'll be able to see better uses of company resources. Maybe you can't find money in your budget to implement a new order tracking system, but with the IT department's help, showing them the value, you can work cooperatively to benefit everyone. Taking a customer approach to working with other departments can often turn poor relations around. Ultimately, you should be doing things that are good for your department, your company, and your internal customers.

✔ **Step up satisfaction.** Now that you can see in cold, hard cash the importance of customer satisfaction, you want to step up the level of customer contentment. Satisfied customers lead to loyal customers, and loyal customers lead to referring customers.

✔ **Support the customers who refer business to you.** The impact of positive word-of-mouth has a multiplying effect in the lifetime value calculation and also in the marketplace.

✔ **Hang your Lifetime Value of a Customer number in your breakroom.** Make sure that everyone understands the value of your customers. Keep this number in mind when you're dealing with disgruntled customers or prioritizing your daily activities.

✔ **Cut out any activity that signals indifference to your customers.** These activities send your clients packing. You know indifference when you're on the receiving end. Examples include sitting on hold for longer than you want to, delayed replies to e-mails or voicemails, lack of follow-through, and general carelessness.

Digging into Why Your Customers Are Your Customers

It's time to uncover why your customers buy products from your company or use your services. If you ask companies what they sell and then turn around and survey their customers to ask what they buy, it's usually not the same thing. Generally speaking, your customers will give you a different answer or express it in a different way. Quickly query a handful of your customers to see it this holds true for your organization. Here is what to ask:

  ✔ Who buys?

  ✔ What do they buy?

  ✔ Why do they buy?

  ✔ When do they buy?

  ✔ How do they buy?

Take Netflix, an online DVD rental service, for example. Employees might say that they sell a service that allows customers to check out and return DVD rentals through the mail. Conversely, customers would say that they're buying convenience. In order to see your business through the eyes of your most valuable customers, you have to understand what your customers think they're really buying from you. You have to think like your customers.

Answers to these questions can be found in information and feedback all around you. Some of that information is easy to obtain and some takes a bit more work. The following sections provide you with a list of methods you can use to find out why your customers are your customers.

Satisfaction by the numbers

Measurements and metrics abound in our companies today. *Customer-focused metrics* are a quick way to determine customer satisfaction. You can benchmark these metrics off industry standards, but more than likely, you know what you want these numbers to be for your company. Are you hitting or missing the mark? Which metrics are the most important to your customers?

Customer-focused metrics are numbers about activities that are important to your customers. You can measure a lot of different parts of your business; some of the data is meaningful and some is garbage. But if you want to see your business through your customers' eyes, track the items that they care about. Here are some ideas to get your wheels turning. Customer-focused metrics are very company-specific. Ask yourself, what do your customers care about? Make sure you are measuring it.

  ✔ **Volume by customer or client:** Track customer sales by dollars or units per month and see if your 80/20 customers are starting to order less frequently.

  ✔ **Growth by customers or clients:** Customers may be growing significantly, but you need to also watch if the number of orders from them is increasing. If it's not, you may be missing a valuable growth opportunity.

- **Referral rate:** This number is the most important for the growth of your company. If your customers are referring you, they're happy. If they aren't, you have a problem.

- **Time to respond to customer questions and inquires:** How long does it take you to respond to a customer request? Studies show the longer the inquiry remains unanswered, the cooler the lead gets by 1 percent each day. Response time is a big indicator of indifference.

- **System-up time:** This factor measures the percentage of time a company's equipment or technology systems are up and running to serve your customers. If the product or service is unreliable, it reduces the value in the customers' eyes.

- **On-time delivery:** If your product doesn't get to the customer when he expects it, the value of your product is diminished.

- **Error rate:** How many mistakes are made when entering customer orders or delivering completed projects? Tracking your error rate is a good indicator of customer satisfaction. If your error rate goes up, likely your customer satisfaction is going down. Clearly you don't want that to happen.

- **Returns/rejects/do-overs:** This indicator focuses on how many products or projects come back to you. Obviously is you have to fix a problem project or a defective product, it costs your company time and money. And you probably have an unhappy customer.

- **Overall satisfaction:** If you collect customer satisfaction data, make sure to monitor it regularly.

Look how you're doing in each of these areas compared with where you want to be. This difference gives you a glimpse of your company's strengths and weaknesses. Determine which customer-focused key indicators you want your business to measure and quantify, and then establish a baseline of current performance, and set goals to increase performance in these critical areas. You can obtain your measures through your internal data sources such as customer surveys, CRM systems, fulfillment systems, and so on. If you don't have a source for a metric you want to track, ask an employee to track it for you until you can set up a system to automate it.

Most organizations know what performance they want to achieve for specific metrics. However, if you are looking for outside validation, check out your industry association. Such associations usually have industry benchmarks.

Obtaining feedback without using a survey

Spending tons of money and months collecting customer feedback can be too overwhelming and cost prohibitive for many companies. But still, obtaining feedback is crucial for the ongoing success of your company. You can easily retrieve information during the normal course of your business day.

Here's a list of easy ways to obtain feedback from your customers without using a standalone survey:

- ✔ **At the point of purchase:** There's no time like the present,. Ask for feedback at the moment when the transaction takes place. This can be face-to-face, on the phone, or over live chat. Customers might not be as honest at this point, but ask a question that is not directly related to the employee and you are more likely to get better answers.

- ✔ **Order forms and invoices:** Include a comments box on your forms and include a business reply envelope for your customers to send back the information.

- ✔ **Online:** Add a "Tell us what you think" link (preferably in the header or footer) on every page of your Web site.

- ✔ **Sales reps:** Set up a easy way for your reps to feed information back into your organization such as through an internal discussion board or intranet that reps access.

- ✔ **Newsletters:** If you send one out, include a question or two. Newsletters can be great tools to find out timely customer information. Instead of asking service questions, consider asking about their industry or business climate. Make sure to only ask one, at most two, questions.

- ✔ **Telephone:** Make sure that your voicemail tells customers how to give you feedback.

- ✔ **Comment cards:** Include comment cards inside your shipments.

- ✔ **Support calls:** Your technical and customer service reps hear tons of information from your customers. Set up a general system to collect the feedback these employees hear every day.

Consider Lexus, the luxury car manufacturer. Management requires that every employee, from the top to the bottom, interview ten customers every month. By doing so, the company creates a culture that regularly puts customer information in the hands of every employee.

Spend time talking to your customers

When all else fails, ask your customers why they buy from you! Ask these questions of your 80/20 customers:

- ✔ What are we doing that's great? What is working?
- ✔ What isn't working and needs improvement?
- ✔ What else would you like to see from our company? What else could we do to make your life easier?
- ✔ If we ceased to exist, what would you do? What would you be giving up?
- ✔ If a friend was in search of <fill in your type of company>, would you refer us? Why or why not?

Sam Walton, of Wal-Mart, reportedly spent five days every month interacting with customers in his stores. This amount of dedicated time kept him close to and in touch with his customers needs and wants. Although I doubt his customer attention was the only reason for Wal-Mart's runaway success, it surely played a big part.

Gathering feedback from a variety of sources results in an objective, comprehensive picture of who your customers are, what they want, and what they value. However, collecting the information is only half of the equation. Ensure that everyone in the company knows what customers are thinking by sharing customer feedback through the organization. By spreading the news, everyone will start to make better, more informed decisions. For your strategic plan, you can use the information you collected over the years to make calculated decisions that have broader implications.

Uncovering How You Deliver Value to Your Customers

For many owners and department managers, focus represents the biggest roadblock to corporate growth. It's not exactly a lack of focus; it's more the tendency to unintentionally focus on the wrong things. Because strategic planning is about focusing on the right things, keep your customers' values in the forefront of your planning efforts. Your company is operating in its sweet spot when you're focused on

✔ What you're good at doing

✔ What you like doing

✔ What the market values you for doing

Connecting the dots between these three elements is critical because organizations can easily lose focus on what their customers and the market truly value.

Unfortunately, the term "value" is one of those undefined and vague business concepts that sounds good and important but isn't easy to get your arms around. When the benefits of a product or service outweigh the costs, you have value. Value makes something sweeter, better, stronger, faster. You can have pancakes without syrup, but what's the point? Value is the icing on the cake. The result of providing superior value is wildly satisfied customers who keep coming back again and again and bring their friends.

Home Depot not only has the best selection on all home improvement products, but also it offers know-how through free classes or on its online resource center. These processes and extras add value and create extremely loyal customers.

Unlocking the value chain

One of the best ways to understand value in your organization is to construct a value chain. A *value chain* is a way to look at your processes through your customers eyes.

A value chain is defined as

✔ A tool to dissect your organization into core and supporting activities

✔ A holistic look at your organization and how departments work with other departments

✔ A way to prioritize resources and activities based on your customer needs

✔ A method to see each and every way you interact with or "touch" your customers through your organization.

You can't get to true customer satisfaction that leads to ultimate loyalty if you don't have an understanding of your processes from the patrons' perspective. And the value chain is the best way to see how your internal process impacts customer loyalty.

Printing up a superior customer experience

When a weekly community newspaper analyzed its value chain, the publisher realized that several of its supporting activities detracted from the overall customer experience. For example

✔ In the general administration area, the newspaper's invoices only offered one method of payment, when there were actually three ways to pay. The publisher immediately revised the invoices to include all options. The cost to the company was next to nothing as they were computer-generated. Decrease in delinquent accounts: 40 percent.

✔ In the human resource management area, the organization's high turnover rate made customers question the viability of the newspaper. The publisher instituted a more rigorous hiring process that included a third-party skills and personality assessment to make sure that the right people were "on the bus."

✔ In the area of technology, the newspaper didn't have an online renewal form. This feature was quickly added, which allowed subscribers to maintain their subscriptions with a click of their mouse instead of calling, faxing, or snail mailing in their renewal forms.

Don't these changes seem obvious and straightforward? It's easier to see the errors of others or after someone points them out to you. Well, it wasn't until the publisher used the value chain that he realized where the links were broken. The organization's core product is highly regarded in the community, but the supporting activities were hindering business growth.

A value chain comprises primary and secondary activities. The links in the chain help you to better understand at what point in your processes you're adding value to the customer's product or service.

The primary activities in your value chain are activities that are directly concerned with creating and delivering your product or service. These activities are as follows:

✔ **Research and development:** Activities such as developing technology, researching product ideas, and finding suppliers and vendors that relate to what goes into the development of a product or service

✔ **Operations:** Activities related to production, assembly, packaging, quality assurance

✔ **Distribution and delivery:** Activities associated with getting the product or service to the customer

✔ **Marketing and sales:** Activities such as advertising, sales force efforts, promotion, and dealer and distributor support that relate to reaching the customer

✔ **Servicing:** Activities associated with after-sales support and assistance to buyers

The secondary activities in your value chain support and strengthen your company's primary activities. These activities aren't directly involved in production but may increase your effectiveness. These processes include

✔ **General administration:** General management, finance, accounting, and legal

✔ **Human resource management:** Recruitment, hiring, training, development, and compensation

✔ **Technology and systems:** Technology systems and telecommunication systems

✔ **Procurement:** Purchasing raw materials and supplies and services

It's rare for a business to undertake all of these activities. For example, an employment agency doesn't have any raw materials, so the procurement area is unutilized.

Developing your value chain

By developing your company's or department's value chain, you'll be able to see where you're adding and delivering value to your customers and where you aren't. This addition is a great way to uncover areas that need improvement in your operations, in your delivery, and in the coordination between departments.

You can develop your value chain by using the framework illustrated in Figure 8-2. Break up your activities into primary and secondary activities and only list the ones that are key to your business.

1. **Break down your organization into its key primary areas using the framework in Figure 8-2.**

   Revise the headings to fit your company. List the areas in order from the first good idea to the finished product or service.

2. **List your key supporting or secondary areas.**

   As with your primary areas, revise the headings in the form to fit your company.

3. **List one or two key activities for each of the primary areas.**

   For each area that your company undertakes that adds value, think about it from your customer's perspective.

4. **List one or two key activities for each of the supporting areas.**

   It can be more difficult to see how these activities contribute to the end product or service. But look critically and think about how an area such as administration can have an impact on your value chain.

5. **Review each area of your completed framework.**

   Are there any links missing in the chain? Are there places where you aren't adding value that you could? Where could your value chain be stronger? Use answers to these questions to develop goals for your strategic plan.

	Research & Development	Operations	Distribution & Delivery	Marketing & Sales	Servicing
Priority Activities					
Supporting Activities	General Administrative				
	Human Resource Management				
	Technology & Systems				
	Procurement				

Figure 8-2:
Analyzing your value chain.

Kicking Your Value Up a Notch

Take out you big-strategy guns and kick it up a notch. To increase your value, you need to create something that is better or different than your competitors. By constructing your value chain, you now know what you can do in specific areas to improve. In this section, you find out how to have a company- or department-wide approach to providing a unique mix of products and/or services to your customers. By having an organization-wide strategy or value-creating strategies, you can consistently provide a product or service that is better than your competition.

Below are three generally accepted organization-wide strategies. Each of the items in italics are explained in greater detail in the following section.

✔ Providing the lowest cost through *operational excellence*

✔ Providing the best products or services through continued *innovation*

✔ Providing complete *customer solutions* through intimately knowing their needs and wants

In case you're tempted to execute all three, think again. That's called being stuck in the middle or riding the fence. Executing a stuck in the middle strategy is like being in the middle seat of a five-seat row on a 747. You don't know whether to crawl over the mom with her sleeping baby to the right or over the guy with his laptop to the left. It's not a good place to be! Companies that find themselves in this position usually end up in a financial crisis or reorganization. That said, this doesn't mean you don't do the other activities well. You just don't focus on them as much as the ones that are central to creating value for your customers.

A value-creating strategy should be selected for each target customer group that you serve. For smaller organizations or departments, select one strategy for your whole company. Managing multiple value propositions can be nearly impossible.

Selecting your organization-wide strategy really comes down to determining what your customers value the most about what you're providing them. The low prices? Your cutting-edge products? Your ability to deliver a service that fits their needs exactly? Take a look at each option to see which strategy is the best fit for your company.

Creating value through excellent operations

Creating value through excellent operations focuses on appealing to a broad spectrum of customers based on being the overall low-cost provider of a product or service because of the company's focus on efficiency. The company implementing this strategy provides superior value to their customers by offering them lowest total cost.

An operationally excellent value proposition sounds something like this: "We offer products and services that are always consistent, on-time, and low in cost." Check out these goals if you're executing this strategy:

- ✔ To continually offer the most attractive prices
- ✔ To purchase and source from the lowest-cost suppliers
- ✔ To offer excellent and consistent quality
- ✔ To ensure that our company has a good product or service selection
- ✔ To make buying from our company easy and fast

To reach your goals, you need to master your operational processes. This process includes monitoring outstanding supply chain management, super efficient operations to control costs, cycle time and quality, and inventory management.

Paul's Plumbing, a plumbing, heating, and air conditioning company, creates outstanding value through a real-time data system. All of the company's technicians have powerful handheld data systems that allow them to accept service orders, respond to them, and close them all in one smooth process. Through this data system, the company cuts down its operational costs by reducing drive time, service order data entry, and error rates due to lost orders and billing costs. The company's customer satisfaction has soared because most service orders are responded to on the same day as requested, there's little surprise in the final bill, and the company's prices are the lowest across the board.

Other companies that continue to offer the best buy or lowest cost through their excellent internal operations include Wal-Mart, Southwest Airlines, Dell, and Ikea.

Creating value through innovation

This strategy concentrates on creating a unique, innovative product or service line. A company implementing this strategy provides superior value by offering its customers a continuous stream of innovative products or services. It seeks to identify emerging opportunities and continuously strives to develop and deliver new products and services.

A product and/or service leadership value proposition sounds something like this: "We offer products and services that expand existing boundaries past what was thought possible." To execute this strategy, your goals may look something like the following:

- ✔ To strive to be first-to-market with new products, services, or functionality
- ✔ To always produce leading-edge products and services that exceed the performance of competing products
- ✔ To maintain higher prices than competitors because of the superior product
- ✔ To reach new customer groups

You need to master your innovation processes and develop an innovation culture to reach your goals. These steps include a pipeline full of new ideas, a conversion rate of ideas to production, excellent and quick product development processes, and marketing and sales departments that can bring the product to market quickly.

Instead of studying Spanish by going to classes or hiring a tutor, students in Guatemala learned from Spanish tutors through Speak Shop, a Web-based application that allows video and voice conferencing. The company was first to market with this innovative method to connect students and tutors in their homes or at work. To maintain its first-mover position, the company continues to add functionality such as quizzes, lesson plans, curriculum, and discussion boards to enhance its core product.

Additional companies that are always on the cutting edge of their industries include Intel, Mercedes, Sony, and Salesforce.com.

Creating value through knowing your customers

Creating value through really knowing your customers concentrates on a narrow market segment by a deep understanding of its customer and their perception of the value of the product or service offered. A company implementing this strategy provides superior value by tailoring its products or services to match *exactly* the needs of targeted customers. It specializes in satisfying unique customer needs through an intimate knowledge of the customers.

A customer intimacy value proposition sounds something like this: "We provide the best total solution to our customers because we make a practice of know exactly what they need." Try to fashion your goals around the examples below:

- To ensure that our customers feel like we understand them by continually engaging in market research and responding to it
- To provide customized products and services to meet their needs
- To stress exceptional customer service
- To install and effectively use a customer relationship management system
- To offer and sell a complete solution (selling multiple and bundled products and services)

Develop a customer-focused culture to attain these marks. These procedures include offering as many products and services that your customers are looking to you to provide — meaning that you completely solve the problem or need that your customers have.

A rapid software development company develops tools for online collaboration. Based on customer feedback, the company develops additional tools and online applications specifically to meet the needs of their growing client base. In fact, this company is so focused on its customers that it provides a *free* online forum and training for customers to develop their own collaboration tools using its platform.

More example of companies that are providing complete customer solutions include Nordstrom, Goldman Sachs, and Cabela's.

Need more help?

Looking to dig deeper into the topic of customer relations? Here is a list of great resources that can help you see your business through your customers' eyes:

- *Marketing For Dummies,* 2nd Edition (Wiley) by Alexander Hiam: This reference provides a no-nonsense approach to growing revenue from your current customers.

- Creating Customer Evangelists is a free resource of articles, newsletters, and blogs by Ben McConnell and Jackie Huba. Check it out online at www.creating customerevangelists.com.

- The Center for Customer Focus is an organization that offers customer-focus training and workshops. Several free articles are also available on this topic at www. customerfocus.org.

Chapter 9

Assessing Your Strategic Position in a Dynamic Environment

. . . .

In This Chapter

▶ Classifying opportunities for and threats to your operating business

▶ Capitalizing on opportunities in your operating environment

▶ Predicting your industry shifts

▶ Sizing up your competition

▶ Rounding out your SWOT analysis

. . . .

*Y*ou're headed down your strategy road with a bus that is primed and tuned. It's time to look out the windows and check out what is going on around you. How's the landscape? Is it breathtaking or gray? What's happening with the weather and how is the condition of the road? All of these factors influence how smoothly you travel down your path to success.

Assume there are several storms brewing on the horizon. Three to be exact. Each one of them is a little further away from the next. The closer the storm, the more potential impact it will have on your trip. The ones furthest out may or may not impact you, but you keep on eye on them nevertheless. The landscape your company operates in is exactly the same. If you are the bus or at the center, there are three influences on your business. Starting with the outer ring of Figure 9-1, they are

✔ Your operating environment

✔ Your industry, which includes your competitors

✔ Your market

Your Operating Environment

Your Industry

Your Market

Your Organization

Ecological and natural issues

Power suppliers or vendors

Current markets

New markets

Power of buyers

Economic indicators

Customers

Market size

Current competitors

Substitute products

Social and cultural shifts

Global forces

Growing or declining

New competitors

Competitive rivalry

Demographic movements

Technology trends

Political winds

Figure 9-1:
A view of your environment.

Some external influences or factors have more direct impact on your business than others. Others just take a little longer to get there. By looking at your landscape in four areas, you won't miss anything that might be hiding on the horizon.

The success or failure of your organization depends not only on your internal capabilities and resources (strengths and weaknesses, discussed in Chapter 7), but also on things that happen outside of your control (opportunities and threats). All of the information in this chapter helps you identify the forces, issues, trends, and events that can positively or negatively impact your business. What possibilities do you see on the horizon and where are the minefields?

In this chapter, you identify potential opportunities and threats that may impact on your business. You discover some of the larger trends likely to impact all businesses over the next ten years as well as how to spot the ones not covered. Lastly, you bring all the pieces of your SWOT together to create a complete picture of your company's strategic position.

Identifying Opportunities and Threats

When responding to opportunities and threats in your environment, you need to react proactively rather than reactively. Being ready for what ifs can help you determine your strategic position. Figure 9-2 illustrates how these elements fit into your SWOT (also covered in Chapters 7 and 8).

Figure 9-2:
Part of the SWOT analysis determines your strategic position by evaluating external opportunities and threats.

Internal	External
Capabilities:	**Operating Environments:**
☐ Human	☐ Political/legal
☐ Organizational	☐ Environment
☐ Knowledge	☐ Social
	☐ Technological
Resources:	
☐ Financial	**Industry:**
☐ Physical	☐ New competitors
☐ Intangible	☐ Substitute products
	☐ Power of suppliers
Processes:	☐ Power of buyers
☐ Operational	☐ Competitive rivalry
☐ Customer management	
☐ Relationship management	**Market:**
☐ Innovation	☐ Growing, shrinking
	☐ Size of markets
Other:	☐ New markets
☐ Technology management	
☐ Communication	**Competitors:**
☐ Productivity	☐ Who they are
☐ Profit margins	☐ Strengths, weaknesses
	☐ Strategies
Current Customers:	☐ Objectives
☐ Customer mix	
☐ Satisfaction	
☐ Loyalty	
☐ Strength of your value chain	
☐ Strength of your value prop	

Strengths / *Weaknesses* (Internal) · *Opportunities* / *Threats* (External)

You need to take a quick pulse of your company's opportunities and threats to assess your external situation. To do so, investigate the various areas listed in Figure 9-2 to get more specific about what is happening in your operating environment.

After you assess your situation, check out Figure 9-3. The questionnaire can help start your list of opportunities and threats if you're having trouble getting going.

When will this trend impact our company... ?	Now	1-3 years	5-10 years	Never	Opportunity or Threat
Increasing price of oil					
Shrinking middle class					
Potential for more natural disasters					
Declining birth rate					
Customers demanding more customization					
Independence of employees (working from home, changing jobs, etc.)					
Growth of all products related to improving physical appearance					
Use of the Internet to streamline business processes					
Growth of robot and automated technologies					
Growth of open source software					
Changing healthcare policies					
Increased security and terrorism					
Labor shortage and outsourcing					
Graying of America					
Increasing diversity					
Increasing economic achievement of women					
Growth of China as a major economic force					
Shortage of raw materials, creation of new ones					
Increasing population					
Growth of environmental sustainability					

Figure 9-3: The opportunities or threats in your operating environment.

Don't forget to ask for help — getting objective input from others helps you see parts you may have missed. The section "Finishing Your SWOT Analysis" later in this chapter gives you ideas about how to proceed, too. Additionally, use Figure 9-4 to spark some ideas.

When will this force impact our company?	Now	1-3 years	5-10 years	Never	Opportunity or Threat
Increase in the number of competitors					
Potential for substitute products					
Increase in the power of our suppliers or vendors					
Increase in the power of our buyers or customers					
Greater intensity of rivalry between us and our competitors					

Figure 9-4: The opportunities or threats in your industry.

To capture all your thoughts and keep them in order, create a note page with a line horizontally in the middle. Label the top section *Opportunities* and the bottom section *Threats*. Jot down thoughts about a new market under the opportunities section and ideas on a competitor's action under *Threats*. (I use this same notation in other chapters when referring to notes.)

Seeing the Future

How much time do you spend thinking about your company's future? Chances are, not much. For the most part, putting out fires and taking care of the day-to-day tasks consume most of your time. But to be strategic in your business, you must discover how to spot future opportunities and threats as soon as possible. Yes, you do need to identify the immediate forces at work, but you also want to think about and plan for the future operating environment and industry trends. The value lies in anticipating change before it happens, instead of mindlessly reacting to whatever comes at you next.

What changes should you be thinking about? Answering these questions should get you started:

- ✔ Who will your customers be five years from now?

- ✔ How will you reach these customers?

- ✔ Do you regularly improve your product quality and customer satisfaction?

- ✔ What is your company's status as a trendsetter within your industry?

- ✔ Are you aware of new competitive threats on the horizon?

- ✔ Are you focused on catching up to the competition or on innovations in the marketplace?

- ✔ Is management flexible enough to alter your business model as necessary?

- ✔ How does your approach to forward thinking compare to your competition?

Your answers to these broad-reaching questions can tell you a lot about who you are today and what may need to change within your business. The response can also give you a better sense of the type of resources you need to commit to reaching your organization's future. Make sure to push the boundaries. Think about each area in this chapter in terms of the present but also how it affects you five or even ten years down the road.

Finding Opportunities in Your Operating Environment

No one has a crystal ball into the future, but certain trends appear to be in the making, and are worth considering now. Although it's sometimes difficult to know how environmental forces are going to impact your business, they really do matter. Like the weather – you are subconsciously aware of the force, but it's not until a big storm comes that you really pay attention. The important part, like everything in strategic planning, is to figure out which trends matter to your business. Huge successes can come from being aware of environmental forces, as you will see in this section.

Your operating environment is influenced by several general areas. These areas summarize the external environment every organization operates in. Refer back to Figure 9-1 to get a clear picture of influences in your operating environment.

Remember your operating environment is the outside circle influencing your business. Some of these trends and issues may even appear to come and go in slow motion. You may not need to watch them religiously, but having an eye on them could be the key to your company's boom — or bust. Also, some of these issues may seem ridiculous to you or doomsdayish, but what's ridiculous to you, someone else may be experiencing.

In the next several sections, you discover many opportunities in your operating environment.

Identifying your economic indicators

Movements and shifts in the economy affect consumer purchasing power and spending patterns. The state of the United States and world economies can be either an opportunity or a threat for any business depending if your company improves and declines with the economy (real estate) or if the opposite happens (price of gold). Economic indicators can be frustrating to watch because it seems as though today's news contradicts yesterday's report. Nevertheless, the economy is probably one of the biggest influences on your business.

There are many economic indicators that affect businesses. These areas may not be of the utmost importance for every business, but consider this list of common economic indicators:

- Overall economic growth or by industry
- Interest rates
- Government spending
- Changes in employment policies and minimum wage
- Housing costs

✔ Exchange rates, which impact demand from overseas customers

✔ Availability of capital

✔ Consumer confidence

Even outside trends tend to impact economic indicators. Some of these areas are out of our control and are likely to be huge factors over the next ten years. Check and see if you can identify any opportunities or threats for your business in the list below:

✔ **Increasing price of oil:** The general consensus is that the era of cheap oil is probably over.

✔ **Shrinking middle class:** Rich people are getting richer; the number of people in the middle class is shrinking, and the underclass is growing and getting poorer. The result: A larger gap between rich and poor.

✔ **Increasing natural disasters:** The possibility of more natural disasters is a growing concern. These occurrences not only take a human toll but also upset local and national economies.

✔ **Decreasing birth rate:** Some of the world's most powerful economies, Europe and Japan, are losing people faster than they're replacing them. The U.S. is barely hanging on. This means fewer consumers with the money to spend. The implications of this consumer shortage may play out over the next 10 to 20 years.

World Prep sells 30 different types of survival kits, which include items such as thermal blankets, hand warmers, water, and food bars. The company was perfectly positioned to make a profit when natural disasters such as the tsunami, hurricanes Katrina and Rita, and the earthquakes in Iran occurred in 2004 and 2005. In business for six years, World Prep grossed $1.6 million in 2005.

Watching important social shifts

Cultural and societal shifts are probably the hardest to spot because the result of these forces affect a society's general attitudes, preferences, tastes, and beliefs. Catching, or even better, predicting, a social trend can be a home run for your business. Think about the low-carb craze, the reinvention of coffee as a lifestyle, digital music, outsourcing, offshoring, and so on.

Social indicators include issues such as

✔ Labor availability and types

✔ Lifestyle changes such as working from home or single households

✔ Attitudes about work and leisure

✔ Education

✔ Health

✔ Fashion and fads

✔ Business model changes

✔ Living conditions

Here's what to watch for or capitalize on:

✔ **Giving power to customers:** Customers have the ability to dictate product quality, price, service, and delivery standards to retailers and manufacturers.

✔ **Changing the face of a career:** Tomorrow's employee makes more career changes, works a shorter time in each position, demands more independence, and requires greater retraining. More than 45 million people currently work from home.

✔ **Becoming more and more beautiful:** America's obsession with looking beautiful is growing. Products and services around gene therapy ($6.5 billion market in five years), dietary supplements ($16 billion in 2004), and cosmetic procedures (one of every 25 people in 2004) are bound to keep growing at a stratospheric pace.

Staying on top of technology trends

Many people believe that the revolutionary impact technology has had on products, processes, and communication systems has just begun. New technologies and processes continue to change the way organizations operate daily. The problem for most companies is evaluating which advances are truly opportunities and which are distracting.

Failure to monitor and address advances may negatively impact your financial position in the market. Areas to watch include government spending on technology, big new discoveries or products, speed of technology transfer, and changes in business processes as a result of technology.

Here are some trends over the next ten years that may be opportunities or threats to your business:

✔ **Embedding the Internet in every part of our lives:** Internet technologies make it easier to have strategic partnerships; put the customer more in control of the buying process; reduce the costs of customer service; offer new ways to recruit, train, and retain employees; and provide new communication tools.

✔ **Growth of robots:** Robots and other automation-based technologies handle most repetitive tasks.

✔ **More open source programs.** Open source software — where the programming code that runs the application is accessible to anyone — is expected to grab more than 20 percent of the world-wide software market in five years. The estimated cost to software makers is $100 billion in revenue, according to the Gartner Group.

With more than 63 million Americans expected to be hooked up to broadband by 2008, companies large and small are making serious money by doing everything from working virtually, to offering online services, to distributing anything that is digital. Skype, the world's fastest growing Internet telephony provider, was sold to eBay for $2.6 billion. Why the large price tag? It boasted more than 54 million customers worldwide using its service, virtually free.

Monitoring political winds

Keeping tabs on your government's policies and legislation on business related issues is crucial. Decisions made at the federal, state, and local level can have significant impact on how you do business. For example, new taxes can cut into already thinning margins, or cuts can improve them. Or changes in labor laws can impact how you handle your employees.

Naturally, legislative threats or opportunities can occur on the local, state, and national levels. Monitoring the political winds includes taxes, international trade regulations, consumer protection, environmental policies, the pro- or anti- business attitude of the president, and the biggie — healthcare legislation.

Here's what is blowing in over the next ten years:

✔ **Increasing costs of healthcare:** Government policies regarding healthcare coverage are important for business owners to monitor. Right now, benefits are estimated to be 40 percent of compensation costs and healthcare costs are clearly on the rise. This burden is big for businesses, especially if you're watching your margins.

✔ **Increasing security measures:** How the government deals with the security issue isn't going to be solved anytime soon. From wiretapping to hellish airport lines, our lives continue to be invaded for our protection.

The CEO of Verified Identify Pass Inc. took one look at the current security situation and saw a major opportunity. He created the Clear Card, which is a one-stop clearance card with data including a set of fingerprints, iris scan, and a Transportation Security Administration threat assessment. With this card, the owner can easily pass through any private security checkpoint — like the airport. Currently, the company is beta testing its product at several airports.

Flexing with demographic movements

Futurists say that you can't understand the future without demographics. Knowing what is going on with demographic changes and movements helps you plan for the demand for your company's products and services as well as labor issues. For instance, sometimes seemingly unexplainable lulls or growth spurts, especially in the retail and restaurant industries, can be explained by understanding the changes in the demographics.

Here are the big movements that may impact every business in the United States:

- **Labor shortage:** The lack of highly-skilled people is a growing concern. Knowledgeable workers are going to be increasingly in demand.

- **Graying of America:** Right now, the baby boomer generation represents a market of about 36 million people. In five years, the 65+ population will be growing faster than the population as a whole. Opportunities abound for businesses working on producing products and services to meet the needs of older consumers.

- **Increasing diversity:** Minorities, primarily of Latin American and Asian descent, will make up one-third of the U.S. population in ten years. Right now, one in every seven people is Hispanic. In ten years, one in every four people in the U.S. will be Hispanic.

- **Greater economic achievement by women:** By 2016, three million more women can be attending college than men. Education is connected with economic status, therefore women will gain more influence, purchasing power, and leadership.

Senior Insight Inc., a small Denver-based company, is poised to help the Baby Boomers through their later years. The company developed a software package for assisted living facilities, nursing homes, and adult daycare. Unlike a traditional hospital, these facilities need patient records that any caregiver can access for daily instructions on eating, bathing, exercise, and medications. Senior Insight's system is built specifically around long-term care. Revenues have doubled over the past two years and the company knows this is just the beginning.

Going global

Globalization, or doing business with companies and customers around the world, is increasing as quickly as the Internet is growing. The impact of globalization has been felt in every part of our businesses and our lives. These trends stand on their own because of the magnitude of the opportunities or threats that they pose.

Here's what can change the global landscape over the next ten years:

- **Shift of labor:** Money and jobs are still flowing into India at a rapid rate. The National Academy of Sciences stated that India graduated 200,000 engineers in 2004 versus 20,000 in the U.S.

- **Growth of China:** The sheer might of the Chinese economy may force every business to rethink its approach. The World Economic Forum predicts that China will become the second-largest global economy by 2020.

- **Terrorism on the rise:** Society can't be lulled into thinking that terrorism efforts won't increase. It is here to stay. The business opportunity lies in providing security services and products. The threat lies in protecting your assets: physical, financial, and human.

Growing natural

All the government legislation doesn't hold a candle to the impact businesses are having on environmental progress. The resources, constraints, overpopulation, and pollution are just a few of the trends driving environmental products, services, and business practices. The big change in the trend is that the environmental services are now becoming profitable.

Here's what's growing:

- **Shortage of raw materials** and **development of new materials:** With the cost of oil on the rise, demand for non petro-chemical-based materials is increasing. Same goes for other natural resources.

- **Increasing population:** By 2050, the global population is estimated to reach 9.2 billion people.

- **Environmental sustainability:** Huge opportunities exist with reusing, recycling, and creating biodegradable products. Clean energy is booming with solar cells, wind turbines, and eliminating preventable energy loss.

Leave it to DuPont to develop a product to replace plastic. Its newest product is called Sorona, a corn-based version of plastic. DuPont clearly identified the growing threat of high oil prices, and turned it into an opportunity by creating a solution. Sorona, referred to as the new nylon, is expected to hit the streets in a few years and could soon be in everything from underwear to carpet.

Monitoring Your Industry

An industry is a group of companies that sell products or services that are close substitutes of each other, such as the furniture industry, the car industry, or the financial services industry. Knowing the type of industry you're competing in helps you predict changes, movements, or shifts that may impact your business. It's also helpful to know how competitive your industry is because some are more cutthroat than others.

What industry does your company operate in? You can most easily identify it by answering the question, *"If customers were to purchase elsewhere, what are all the potential options that exist?"*

Classify the different types of companies you identify with in small groups until you have a big enough circle to define the entire set. For the most part, identifying your industry is intuitive, but sometimes the nets aren't cast wide enough. For example, a charter sailing company isn't in the cruise industry. Instead, the company is swimming in a bigger pond called the travel and tourism industry.

In an effort to understand the dynamic nature of an industry, you can break any industry into five components or forces: new competitors, substitute products, power of suppliers, power of buyers, and competitive rivalry. These five forces impact every industry in some form or fashion and determine your industry's attractiveness and long-run profitability. Each force is discussed in the next sections.

Looming new competitors

Obviously, the more companies swimming in the same pond, competing for the same customers, the more competitive the industry. Often some competition is better than none. But if it's easy for someone to jump into your industry (for example, restaurants, online services, advertising agencies, and so on), the threat of new competitors is very high. Conversely, if big startup costs and regulatory hurdles have to be crossed —like the construction, airline, and manufacturing industries — your may not feel as threatened. The barriers that exist determine how big of a threat this force is.

Key barriers include

- ✔ Economies of scale (when more units of a good or a service can be produced on a larger scale, yet with, on average, less input costs, economies of scale are achieved)
- ✔ The size of the capital or investment requirements
- ✔ The ease or difficulty of switching from one company to another
- ✔ The ability to access distribution channels
- ✔ The likelihood of retaliation by existing companies

The number of companies developing and selling Customer Relationship Management (CRM) systems seems to grow every year. Companies in this space include Salesforce.com, Siebel, ACT, Microsoft with its Business Contact Manager, Intuit, and Oracle. As more and more companies join the party, the current players see the threat of new competitors increasing. The entry barriers are relatively low except one: the difficulty for customers to move from one platform to another. In fact, anyone who's implemented a CRM system knows that the biggest challenge is getting people within the company to adopt the new system. Moving around from one platform to another is a time-consuming process and can kill your business. Because this barrier is so high, the threat of new competitors to established companies is slightly diminished. The opportunity for the established companies is to grab as much market share as quickly as possible.

Threatening substitute products

With the continual flux of technologies and the speed of development, the threat of a substitute products taking the place of yours is greater than ever before. Substitute products can be an area of opportunity or an area of threat depending on when you catch wind of the change. If you're on top of it, *you* could produce the new product. If you're behind the change curve, you may likely see a decline in demand. The probability that customers will move to a new product or service is based on three areas:

- ✔ The customer's willingness to change
- ✔ The price and performance of the new product
- ✔ The cost to switch

The popularity of satellite radio has exploded over the past several years, with the two main companies, XM Radio and Sirius, grabbing market share as fast as possible. With more and more consumers tuning into satellites instead of radio tuners, traditional radio stations are finding their listener base declining rapidly. Who knows the ultimate fate of AM and FM, but media companies are scrambling to reposition themselves because a substitute product is whisking its customers away.

Bargaining power of suppliers

Suppliers or vendors are any company that provides raw materials, components, or services into your industry. The amount of control your suppliers have over the price of goods you purchase dictates whether this area is an opportunity or threat. The more suppliers, the less control any one company can have over controlling your costs. The power of your suppliers is high when any of the following factors exist:

- ✔ Few suppliers and many buyers
- ✔ Similar products or services but with higher value or cost
- ✔ Suppliers or vendors threaten to integrate forward (like Nike opening its own retail stores called Niketown)
- ✔ Your industry isn't a key customer group for the supplier

AT&T sells many of its telecommunication services through independent sales agents. This distribution channel has facilitated the growth of many small telecommunications consulting companies that resell AT&T products. The commission earned off these products was a primary source of revenue for these agents' businesses. AT&T is one of only a few suppliers of telephony. Because of this fact, losing one of the only suppliers was a huge threat to these companies. And AT&T took advantage of that power by terminating many agent contracts and bringing the accounts in-house. This action was completely legal but destroyed many agents' businesses.

Bargaining power of buyers

The power of buyers can be summed up in one word – Wal-Mart. Because 10 cents of every consumer dollar is spent at Wal-Mart, any company in the consumer goods industry must contend with the force of its buying power. Buyers in this analysis are anyone who creates demand in your industry. The power of buyers is great when any of the following factors exist:

✔ Many sellers, few buyers

✔ Buyers threaten to integrate backwards (a computer manufacturer deciding to produce semiconductors or another component they would normally purchase)

✔ Your industry's products are standardized with little differentiation between competing products

✔ Your industry isn't a key supplying group for the buyers

Duking it out with your competitors

The rivalry or intensity at which you compete against your competition can move and change over time as the dynamics of the industry change. Competitive rivalry is an opportunity or a threat depending on how you handle it.

Do you recognize the intensity of the competition and are positioning yourself accordingly? Or are you feeling the pressures, but don't know where they're coming from? The following aspects have an effect on whether you feel the pressure of your industry more or less:

✔ **The structure of the competition:** Rivalry is greater when there are many small companies and less when there's a clear market leader.

✔ **Growth objectives:** Rivalry is greater when everyone is focused on growth (like biotech) and less when the industry is mature (like publishing).

✔ **Exit barriers:** If leave an industry is expensive or difficult, rivalries tend to be higher.

✔ **Degree of differentiation:** This factor is present in industries where products are commodities. *Commodities* are products and services that have no obvious differences and companies compete on price (like computers, steel, and so on). Rivalry is higher than when competitors can differentiate their products.

✔ **The structure of the industry costs:** In industries that have high fixed costs (like manufacturing), competitors tend to cut prices to fill unused manufacturing capacity, which leads to higher rivalry.

Analyzing Your Competition

It's easy to swing from one extreme to another when it comes to analyzing your competition. Some organizations don't worry about what their competitors are doing and just charge ahead. Others track every move and assess how to react. You want to fall somewhere in the middle.

The reason to even do a competitive analysis is to assess the opportunities and threats that may occur from those organizations competing for the same business you are. You need to have an understanding of what your competitors are or aren't offering your potential customers. Here are a few other key ways a competitive analysis fits into strategic planning:

✔ **To help you assess whether your competitive advantage is really an advantage.** Your competitive advantage, by its definition, means you have an advantage over your competition. (Flip to Chapter 5 for more on competitive advantage.) If you don't know your competitors well enough, you won't know if you really are better than they are in the areas you've isolated as your competitive advantages.

✔ **To understand what your competitor's current and future strategies are so you can plan accordingly.** You don't want to being crafting the same strategy as they are or you won't be successful. Remember, you want to be unique in the value you provide to your customers.

✔ **To provide information that will help you evaluate your strategic decisions against what your competitors may or may not be doing.** It's nice not to make decisions in a vacuum. By looking at what your competitors are and aren't doing, you might find out if you are missing something they have already identified. Or, conversely, if you are on to a trend that they haven't noticed, you might need to move faster.

The process of gathering competitive intelligence is like putting together a big puzzle. Each piece individually may not seem that interesting, but when all of the pieces are put together, you have a complete and useful picture. In the same vein, if you don't have enough information, the picture will be incomplete.

Before conducting your competitive analysis, decide your basis of comparison. In other words, are you doing the analysis on a product or service? A product or service line? Or on the company as a whole?

Identifying your competitors

If you're gearing up for a big athletic competition, your training regimen is directly proportional to who you're competing against. You really don't want to work harder than you have to, right? Well, it's the same thing for your business. Certainly, if you're running a for-profit business, you're competing to win. If you're a nonprofit or a department head, you're competing for scare resources, usually funding. In all cases, you need to know who you're trying to beat so you can position yourself properly.

The clearest way to identify your competitors is to figure out if you weren't around, who would supply your customers to fill their needs and what customer would buy to solve their problem?

Competitors come in three flavors, as discussed in the next sections.

Direct competitors

These companies are the ones you need to find out the most about because they're your fiercest competitors. When customers are making purchasing decisions, their products or services always end up on the short list. With this group, you're vying for the same customer dollar. More than likely, you have three or four companies that fall into this category.

Indirect competitors

These companies offer alternative products and services than your offering. Usually, you don't worry about these companies too much, but you should keep tabs on what they're up to. Sometimes an indirect competitor can become a direct competitor.

Substitutes or new entrants

While conducting your competitive analysis, determine if there are substitute products or potential new entrants. A substitute product is anything that delivers the same set of benefits to your customers as you do, but is not a competing product. For example, DVD rental is a substitute service to cable TV. There could be new companies or entrants coming on the scene that might change your industry completely, such as satellite radio has done to the radio industry.

Don't restrict your thinking only to companies similar to your own. Consider firms outside of the realm of possibility such as those who compete in the industry from a corporate strategic viewpoint. When contemplating the future, it's necessary to envision any number of possibilities.

Gathering competitive intelligence

In the past, it was often difficult to collect data on your competitors. Today's overabundance of information makes this important analysis much easier. Not only can it be done legally and ethically, but also there are a plethora of sources available to you. Check out Table 9-1 for a list of sources.

Table 9-1	Sources for Competitive Intelligence	
Online Sources	*Direct or Physical Sources*	*Undercover Sources*
Corporate Web site	Pricing, pricing lists	Hire an ex-employee
Annual reports	Advertising campaigns	Talk to vendors
Press releases	Special promotions	Interview customers
Newspaper articles or stories	Brochures, sales kits conferences	Attend their seminars or
Analysts reports	Purchase their products	Attend social events or networking where they are present
Government reports	Trade show booth	
Online presentations		
Blogs		
Newsgroups		
Patent applications		

The sources for our competitive analysis are broken into three groups – online, physical, and undercover. Information online is the easiest to secure, followed by physical, and then undercover.

Isolating what you really need to know

Undoubtedly there are some things you probably know or someone knows about your competitors. You really don't need to know about the CEO's favorite lunch spot or the receptionist's name.

Here's what you do care about:

✔ What is the profile of your competitors? Who are they? What products/ services do they sell? How many employees are in the company? See Table 9-2 for more ideas.

✔ What are the company's strengths and weaknesses?

✔ What are their competitive advantages?

✔ What are their strategies and objectives? Where are they headed and how are they going to get there?

Take the time to formalize what you know and what you *want* to know in writing. With this list in mind, you can more easily sort out what's important from what's unimportant when you conduct your competitive analysis. You can also make a small SWOT grid for each of your competitors (see Figure 9-2 at the beginning of this chapter for an example of a SWOT grid). See Table 9-2 below for more specifics on what you need to know about your competitors.

Table 9-2	Sleuthing Out Your Competitors
What You Probably Already Know	*What You Want to Know*
Overall sales and profits	Sales and profits by individual product or service
Expenses levels	Cost of goods sold
Organizational structure (number of employees and positions)	Customer profiles
Distribution of products or services	New product or service ideas
Identity and profile of the senior management	Size of customer database
Marketing strategy and messaging	Effectiveness of marketing campaigns
Customer retention	Future investment plans
	Terms and partnerships with vendors

Competing to win

After you collect data on your competition (see the previous section), what do you do with it? Follow these steps for weeding out the info:

1. **Narrow down your playing field if at all possible.**

   Look closely at your three top competitors.

2. **Determine what your competitors' strengths and weaknesses are.**

   The factors can be customer service, pricing, quality, operations, resources, personnel, and so on. Develop a good understanding of likely changes your competitors might make in the near future.

3. **List the strengths and weaknesses that are an opportunity or a threat to your company.**

Add your thoughts to your list of opportunities and threats you started at the beginning of the chapter. You will use this information to develop strategies, strategic objectives, and goals in Chapter 12.

If you find your competitors are lacking or missing some obvious opportunities, this opening is a perfect chance for your business to fill the void. To do so, you need to figure out the best strategy. Review the different strategies listed in Chapter 8 for ways to differentiate yourself from your competition. Your competitive analysis guides you to select the one that gives you an edge on your competition.

Analyzing Your Market

Referring back to Figure 9-1 in the beginning of the chapter, your market is the ring that is the closest to your company. Trends, changes, and shifts that occur in your market likely have the biggest impact on your company. Your market is a group of customers that you can easily identify who respond to your products or services in similar ways. Your offering satisfies the needs and wants of the whole group.

You need to have a complete picture of your company; it's important to take a high-level look at your market. Based on the information you have available today, you can quickly determine the opportunities and threats that exist in your markets by following a few steps:

1. **List the three to five main markets you compete in. Also list one or two that are new potential markets.**

2. **For each market, determine if it is growing, shrinking, or staying the same.**

3. **Determine the size of each market.**

4. **Determine if serving the market presents an opportunity or if the market is not worth focusing on.**

5. **Summarize the markets you want to focus on in your opportunities section of your SWOT.**

Don't worry about being exhaustive in your list because this can cripple your planning effort. You need to have enough information to feel comfortable with making decisions based on what you've collected. If you don't feel comfortable with the information you have available today, select one or two items to research further.

Summarizing Your Opportunities and Threats

Opportunities and threats are external factors, forces that you don't control but *can* take advantage of if appropriate. For example, an opportunity may be that the rising number of Hispanic consumers could lead to an increased demand for your product if your company is positioned correctly. A threat might be the proliferation of technology is making a current product obsolete.

If you answered the questionnaires in the previous sections, you have a good starting point to summarize and add to your key opportunities and threats. You can translate those thoughts into a grid like Figure 9-2. Right now you have developed thoughts to fill in the two right-hand quadrants on the grid.

Finishing Your SWOT Analysis

If you've been working through the last three chapters and collected all of the data I've discussed, it's time to make some sense of your list by organizing it in a SWOT format. Remember, the purpose of a SWOT is to help produce a good fit between your company's resources and capabilities and your external environment.

Your SWOT analysis is a balance sheet of your strategic position right now. In the analysis, you bring together all your internal factors, strengths, and weaknesses, as well as your external factors, opportunities, and threats. Strengths and weaknesses are factors that you can control and affect. These are identified in Chapters 7 and 8. Opportunities and threats, which are identified in this chapter, are outside of your control; you can either try to take advantage of them or try to minimize them. Follow these steps to complete your SWOT analysis grid:

1. **Construct a grid with four quadrants.**

   See Figure 9-2 for help.

2. **Review your list of strengths, weaknesses, opportunities, and threats you developed over the last three chapters.**

   Condense similar factors. Eliminate the ones that are nonessential. You want to be able to see a clear picture of your strategic position. If there are too many factors, it is impossible to draw any conclusions.

3. **Place your company's strengths and weaknesses in the left-hand boxes.**

Make sure to include only the factors that are internal and controllable.

4. **Place your opportunities and threats in the right-hand boxes.**

   Make sure to include only the factors that are external and out of your direct control.

Before you move on, consider pulling in other people to get an objective perspective of your opportunities and threats. Here are a few approaches to consider:

- ✔ **Hold a SWOT meeting.** Bring in your key employees and managers to help you complete your SWOT. You can either facilitate the meeting by asking them to think about the areas explained earlier in this chapter, or you can have a free brainstorming session. At the end, get your groups to come to a consensus as to what the top five strengths, weakness, opportunities, and threats are. You can use this to guide your short-term goal development for your strategic plan.

- ✔ **Form a SWOT team.** Pull together a group of employees and outsiders, such as advisors or industry experts, to do a SWOT analysis. Ask this team to pull in ideas not only through talking to co-workers but also to see what you may be missing by assessing the competition and your industry.

- ✔ **Go stealth.** Not everyone feels comfortable sharing their ideas in front of a group, especially if the opinion isn't a widely shared one. Develop a Web-based survey, such as Zoomrang or Survey Monkey, with open-ended questions about the strengths and weaknesses of your company. Make sure that the survey is anonymous and that everyone knows it. I do this with all my clients, and the information people provide is invaluable. You couldn't pay a consultant enough to give you the same ideas.

A well-thought out SWOT helps you weigh factors against each other to determine what your company should do and when you should do it. In Part IV, you take action on your SWOT analysis by developing goals and objectives around your findings. In the meantime, if you want to take action now, here is how to use your SWOT today:

- ✔ Build on your strengths.
- ✔ Shore up your weaknesses.
- ✔ Capitalize on your opportunities.
- ✔ Recognize your threats.

Change is the only constant in business. Therefore assessing your strategic position is as dynamic as the environment you operate in. Know that your SWOT just captures a moment in time, like your balance sheet. Take this tool out every time you go into your strategic planning cycle. I promise, it never gets rusty.

Part IV
Moving Your Organization into the Future

"Business here is good, but the weak dollar is killing my overseas markets!"

In this part . . .

Undoubtedly (or at least I hope) opportunities for your organization abound. More often than not, you have more to do than you have time to do it. In order to move your organization into the future, you need to select the right opportunities and the right strategy to go with them. In this part, you identify, evaluate, prioritize, and execute against your opportunities. You determine how to grow and establish your strategic priorities. I also provide a chapter on finding new customers.

Chapter 10

Growth: It's Not Just for Kids Anymore

In This Chapter

▶ Growing your business using current products and developing new ones

▶ Exploring and assessing new market potential

▶ Looking at various partnership strategies

▶ Finding out about growth through mergers and acquisitions

At the end of the day, what's every business trying to do? Grow. More customers, more sales, positive cash flow, larger deal sizes, higher volume, more billable hours, justification for higher prices, and so on. Ask any hardworking entrepreneur what he or she is working on and you're bound to hear a comment related to growth. Growth is why you're in business — to build or create something bigger than yourselves. Because if you're not growing, you're shrinking.

With that said, you don't want to focus on growth for growth's sake because growth is just the means to an end. Your desire to grow must match up with your vision for your organization. Rapid growth, incremental growth, or maintaining your current position require specific strategies.

In this chapter, you discover the different paths for growth strategies. You understand how to travel in more than one direction to find partners and acquire others. Lastly, you look at how to evaluate the different growth strategies against each other to get a clear picture of your strategic choices.

Strategizing How to Grow

Successful growth stems from matching up your strengths and weaknesses with the opportunities that exist in your business environment. Your growth strategy is the way in which you position your company to exploit your strengths and opportunities and mitigate your weaknesses and threats. By strategizing how to grow, you're actively deciding how to connect your mission with your vision (see Chapter 6 for more on missions and visions). Your growth strategy answers the question: *How do we get there?*

Keep these key points on growth in mind as you move through this chapter:

- ✔ Growth begins with your customers in mind.
- ✔ Growth focuses on opportunities.
- ✔ Growth looks forward by learning from the past.
- ✔ Everyone can grow.

Growth comes from either leveraging your market knowledge or leveraging your product knowledge. Figure 10-1 illustrates how you can leverage your market and/or product knowledge to create four different strategies:

- ✔ Market penetration
- ✔ Product development
- ✔ Market development
- ✔ Innovation

In Part III of this book, you identify your strengths, weaknesses, opportunities, and threats. If you've covered that information, use it to guide your strategy selection in this chapter.

Market

	Existing	New
Existing	Market Penetration Focusing on your market and product by niching	Market Development Leveraging your product knowledge to reach new markets
New	Product Development Leveraging your market knowledge to develop new products	Innovation Diversifying by offering new products in new markets

(Products)

Figure 10-1: The four squares of growth.

Market penetration

The most common growth strategy is to focus on what you do best by emphasizing your current products in your current markets. This strategy is also called the *concentrated growth strategy* because you're thoroughly developing and exploiting your knowledge and expertise in a specific market with known products.

How do you grow if you're doing what you're already doing now? Here's how:

- ✔ **Increase present customers' rate of use:** You achieve this goal by
  - Increasing the size of purchase
  - Maximizing the rate of product obsolescence
  - Finding new uses for your product
  - Advertising other uses
  - Offering incentives for increased use

- ✔ **Attracting your competitors' customers:** You lure customers away from your competitors by establishing differentiation between yourself and them, increasing advertising efforts, or cutting your prices. Look at Chapter 5 to find ways to differentiate yourself from other companies.

- ✔ **Attract nonusers to buy your products:** This process can be done by offering trial uses of your products, adjusting the price up or down, and promoting other uses to attract these customers (check out the following Example icon for details).

Think about Arm & Hammer Baking Soda. You could easily argue that it's not the most exciting product; in fact, it's almost boring. Agree? It's white powder in a box, but the company dominates the market as the number one baking soda for cooking year after year. But with such a large market share, you may be wondering how the company grows by using its current products. *It finds a new use for an existing product.* The company launched a year-long marketing campaign promoting the use of baking soda as a refrigerator deodorizer, which resulted in a 57 percent increase in sales! Arm & Hammer has not stopped there. Check out the company's Web site at http://armhammer.com for a timeline of how it continues to reinvent uses for its core product.

Product development

If you have a good understanding of your market, another way to leverage your knowledge is to develop new products and services to meet this market's needs. If you hear the term *product development,* you may think about brand new products, but that's not necessarily the case. Executing a product development strategy can happen by adding more value to your existing product through features, upselling, or cross selling. The best thing about this strategy is you've already established yourself in your current markets and you know what your customers want. You have the distribution channels, and you know how to reach them.

Consider the following questions if you're thinking about expanding your product line or developing new products:

- ✔ Will your customer benefit from the added value or new feature? Are they asking for additions to the current product line?

- ✔ Do potential manufacturing, marketing, and distribution cost efficiencies exist from an expanded product line? Can you share current costs across the new products or services?

- ✔ Can your current assets, brand, marketing, and distribution be used with the new product?

- ✔ Do you have the skills and capabilities to develop and produce the products proposed?

After you've given product development some consideration, and you've decided to proceed full steam ahead, here's how to develop new products and services to meet your market's needs:

- ✔ **Add new features or services by extending your current products.** For example, cell phone companies add on media packages for text messaging, additional ring tones, and Internet access. Here are a few ways to extend your current offering:

  - • Adapt (to other ideas and developments)

  - • Modify (change color, motion, sound, odor, form, shape)

  - • Magnify (more for a higher price, stronger, longer, extra value)

  - • Reduce (smaller, trial version, shorter, lighter)

  - • Substitute (other ingredients, processes, power)

  - • Combine (other options, products, ideas, assortments)

- ✔ **Develop additional models and sizes of your current products.** For example, the iPod expanded to the iPod mini and the iPod nano.

- ✔ **Develop totally new products.** In this case, you usually leverage your brand recognition. Some good examples of this development are Gerber producing baby clothes and a CPA firm expanding from tax work into financial planning.

Just because you're successful with your current products in a market, doesn't guarantee success with new ones. The classic failed product development strategy was New Coke, which Coke introduced in the '80s as a replacement for Coke. Coke assumed that its customers would gravitate toward a newly-developed formula only to realize, too late, that its cola drinkers were fiercely loyal to the traditional flavor. Needless to say, the new product fizzled.

Nowadays, it seems like Coke tries to introduce new products along with existing products, even if they overlap (like Coke Zero and Diet Coke — both diet sodas, but one isn't replacing the other). The lesson here is don't trash what's been working just fine when trying something new.

Market development

You can grow by leveraging your product knowledge to reach new customers. More than likely, you have spent time and money developing your product and service offering. Assuming you're happy with your current offering, extending it into new markets is a logical next step. This is aptly called a *market development strategy*. If, in Chapter 9, you identified potential new markets as opportunities, use these strategies to reach them.

Here are some quick considerations to make before executing a market development strategy:

- ✔ Is the market attractive? (To really answer this question, I recommend some form of market research to validate your gut feeling.)
- ✔ Are you willing to commit the required time and resources to reach this new market?
- ✔ Can your business be adapted to the new market?
- ✔ Will you maintain your current competitive advantage in this new market?

In the next two sections, I cover the two types of market development strategies.

Expanding geographically

When you're thinking about expanding, first think about where you want to cultivate new business. You have options: other regions, nationally, or internationally. Geographical expansion works well for a company that wants to expand its service territory because it needs a physical location to serve its customers. Clearly your ability to expand is subject to your ability to finance such as expansion. See "Executing Your Growth Strategy" later in this chapter.

Many of the big boys of business, including McDonalds, Wal-Mart, and Home Depot, have exported their operations to other countries. On a smaller scale, many microbreweries have opened up new locations in various metro areas and airports in the United States as a way to expand their geographical reach.

Reaching into new market segments

You can also grow by reaching a completely new set of customers or market segments. This area is such a popular growth strategy because you leverage the products and services you already have developed. (Flip to Chapter 11 for the entire story on new market segments.)

Examples of this strategy abound, such as Bayer aspirin now being sold not just for aches and pains, but also for heart attack prevention if taken daily.

Something totally new

Sometimes you just need to bust out and try something new — like learning the polka. Or if you are a tobacco firm, buying a packaged-food company; a cola firm entering the water business; or a chemical company going into the spa supply business. All these moves, except the polka of course, are examples of diversification. (The polka would be diversifying your dance portfolio, but that's another book all together.) *Diversification* is entering new markets with new products. Refer back to Figure 10-1 for how this strategy relates to the others.

You can also refer to diversification as *innovation.* Many companies appreciate the need to be innovative, but few use it as a way of relating to their markets. Fundamentally, this strategy is about creating new products, with new product life cycles, making the existing ones obsolete. By doing so, firms launch new products that are developed not just for current customers but for new ones, too.

To execute this strategy, you usually manage a merger, an acquisition, or a completely new business venture. See "Executing Your Growth Strategy" later in this chapter. Well known, highly innovative companies include Intel, Google, DuPont, and all of the pharmaceutical companies.

A company's diversification strategy can be either related or unrelated to their original business. *Related diversification* seems to make more sense than unrelated because the company isn't sharing assets, skills, or capabilities. But there are many successful companies such as Tyco and GE that continue to buy unrelated businesses.

Check out the next two sections for more information. Figure 10-2 also summarizes the reasons for related and unrelated diversification.

Related diversification

In related diversification, there's a strategic fit between the new venture and the existing company. You capitalize on the strengths or competitive advantage you've already established to make this strategy work.

Richard Branson, famous for his company Virgin, has more than 300 companies that carry the Virgin name: Virgin Atlantic, Virgin Mobile, and Virgin Galactic — his most recent venture into space travel — are just a few examples. This related diversification strategy works because all the companies share the brand, marketing, public relations, and corporate knowledge.

Unrelated diversification

Unrelated diversification has nothing to do with leveraging your current business strengths or weaknesses. It's more about not putting all your eggs in one basket. For example, an investor diversifying his financial portfolio to protect against losses. Many entrepreneurs execute this strategy unknowingly by becoming involved in multiple, unrelated businesses.

Hypothetically, say the owner of a local IT consulting company also decided to take over a failing sandwich shop because he always wanted to be in the restaurant business. Clearly these two businesses are unrelated. But by accident, the business owner is executing a diversification strategy. He is now in the IT industry and the dining industry.

Related Diversification	Unrelated Diversification
Sharing skills and competencies	Interest to the owner or executives
Leveraging a brand name	Reducing risk by operating in various markets and product lines
Using a shared marketing skills and knowledge	Refocusing the company
Using sales and distribution capacity	Tax benefits
Exchanging manufacturing skills and know-how	Defending against a takeover
Access to research and development and new product capabilities	Obtaining liquid assets or other assets needed by the main company
Realizing economies of scale	Defending against a takeover

Figure 10-2: Choosing between related or unrelated diversification.

Growing up (and down)

Another potential way to grow is through *vertical integration* — moving up and down your supply chain. You can integrate forward by setting up operations closer to your customer, such as a clothing company opening up retail stores. Or you can integrate backward, moving closer to your raw material source such as the clothing company opening a manufacturing plant. Although these strategies are less common that the others, they do have some benefits:

✔ **Direct access to supply and demand:** Eliminating the middleman in both directions is forward and backward integration. Getting direct access to your vendors and customers can be a huge benefit for many businesses.

For example, many of the auto manufacturers moved forward by investing in the big car rental firms. Many companies seek backward integration because there is no source for a component they need. For example, when refrigerated warehouses were needed by meat packers, they built them.

✔ **Better control over the quality or availability of the product or service.** Many times, manufacturers need specialized raw material that is a key component in the end product. To gain better quality control and eliminate the risk of not being able to acquire the product, the company buys the vendor. This is backward integration.

So Sony could guarantee content for its products, the company purchased Columbia Pictures, Tri-Star Pictures, and CBS Records.

✔ **Entry into a potentially attractive business area.** Manufacturers continually fight margin pressures. The best way to get control is to go directly to customers instead of through retailers, also known as *forward integration.*

Companies like Nike have been successful in this area, whereas a company such as Universal Pictures hasn't.

Executing Your Growth Strategy

The preceding section lays out different growth strategies. Now you need to evaluate which path you want to take. But in order to choose a path, you must also decide how to execute the strategy.

By matching up your growth strategies with your strengths, weaknesses, and opportunities, you can determine which ones to pursue. The next sections cover the pros and cons of doing it yourself, developing partners, and growing through others.

Going it alone

The most obvious and straightforward approach to implementing your growth strategy is doing it yourself. Most of the time, companies choose to enter new markets or develop new products by providing the necessary capital, equipment, people, and other assets themselves to get the job done. But choices come with consequences — in this case, list your pros and cons.

The pros of doing it yourself can include

- ✔ **Having more control:** You hold all the strings in this scenario. You don't have to wait for the other company to make decisions or take actions.

- ✔ **Reaping greater rewards:** All the revenue and profit is kept in your business.

- ✔ **Saving more money:** You realize all of the cost savings through economies of scale (spreading costs out across products and services) and shared resources (sharing assets across product and service lines).

Going it alone also comes with some drawbacks:

- ✔ **Limited resources:** Everyone has limited time and money, which restricts the number of strategies that can be pursued at the same time

- ✔ **Lack of skills:** You may not have the skills and capabilities within your company to execute the strategy successfully.

- ✔ **Greater risk:** Of course, with all the rewards, comes all the risk. Your neck is on the line if your strategy bombs.

More than likely, doing it yourself may come down to the money. You aren't able to finance the entire endeavor on your own. If you want some suggestions on how to help pay for growth, flip to Chapter 14. You can also check out *Raising Capital For Dummies* (Wiley) by Joseph W. Bartlett and Peter Economy (yeah, that's really his last name!).

Video Gaming Technologies (VGT), named the fastest growing small company by Inc. Magazine in 2005, made it to the top through its own business model and focusing on a single market. VGT produces touchscreen gaming machines and leases them to Indian casinos in Oklahoma. Yep, just Oklahoma. Since landing its first games in casinos in 2001, the company's growth has skyrocketed to a total of 9,720 percent, nearly reaching $100 million in revenue in 2004. VGT has captured 30 percent of the Oklahoma market and plans to continue its growth by taking its products to China and South America.

Playing well with others: Developing partners

As you evaluate the different growth options against your resources, you may discover that you come up short – like the money. You have the vision, but you don't have what it takes to get the job done. That's when you should check out strategic partnerships as a growth option.

Strategic partnerships are also known as strategic alliances, joint ventures, licensing, franchising, and private labeling, and I use the terms interchangeably. In this section, I use the words *strategic partnership* to mean any type of agreement that results in a synergy between two cooperating organizations resulting in the sum of their efforts being greater than the parts.

Alliances between companies are incredibly popular in today's business climate because, when done correctly, they enable you to take advantage of more market opportunities. Alliances require less capital, are more responsive to the market, and spread the associated risks.

A Booz Allen Hamilton study provides CEOs with statistics that can't be ignored:

- ✔ For nearly ten years, strategic alliances of the world's top 2,000 companies have consistently produced an average annual return on investment of nearly 17 percent. This is a 50 percent higher ROI than their non-alliance activities produce.

- ✔ The percentage of annual revenue that the 1,000 largest U.S. companies earned from alliances grew to 35 percent by 2002.

A strategic partnership allows both organizations to realize their respective growth goals while sharing resources and profits from success. The key is leveraging your own company's strengths while shoring up your weaknesses with your partner's strength.

Identifying the types of strategic partnerships

Strategic partnerships come in as many flavors and colors as there are businesses in this world: Some are conventional and unconventional; some strategic, some transactional; some done on a hand shake and others with a100-page contract.

To make sense of the variety of strategic partner arrangements, see Figure 10-3. Notice the vertical continuum represents the length of the commitment — from shorter term to longer term — between the partners. The horizontal continuum illustrates another variable: the degree of shared resources, from no shared resources to wholly owned.

	Licensing	Collaborating marketing	Franchising	Strategic alliances	Joint venture	Acquisition
Longer Term	A company acquiring the rights for usage of Web-based software such as NetSuite.	Rubbermaid and Home Depot sharing marketing dollars to promote products.	An individual purchasing the rights to open a McDonalds.	Wal-Mart and Cifra join assets and money to open stores in Mexico.	KFC entered Japan through a joint venture with Mitsubishi.	GM purchasing Saab. eBay's purchase of PayPal.
Shorter Term	**Outsourcing** Amazon runs Borders.com. **Joint bid** Two firms come together to win a government contract.	**Private label** Costco creating a private label line of products called Kirkland Signature.	**Distribution agreement** Port of Subs and Baskin & Robbins opening locations together. Airlines code sharing and gate sharing.	**R&D partnerships** Lockheed and Boeing developing new products with joint funding.		
	No shared resources	Shared information	Shared assets	Shared funding	Shared equity	Wholly owned

Commitment (y-axis) / *Degree of shared resources* (x-axis)

Figure 10-3: The partnering continuum.

Here are some other types of partnerships not included in Figure 10-3:

- Collaborative advertising
- Cooperative bidding
- Cross licensing
- Cross manufacturing
- Lease service agreements
- Resource venturing
- Technology transfer

Knowing when to buddy up

The value of a strategic partnership lies in the growth it offers companies who are strong in one area but not another. In other words, partnerships must be mutually beneficial. But how do you know when to consider partnering as a viable growth option? Explore the following reasons for joining forces with another organization:

✔ **Increased market reach:** Through partners, you can expand your market reach by selling your products and services into their markets. You can also realize broader geographic expansion.

✔ **Faster product development:** By combining forces, partners can share areas of expertise, defray the typically high costs of product research and development, improve quality, and hopefully realize a higher return.

✔ **Purchased access to a customer base:** Your partner may have customer relationships with larger accounts you're seeking access to.

✔ **Facilitated international trade:** Partnering opens up new markets and export opportunities on a global scale. Inexperienced partners can quickly gain knowledge, skills, and sales expertise of an experienced export partner.

✔ **Gained access to needed technology:** You may be able to gain quicker and faster access to technology than if you built it yourself.

✔ **Enhanced purchasing power:** Partnering with other firms to purchase raw materials, distribution, and other goods and services can result in substantial savings for an individual organization because you buy larger volumes and can negotiate better prices. Typically, the more you buy, the better the price.

✔ **Shared marketing:** Partnering to pool market research knowledge, customer databases, campaign dollars, and other promotional expenses can be a huge reduction in expenses for businesses. The key is to partner with a company that truly meets the needs of your customer base. (See "Determining who to buddy up with" later in the chapter).

✔ **Shared logistics, distribution, and operations:** Economies of scale can be realized if two companies partner to coordinate product management from contract to delivery.

✔ **Shared administrative/human resources:** This area is slightly more difficult to share, but it's possible. Human resource knowledge, expertise, and even staff can be shared because as the labor shortage grows, this may become a competitive advantage for those companies that can effectively share human resources.

The main rationale for setting up a strategic partnership is that by sharing resources, you can execute your plans more quickly, cheaply, and with better quality.

Defining how to buddy up: The Partnership Criteria Sheet

If you've decided that partnering is the way you want to achieve your growth (or part of your plan), you need to define clearly what the partnership looks like and how you will go about structuring it. With as many details as possible, put together a one-sheet document, called a Partnership Criteria Sheet, that answers the following questions:

- ✔ What is the goal of the partnership for your company? (See the list of reasons to set up a partnership in the previous section.)

- ✔ Will a partnership fill a goal better than in-house development or acquisition?

- ✔ What type of partnership are you looking for? What length of time and what level of shared resources? (Refer back to Figure 10-3 if needed.)

- ✔ What resources does the partnership require? Is your business able and willing to deliver those resources?

- ✔ What resources does the partner need to deliver?

- ✔ How should you divide partnership ownership? (Who owns what?)

- ✔ What value do the partnership's proposed products or services bring to your customers?

- ✔ How will the partnership be measured and how will it be managed?

- ✔ What are the specific revenue goals or cost savings you expect to realize?

Use the Partnership Criteria Sheet to help you evaluate potential partners as well as develop the deal when it comes time. The sheet helps you and your team focus on putting together the right partnership for the right reasons.

Determining who to buddy up with

Chances are, you already have a general idea of who you should be partnering with. The best candidates are those whose assets, experience, customer base, and distribution best support your weaknesses.

Start by looking at your supply chain — from development all the way to the end user, and especially the businesses involved in transporting your product to market. Also look at other companies that reach the same market you do or markets that you want to tap into.

After scanning the possibilities, come up with a list of three or four likely candidates that meet the criteria listed on your Partnership Criteria Sheet. And then follow these steps:

1. **Do your homework.**

   What are the candidate organization's key strengths, market position, and financial status? Try to find out how this organization has behaved in the past toward vendors, customers, and in alliances with other organizations. A great place to start is the Dun and Bradstreet directory of businesses (http://dnb.com).

2. **Estimate the profitability of the partnership.**

   Determine if the estimated partnership profits justify the investment in developing the alliance. Put together a small financial projection of just this partnership. See Chapter 13 for guidance on how to put together projections.

If you're unprepared or lack initiative — no matter how good the potential partner or deal — a strategic partnership can blow up, wasting everyone's time and resources. Before you seal any deals with your new partner, make sure to avoid the hidden pitfalls of partnerships:

- ✔ Lack of trust between the two parties

- ✔ Moving too fast into the agreement

- ✔ Lack of buy-in from senior management in both organizations

- ✔ Failure by one or both partners to clearly articulate the alliance's "value proposition" to managers or employees

- ✔ Failure to define who owns what

- ✔ Getting bogged down in bureaucracy in one of the two companies

- ✔ Lack of consistent, regular communication

- ✔ Failure to establish the exit clause before the partnership starts making money or goes south

Combining forces: Mergers and acquisitions

A popular and legitimate growth strategy is through a merger or acquisition. A *merger* is combining two separate businesses into a single new business, whereas an *acquisition* occurs when one company purchases the assets and majority ownership of the other company. According to Securities Data Corporation, mergers and acquisitions (M&As) grew 15 percent from 2004 to 2005.

Seasoned business folks say that true mergers don't exist. In nearly every situation, there's an *acquirer* and an *acquiree*, where the acquirer maintains majority control. See Figure 10-3 for a visual on how M&As relate to the partnering continuum. Because this is a large topic, I only provide key considerations about M&As as a growth option. Therefore, we only look at the deal from the acquiring company side.

Partnering through franchising

Franchising is exploding in popularity as a way to grow your business potential very quickly. Franchising is a partnership of sorts between the two parties because they're sharing assets for a mutually beneficial outcome. You can license your intellectual property to wanna-be business owners in exchange for their cash in the form of a franchise fee. The benefit to the franchisor is to expand through quick access to capital and human resources. The benefit to the franchisee is the ability to buy a proven business model with no time or money needed for research and development.

Want a good example of franchising? Great Harvest Bakery has successfully opened 206 franchises nationwide with an unusually loose model. The company encourages entrepreneurial spirit and open communication between storeowners, who enjoy the freedom to run their businesses their way. In fact, the Uniform Franchise Offering reads: "Anything not expressly prohibited is allowed." Because the company is privately held, financial information isn't available, but its continued growth, with 13 stores expected to open this year, is an indicator that the company developed a very successful partnership model.

Wonder why you *wouldn't* want to franchise? Check out Jamba Juice, the maker of fruit-juice smoothies. They backed away from franchising as a growth strategy specifically because of the inability to control product quality. At the time the company was making the critical decision about how to grow, founder Kirk Perron decided that consistency in location, store design, in-store merchandise, and smoothie ingredients was what would lure repeat customers. By franchising, Jamba Juice didn't have the ability to monitor the quality so important to the company's distinctiveness. Opening wholly-owned stores funded by a handful of big name venture capitalist proved a winning strategy for the company. The company now has 500 stores nationwide with net sales of $300 million in 2005.

Although M&As are growing in popularity, so is their failure rate. According to *Mastering the Merger: Four Critical Decisions that Make or Break the Deal* by David Harding and Sam Rovit, 60 to 70 percent of acquisitions fail. To make matters worse, about 90 percent of all acquired businesses lose market share. Given the high failure rate, it's imperative that all of your i's are dotted and t's are crossed and double-checked before making an acquisition.

Keeping your motivations clear

What makes a good acquisition deal? At the end of the day, a good acquisition improves your income statement and balance sheet within two to three years. If you think it may take longer, you don't have a good deal.

Before making any M&A deals, ask yourself the following questions (if you can't answer yes to all of them, you're not likely to grow):

- ✔ Will the acquisition increase profit?
- ✔ Will the acquisition improve the balance sheet?
- ✔ Is the risk level acceptable for all stakeholders?

It's easy to lose sight of the end goal by getting caught up in the trivial details of the deal. Ultimately closing the deal is only half the battle. A successful acquisition yields the returns you anticipated on purchase. Not until you realize those profits can you say your acquisition was successful.

Weighing the pros and cons

If M&As were never successful, they wouldn't be so popular. Clearly there are plenty of companies acquiring successfully, so pros do exist in mergers and acquisitions. Here are a few:

- ✔ **Expanding your markets:** Overnight you can acquire new products, services, and customers for your current lines of business in your same market or even new markets. Additionally, you may acquire new distribution channels and vendor relationships.

  Oracle's $10 billion buyout of PeopleSoft yielded new customers, services, and thousands of new distribution outlets for the high-tech company.

- ✔ **Acquiring people, systems, technology, equipment, intellectual property, or processes:** If you can't build it, buy it. A huge benefit to an acquisition is the rapid ability to have new operations up and running quickly.

- ✔ **Acquisitions may also improve your economies of scale:** Microsoft and Google continually purchase smaller companies as a way to expand their product portfolios and spread their assets out over more revenue sources.

- ✔ **Reducing expenses:** You can generate more money with less overhead when you trim out some of the excess details.

  Any of the auto manufacturers' mergers, such Ford's purchase of Volvo, are an example of reducing expenses through an acquisition.

- ✔ **Eliminating competition:** If you can't beat them, buy them.

  HP's purchase of Compaq is a good example.

Oh, did you really think that I would have a pros list without the cons? Following right behind the list of pros are the cons:

- ✔ **Having a cultural mismatch:** Don't underestimate the importance of cultural harmony. Shared beliefs, values, goals, and business models ensure the culture is complementary to yours.

- ✔ **Overvaluing expense savings:** Many companies think they can significantly decrease expenses by consolidating functions like sales, administration, and service into one location. However, your acquiree's competitive advantage may well be a function of these field functions. If you go through with the consolidation, you risk losing that benefit.

- ✔ **Misreading your customers:** Will your customers really buy the products or services you assume are complementary to your own? Do they need or want the acquiree's products or services? If you misunderstand your customers, you may end up with two completely different customer groups and unrelated product lines — an expensive and unwieldy proposition.

- ✔ **Underestimating customer retention:** Any time you acquire, you're likely to lose some of the acquiree's customers. Don't automatically assume that sales will continue at the same level after the purchase as they were before it.

- ✔ **Misreading the company:** You're trying to understand the operations of a business that's been around for 10 or 20 years (or more or less) in a matter of a few weeks or months. Even when you buy a company similar to yours, you can never know everything about it before you make your decision.

Using M&As to grow

Ultimately, the primary reason for considering an acquisition is the desire or need for quick and substantial growth. No matter what the secondary reasons — expanding into another geographical area, acquiring systems and assets, or obtaining new products or new distribution channels — M&As still comes down speed. If you want to grow incrementally, an M&A isn't for you.

To determine whether an M&A may help you realize your growth goals, answer these three questions:

- ✔ What are the different ways you could grow your business?

- ✔ Is an acquisition the best way to achieve that growth? Do any of the other alternatives meet your needs? (Check out "Playing well with others: Developing partners," for more info on alternatives.)

- ✔ What other strategic goals will the acquisition help you accomplish?

Improve your chances of success by integrating these tips into your acquisition strategy:

- **Understand *how* you reach the goal of your M&A.** Figure out what part of the M&A drives the growth you're looking for. Different areas such as customers, costs, and processes can all be factors. If you haven't defined your goals, you can't begin to execute an effective acquisition campaign.

- **Never risk the stability of your company on the acquisition.** Make sure that you're never risking more than you can afford to lose if the purchase doesn't work out.

- **Only buy profitable companies.** Sick companies are almost always more difficult to fix than expected. Of course, companies that have obvious areas for improvement that you can pinpoint are perfect acquisition targets.

- **Don't set your acquisition strategy up to fail.** Put your best people in charge and fund it accordingly.

Outsourcing your outsourcing

Outsourcing is here to stay because of the numerous environmental pressures companies are dealing with. Basically, why keep non-core functions in-house when you can get them cheaper overseas? The problems arise when companies have tried to put this into practice. It's not as easy as it sounds, so outsourcing brokers and consultants should be used. This new crop of companies is helping organizations of all types locate, contract, and manage their outsourced projects.

For example, Business Health Services needed to either cut costs or cut jobs. One area for cost cutting was reducing its costs to transcribe doctor's notes and other medical documents. At the time, the company was paying 16 cents a word, but through the help of an outsourcing broker, it was able to locate a vendor in India who would do it for 11 cents. Add on the 25 percent premium that the broker gets, and the company now only pays 11.5 cents a word — a $7,000 per month savings.

Is outsourcing in your future? Here are some guidelines to determine whether outsourcing is the right move for your company:

- You need a higher level of expertise than you currently have, or you only need that expertise periodically.

- You have a set of activities or functions that need rapid change.

- Departments or functions are performing subpar when compared to others in your company.

- Outsourcing is cheaper without a decrease in quality.

- You need better performance but lack the resources to do it yourself.

- You have a non-core area that's giving you a headache.

Check out the National Association of Software and Service Companies (www.nasscom.org), India's trade group, for help with outsourcing.

In 2004, FedEx purchased Kinko's for $2.4 billion with its main goal of attracting more customers in smaller and mid-sized companies as well as fending off competitors. The 1,200 Kinko's stores give FedEx a direct line into businesspeople who work out of their home or own small businesses. FedEx can also target on-the-road employees. Additionally, the acquisition provides a much stronger distribution channel than FedEx had previously.

Evaluating What Path to Take

If you've read through most of this chapter and are now familiar with the different growth strategies and the approaches to implementing them, now it's time to figure out what to do and how to do it.

The best way to visually see your strategic choices is by creating a Product/Market Grid. By developing this grid, you can prioritize and sort your options. See Figure 10-4 for help in developing your grid, and then follow these steps:

1. **In Excel or Word, create a table that lists all your current and potential products down the left-hand column and all your current and proposed markets across the top.**

   Refer Figure 10-4 for an example of the layout.

2. **Estimate the demand for your current and new products in each of the markets by filling in the cells different shades of grey.**

   For example, if there's a potential high demand for the product, shade the cell dark gray. If there's low demand, fill the cell with light grey.

3. **Based on your demand estimations, select your growth strategy.**

   Look at whether you're leveraging your product or your market knowledge in each market. For example, in the column titled *Current Market #1,* there's high demand for the two current products and one new one. To increase sales for the new product, the company will continue to serve the market by executing a product development strategy.

4. **Decide how to execute the growth strategy.**

   You need to base this decision on your knowledge and judgment of the resources you have to execute each strategy. Will you do it yourself, find a partner, or acquire a business? (See previous sections in this chapter on these endeavors.)

5. **Prioritize each group based on which is the best opportunity for your company.**

   Use this information to guide the development of your Customer Goals and Objectives in Chapter 13.

	Current Market #1	Current Market #2	New Market #1	New Market #2
Current Product #1				
Current Product #2				
New Product #1				
New Product #2				
Growth Strategy	Product Development	Market Penetration	Market Development	Innovation
Strategy Implementation	Do it myself	Do it myself	Find a partner	Look at an acquisition
Priority	1	2	3	4
Legend – Projected Demand:	High demand	Medium demand	Low demand	None or N/A

Figure 10-4: Your growth options.

Basing your project demand on market research and past sales is the best way to construct this grid. Because this isn't always available, do your best to fill in the grid because it provides you with a good idea of how likely one strategy is compared to the others. If you have the time, jump online, talk to your sales people, or hire a market research firm to get the real data to fill in your Product/Market Grid.

Keep your Product/Market Grid handy. You use it again in Chapter 13 to develop your goals and objectives in your strategic plan.

Chapter 11

Finding New Customers

· ·

In This Chapter

▶ Investigating new customer markets and picking the best ones

▶ Writing position statements

▶ Keeping a focus on the market

▶ Deciding how to reach your new customers

· ·

*E*very business wants to find new customers. It's like asking if you want to make more money. Of course you do! There are two ways to grow your top line: Increase sales from your existing customers (see Chapter 8) or generate sales from new ones (this chapter).

Finding new customers is the role of marketing. When you sift through all the semantics, misused business lingo, and fuzzy concepts, marketing is really pretty simple: Identify who you want to sell to; figure out how to get those people to notice you; and when they do, get them to buy from you. If it is this simple, why does marketing continue to be confusing? Mainly because most people make it too complicated. At the end of the day, nothing matters until there's a sale. And the only person who can make that decision is the customer. As management guru Peter Drucker says, "The purpose of a business is to create a customer." Period.

 The primary reason marketing campaigns fail is because customers weren't offered something they wanted, needed, or valued. The components of a campaign — your product, its price, the advertising, sales channels, your salespeople, customer service — can contribute to the failure. But ultimately, the problem comes down to the fact that the customer wasn't satisfied.

This chapter focuses on marketing planning elements, which are part of your strategic plan. Additionally, the chapter helps you create a market-focused organization. In Chapter 10, you may have selected either market development or market penetration as potential growth strategies. If so, implementing either of these requires reaching new markets. This chapter also explains how to give those strategies life.

Researching New Markets

Good market research ensures that you don't spend a lot of money on marketing campaigns that customers don't jibe with or new products that they won't pay for. To be effective, organizations need good information about their customers' needs, wants, and characteristics. Generally, if the result of your decision impacts the customer, you should ask the customer for input into your decision before you make it.

Market research is an entire discipline, which is too overwhelming to cover in depth here. Instead, this section focuses on how to conduct market research for the purpose of making strategic decisions about which target markets to enter. Those markets result in actions within your strategic plan.

Identifying your information needs

Before beginning any research effort, clearly state your information needs. Undoubtedly there may be some holes and unknowns about new markets you want to pursue, but you also want to have a better idea of how attractive the potential target market is and if it identifies with the need you're trying to solve. Ask yourself the following questions about each market you're considering:

- ✔ What market am I trying to serve? How big is my market in terms of number of customers, units sold, or dollar volume?
- ✔ Are there obvious segments in my market?
- ✔ What are the overall trends and developments in my industry?
- ✔ What is the rate of market growth or shrinkage over time? Are there any differences in market growth by time of year?
- ✔ How big are my competitors? What companies have what portions of the market?
- ✔ What products or services do my competitors offer? How do they differ from mine?
- ✔ How does competitors' pricing compare with mine?
- ✔ What marketing strategies and tactics does the competition use and to what degree of success?
- ✔ What are the key factors for success in the market I'm trying to serve? Are there any specific media outlets that reach this market directly?
- ✔ How do customers perceive the problem the offering is intended to solve? How serious do they believe the problem is? What benefits of the proposed offering would be of most importance to them?

✔ How do customers solve the problem today?

✔ What costs do customers incur now to solve the problem?

It's a pretty long list, I know. But don't feel overwhelmed. You don't need to answer all these questions. Just focus on these key steps in processing your answers:

1. **Use the questions listed above to help identify what specific information you need about potential new markets.**

2. **Then clearly state these needs in one or two objectives.**

3. **Use these objectives to guide your research efforts.**

4. **If the information you locate doesn't achieve the stated objectives, file that info somewhere else or delete it.**

Locating information sources

You know your information needs, but now you've got to go out and find the answers.

Doing market research can be like pulling on a never-ending spool of thread. Sometimes you reach the end of your search and sometimes you don't. At some point you need to decide if you've collected enough information to make a strategic decision about which markets to pursue. Weigh the cost of perfect information against the risk of a less-than-perfect decision.

The following subsections provide a list of potential sources. I admit that the sources aren't exhaustive, but I do cover the most popular research sources available. Some of the sources are free, while others are quite expensive. I always evaluate the cost of research against the "cost" of decision. Or, in other words, how much insurance do you need or want to buy?

Internal company information

You may be amazed how much information you have stored in your company databases, customer relationship management systems, employees, vendors, and distributors. Before you spend any time surfing databases or spend any money on a research study, start with your internal company information. Look for data that answers the questions in the earlier section "Identifying your information needs."

Secondary data

Information or data that's already compiled, such as reports, statistics, and white papers, is considered *secondary data.* To get a general understanding of the market and to begin to develop customer profiles, you can easily tap into secondary sources. Here is a list of some of the best:

- ✔ **Google Answers or Yahoo! Answers:** This services are provided by Google and Yahoo! and allow you to post a question to a stable of qualified researchers. At the time of posting, you set the price you're willing to pay for the information. Average bids range from $5 to $100 dollars. Visit the site online at www.google.com/answers or www.answers.yahoo.com.

- ✔ **STAT-USA/Internet:** This service of the U.S. Department of Commerce provides information about business, trade, and economic information from across the Federal Government. Check out the Web site www.stat-usa.gov.

- ✔ **eMarketer:** This service (www.emarketer.com) provides market research on e-business and online marketing; objective analysis of online market trends; and data from over 2,000 worldwide sources.

- ✔ **MarketResearch.com:** This source sells market research reports for a variety of industries. They also have the most comprehensive collection of published market research available. Check it out online at www.marketresearch.com.

- ✔ **Demographics Now:** This company has numerous tools for both business and consumer markets such as segmentation, customer profiling, site selection, demographic data, and competitive analysis reports. The company's Web site is www.demographicsnow.com. (See the coupon in this book for a discounted price on their reports.)

- ✔ **Frost & Sullivan:** They are a business consulting firm that provides industry specific, B2B research and reports for a variety of different fields. The online sources is www.frost.com.

- ✔ **The U.S. Census Bureau:** The Bureau (www.census.gov) gives you free access to all Census data about people, businesses, trade, and much more.

A variety of other Web sites provide business specific information. Here are a few:

- ✔ Dow Jones Interactive: www.dowjones.com

- ✔ Hoover's Online: www.hoovers.com

- ✔ Factiva: www.factiva.com

- ✔ Lexis/Nexis: www.lexisnexis.com

- ✔ FISonline: www.fisonline.com

- ✔ Value Line: www.valueline.com

- ✔ Investext: http://research.thomsonib.com

- ✔ S&P's Industry Surveys: http://sandp.ecnext.com/coms2/page_industry.

Want to get more specific in your secondary research efforts? The University of California Berkley Library publishes a guide entitled *Finding Information on the Internet: A Tutorial*. Check out this free resource at `www.lib.berkeley.edu/TeachingLib/Guides/Internet/Strategies.html`.

Primary data

If you have a specific research question, want to evaluate a specific need, or want test market a product, you may need to go directly to the information source: your customer. This research is called *primary research*. You may also need to conduct primary research if you can't locate a critical piece of information through secondary sources. Primary research includes surveys via e-mail, phone, direct mail, in-depth interviews, focus groups, usability testing, and direct observation.

You can conduct primary research yourself or hire an outside market research agency. Check out the GreenBook directory — `www.greenbook.org` — for a list of market research agencies.

Defining Your Target Markets

Think about your market as if you're someone who's interested in buying your product or service. You might have some luck reaching some of them with a widespread approach. But wouldn't a more targeted approach be more effective? In order to use this approach, you have to aim at a clear target, which is your ideal market. To create a target, you need to be able to take a sea of customers and group, or segment, them. You can do this by creating groups of customers based on similarities. This is a *target market*.

The goal of creating target markets is targeting specific customers that have similar needs and wants with the same message, products, and pricing and through the same distribution channels. When done correctly, your target market responds similarly to your marketing efforts.

Here is an example. Look at two 24-Hour Fitness customers:

Tim is a health nut. Working out is his life. He typically uses the facilities five times a week. He's on a program established by his personal trainer and has referred two people to the gym this year already.

Sheila, on the other hand, hasn't set foot in the gym since she joined six months ago.

Membership renewal fees for both Tim and Sheila are due next month. If 24-Hour Fitness uses the same strategy to encourage Tim and Sheila to renew, their tactics may fail. Tim already understands the value and is a satisfied customer. However, Sheila needs substantially more communication to see the benefit. The company may likely lose her.

Clearly, utilizing the same marketing campaign in the examples above causes a decrease in potential sales and profitability. The same is true with your approaches in the real world. Therefore, a more targeted approach to sales and marketing is needed. In the following sections, I show you how to take that approach.

Dividing up your market into groups

What's the best way to divide your large customer base? Find a variable that splits the market into actionable groups.

Most companies first make a product, then figure out who to sell it to. The focus is on the product and not on what the customer wants to buy. By flipping your thinking around, you first look at what customer needs you're trying to satisfy, and then which products fit that need. This process helps isolate customer groups and make educated decisions on which segments offer the most attractive opportunities.

Choosing a variable or a base is like selecting what type of knife to use when preparing dinner. A serrated knife is preferable for cutting bread; a paring knife for halving cherry tomatoes; and a chef's knife for dicing an onion. They each have their own specialty. Different knives produce different results. The knife is analogous to the segmentation variable, not the segment itself. You slice and dice markets by using different variables until you come up with the segmentation of your customers that makes the most sense. For example, you can segment a consumer market by product/service benefits sought, demographic variables, geographic variables, psychographic variables, or behavioral variables. But you can't use all of them at the same time, or you'll end up with a market of one.

Segmenting can be confusing and more difficult than it needs to be. Remember, there's no right or wrong way to segment your market. It requires creativity. Take a shot at creating segments that makes sense to you and your business situation. You can always revise your segments at a later date.

The following two sections describe your selection process.

Benefits

Benefit segmentation is based on dividing customers based on their needs. This process is also called *needs-based segmentation*. Simply put, you're trying to solve a need for a customer. Why not group all of the customers that have the same need together?

Some marketers argue that this is the only way to segment a market because people differ only when it comes to paying you for your product based on the benefits your product provides. However, this type of segmentation may not work for your organization, or it may not be as straightforward. Researching your market (check out the info in "Researching New Markets" in this chapter for help) can provide some insight on how you can segment based on benefits.

Netflix, an online, home-delivery DVD rental service, divides its customers into three groups based on needs. Group one needs the convenience provided by free home delivery. Group two consists of film buffs who want to be able to access any movie possible. Group three wants the benefit of cheap rentals. They are the bargain hunters who want to watch a bunch of movies for less than $20 per month.

Descriptors

Descriptors are customer characteristics that are significant enough to divide your market. You don't use all the descriptors together, but you may use one or two together from the list below:

- ✔ **Demographic:** Grouping customers by age, income level, gender, family size, religion, race, nationality, primary language, and so on.

- ✔ **Geographic:** Grouping customers by area such as regions of the country or state and urban/rural.

- ✔ **Psychographic:** Grouping customers into cultural clusters, social sets, lifestyle, and personality type.

- ✔ **Decision makers:** Grouping customers based on who decides to purchase your product.

- ✔ **Behavioral:** Grouping customers by product usage (light, medium, heavy users), brand loyalty (none, medium, high), and type of user.

- ✔ **Distribution:** Grouping customers based on where they go to purchase your product such as in-store, online, or through the catalog.

E*Trade, an online brokerage and bank company, segments its markets in two ways:

- ✔ The company looked at *behavioral* descriptors such as usage. It found a large customer segment of day traders who wanted inexpensive and fast trades. E*Trade developed quick-trade products and bulk pricing to serve this market.

- ✔ The company looked at *demographic* descriptors, specifically income. Through market research, the company discovered that the group of people with $5,000 to $50,000 to invest was a fast growing segment that was underserved.

Through these descriptors E*Trade developed tools to enable the company to profitably serve these customers.

Begin a new notes page for each target customer segment. You may have just a few or you may have a lot. Don't worry about that for now: You can refine your list later. Give each customer group a name and use this to label your page. Then write down the segmentation base. Did you segment by needs? What is the need? If you segmented by descriptors, what were they? Use Figure 11-3 as a guide to guide your notes page structure as you work through the rest of this chapter.

Visualizing your target customer

To visual your ideal customer you want to create a customer profile or detailed description of your target customer. Specifically, you want your profile to be so descriptive that you can visualize shaking your customer's hand.

To do this, you need to know your customers' characteristics because knowing them is beneficial in developing consumer customer profiles. Be interested in their likes, dislikes, needs, wants, birthdays, anniversaries, styles, titles, beliefs, behaviors, perspectives, politics, dreams, shoe size . . . and the list goes on. (Okay, I was just kidding about shoe size.)

Check out this list of generic consumer and business characteristics:

- Consumer characteristics
  - **Demographics:** Age, generation, gender, income, family size, life cycle, occupation, education, religion, race, ethnicity, social class, health
  - **Geographic:** World region, county, state, city, climate, density
  - **Lifestyle:** Innovators, thinkers, achievers, experiencers, believers, strivers, makers, survivors
  - **Personality:** Compulsive, gregarious, authoritarian, ambitious
  - **Usage:** Occasions, benefits sought, user status, usage rate, loyalty status
- Business characteristics
  - **Demographic:** Industry, company size, location
  - **Environmental:** Economic developments, supply conditions, technological change, political and regulatory developments, competitive developments, culture and customs

- **Purchasing approaches:** Location of the purchasing function, decision making structure, nature of existing relationships, general purchasing and payment policies, purchasing criteria

- **Situational factors:** Sense of urgency, need product/service for a specific application, potential size of order

- **Personal characteristics:** Buyer-seller similarity, attitudes toward risk, loyalty

Create a customer profile that requires you visualize your customers with 100 percent clarity. Table 11-1 presents examples of good and bad customer profiles.

Table 11-1	Good and Bad Customer Profiles	
Bad Example	*Good Example*	*Better Example*
Small businesses located Oregon	Small businesses located in Oregon that are in the auto industry	Small body shops seeking rapid insurance reimbursement in Oregon
All agencies in the marketing industry	All agencies in the marketing industry billing less than $10 million annually	An agency focusing on public relations for local and state government community programs
Field sales people constantly on the road	Field sales people earning between $50K and $100K who're looking to purchase a new car in the next year	Field sales people earning between $50K and $100K who are image conscious first movers and are looking to purchase a sports car in the next year

For each one of your target customer groups, begin to list their needs and wants. Think about behaviors, motivations, and potential benefits sought. Then begin to list characteristics. If you have a consumer product or service, the major types of characteristics are demographic, geographic, lifestyle, and usage. If you have a business-to-business product or service, the major types of characteristics are demographic, environmental, operating variables, purchasing approaches, situational factors, and personal characteristics. If you have specific companies that you're targeting, write down their names and main contact information.

More than likely, you need to obtain additional information about these target customer groups in order to complete your profile. If so, use the profiles to guide your market research efforts, as explained in the previous section.

> # The best example: Anthropologie, a nationwide retail store
>
> "A female about 30 to 45 years old, college or post-graduate education, married with kids or in a committed relationship, professional or ex-professional, annual household income of $150,000 to $200,000. She's well-read and well-traveled. She's very aware — she gets our references, whether it's to a town in Europe or to a book or a movie. She's urban-minded. She's into cooking, gardening, and wine. She has a natural curiosity about the world. She's relatively fit. Her identity is a tangle of connections to activities, places, interests, values, and aspirations. She's a yoga-practicing filmmaker with an organic garden, a collection of antique musical instruments, and an abiding interest in Chinese culture.
>
> The Anthropologie customer is affluent but not materialistic. She's focused on building a nest but hankers for exotic travel. She'd like to be a domestic but has no problem cutting corners (she prefers the luscious excess of British cooking sensation Nigella Lawson to the measured perfection of Martha Stewart). She's in tune with trends, but she's a confident individualist when it comes to style. She lives in the suburbs but would never consider herself a suburbanite."
>
> Can you visualize Anthropologie's customers? Without a doubt! Now don't worry if your customer profile isn't this specific. In fact, it probably won't be. Not everyone in this company's market exhibits all of these traits; that would be too narrow. Nevertheless, this example illustrates the power behind really, truly knowing your customers. You can immediately see how this profile helps the company select which products to carry in the store, what messages to use in its advertising campaigns, how to price the merchandise, and what type of customer service drives repeat business.

Targeting the Most Attractive Markets

Choosing which target markets to pursue can be challenging because you may want to target all segments, especially those that are growing and appear very profitable, but resist the temptation. Most businesses can't possibly serve all identified target markets (or at least not well). Try to choose between one and three new markets to target at any given time.

Additionally, you want to make sure that your company doesn't enter into segments that you can't support or don't have the resources to provide excellent customer service. You want to focus your energies on the most attractive segments.

Defining an attractive segment

If you only identified two or three new markets in total, verify that you've identified the most attractive target markets. Use the following checklist to evaluate the attractiveness of each potential segment:

- ✔ **Competitors:** Look at your competitor analysis (Chapter 9 covers this topic in more detail). Are you better than the competition? Are they getting better or worse at meeting the needs of customers in this segment?

- ✔ **Company resources:** Do you have the right strengths to compete in this segment? Do you have weaknesses that need to be improved and are they fixable? In Chapter 7, you can review your company's strengths and weaknesses. Look at the culture of your organization. Is it consistent with serving this segment?

- ✔ **Segment size:** The sales potential of the segment, in terms of number of units of your product that can be sold or number of customers served, is important in making a segment attractive. Is it big enough to bother with? To find out, use the market research resource provided in the section "Locating Information Sources." Remember, size is relative. What may be too small to one company may be huge to another. Evaluate where the segment is big enough based on your requirements.

- ✔ **Segment growth rate:** You want to enter market segments that are growing and not shrinking. While this may seem obvious, many companies enter markets that are shrinking. Ideally, you should create a market strategy that allows you to serve a market for a good length of time, recouping marketing expenses and any product/service modifications. To reduce the risk of losing money when entering a new market, find one that is growing, not shrinking.

- ✔ **Segment profitability:** You need to know if focusing on this customer group is feasible. A segment's profitability is important in making a segment attractive. Knowing how profitable is profitable is only subject to your company's requirements. You can estimate revenue for one year with a simple formula:

    Number of customers × average sale per customer × number of sales per customer per year = revenue.

  To determine profit from the segment, subtract the estimated costs associated with producing the product or service and reaching the segment. (See Chapter 13 for more details.)

- ✔ **Segment accessibility:** It's possible to identify a very attractive segment, but there's no cost effective way to reach them. An attractive segment requires that you can reach this group through clear communication channels. To reach them, you first have to find them. A good indicator of segment accessibility is how easy or hard it is to dig up information in your market research efforts.

✔ **Segment differentiation**: Uniqueness is a characteristic of an attractive segment. Will this group respond to product and service offerings differently than other groups you have identified? If not, consider combining two segments. Segment differentiation tends to be obvious. You either see a clear difference or you don't. But you may need to additionally research or test-market your product or promotional message to make sure.

Evaluating your target customer groups

Choices, choices, choices. It's hard to narrow down options, especially when they all look good. Figure 11-1 provides an excellent tool to help you evaluate how well each group stacks up against the other. You can use this tool to eliminate markets as well as to prioritize them. To use the tool, follow these steps:

1. **In Figure 11-1 or on a separate notes page, write in the name of each segment across the top of the paper.**

2. **On a scale of 1 (poor) to 3 (excellent), rate each segment against the market attractiveness criteria on the left-hand side.**

3. **Add up each column.**

4. **Focus on the segments with the highest total score.**

Take the segments with the highest total score and use them in Chapter 12 to develop your strategic goals/priorities for the coming year or years.

Rate each segment on a scale of 1 (poor) to 3 (excellent)	Segment #1	Segment #2	Segment #3
How do you stack up against the **competition**?			
How are your **company resources** positioned to meet the needs of this segment?			
What is the **size** of this segment?			
What is the **growth potential** of this segment?			
What is the **profitability** of this segment?			
How **accessible** is this segment?			
Will this group **respond differently** from other groups to product and service offerings?			
Segment Totals			

Figure 11-1:
Evaluating your market segments.

Standing Out from the Crowd: Your Positioning Statement

You've determined who you want to market to, what their needs and wants are, and that they, as a group, are attractive enough to get your interest. Now you just have to get their attention! Here's a great analogy about how to get your customers' attention:

> "Cows, after you've seen them for a while, are boring. They may be perfect cows, attractive cows, cows with a great personality, cows lit by a beautiful light, but they're still boring. A purple cow, though: Now, that would really stand out. The essence of the purple cow is that it would be remarkable. Something remarkable is worth talking about, worth paying attention to," writes Seth Godin, author of *Purple Cow* (Portfolio Hardcover).

The world isn't only full of boring stuff (like brown cows), but it's also full of thousands of competitors, which is why so few people pay attention to what you're trying to communicate and sell. If in doubt, measure the level of market noise in your industry by typing in your business description into Google to see how many companies are doing the same thing you are. (*Strategic planning* returns 70 million results!)

Godin's analogy is simply a visual representation of an age-old marketing concept called positioning. *Positioning* is the space your product/service occupies in the mind of your customers. No matter what, companies consciously or subconsciously influence their position in the customer's mind. You may or may not be positioned the way you want to be. You may also just be a brown cow — invisible and boring. Extremely well positioned products or services become nouns or verbs such as Kleenex and Google.

To get customers and potential customers to pay attention, you must clearly position yourself in your customers' mind. To do so, you need a positioning statement that guides all your marketing efforts directed at the target customer group. It's the core message you want to deliver in every medium and everything you do.

In the next few sections, I discuss position statements and how to make yours really shine!

Writing your positioning statements

The purpose of writing a positioning statement is to ensure that all of your marketing activities for a customer groups are consistent and clear. (And it saves you tons of time in the long run.) Initially, focus on writing a positioning statement that's only used internally. In the future, you may end up using it for other purposes such as in your marketing collateral. But if you throw that into the mix the first go around, crafting a statement that makes sense may be more difficult. Ready to jump in?

To write your positioning statements, follow these steps:

1. **Select the target customer group you want to focus on.**

2. **Develop a list of needs your customer group has that you intend to meet (if not already included in your customer profile).**

3. **List your product/service's benefits that uniquely meet these needs.**

4. **Use the lists of customer needs and product/service benefits to finish this sentence:** *When this customer group thinks of my product or service, I want them to think _____.*

5. **Evaluate your positioning statement by making sure it's simple, clear, and consistent.**

6. **Get the word out to everyone by consistently communicating your positioning message in everything your company does for this customer group.**

Don't forget: The customer himself does the real positioning by paying attention and deciding to buy your product/service. What you *do* have control over is assessing what positions exist in the customer's mind and then determining which of those you have the best chance of occupying and defending based on your own strengths.

Perusing examples of positioning statements

Sometimes a positioning statement sounds like a tag line or a slogan. That's fine, but remember that the purpose of a positioning statement isn't to be cute. Instead its purpose is to help guide all your activities associated with a specific target customer group. You can turn it into a marketing message in the future.

If you need some inspiration, read through these positioning statements from large and small companies:

- **Mercedes-Benz:** Engineered like no other car in the world.

- **Wharton Business School:** The only business school that trains managers who are global, cross-functional, good leaders, and leveraged by technology.

- **BMW:** The ultimate driving machine.

- **Southwest Airlines:** The short-haul, no-frills, and low-priced airline.

- **Midwest Express:** All the creature comforts and calm, refined air service at competitive prices.

- **Avis:** We are only Number 2, so we try harder!

- **Famous Footwear:** The value shoe store for families.

- **Miller Lite:** The only beer with superior taste and low caloric content.

- **The Heidel House Resort:** The place to reconnect with loved ones.

- **Northern Nevada Business Weekly:** The only source for local business news.

Reaching Your New Target Markets

No matter whether you're targeting 18- to 34-year-old high-income males or 65- to 85-year-old fixed income retirees, you've got to reach them effectively and efficiently. That means finding the right balance of marketing tools and program elements to create and deliver the right product or service to consumers at the right price, right location, right time, and with the right features and attributes.

The Four Ps: Neither a soul band nor a legume

At this stage, you want to bring in your marketing mix. The marketing mix, or the Four Ps — promotion, place, product, price — are the combination of actions you have to serve your target market.

Think of each P as a leg on a chair. If they don't all support each other, the chair falls over. The same thing is true for your marketing mix. Each element needs to support the other. If there are inconsistencies, your customers *will* notice.

One of the main keys to the success of any marketing program is creating a marketing mix that is 100 percent relevant and resonates with your target market. The following sections cover all four Ps and how they fit into the market.

Product

Your marketing mix is based on and built off your products and/or services. Products are defined as anything that's capable of satisfying customer needs. Make sure that you have a product or service that is geared toward the need of your target market.

Price

Make sure that your price is within the budget of your target market to create that marketing mix that your customers desire. From the customer's perspective, price is the monetary expression of value, and that value is enjoyed by customers. Therefore, value equals benefits minus price. This P is one of the easiest Ps to change. But remember that price really is the only place that actually directly determines revenue generation.

Promotion

It's not enough to just have a good product at a good price. These benefits have to be communicated to the customer. Gear your promotional messaging to solve the problems that customers encounter.

There are hundreds of ways to communicate with your customer and more are being added every day. (Even manhole covers have logos on them!) The high-level channels include advertising, direct marketing, personal selling, sales promotion, and public relations.

Place

This P is also known as distribution. Ensure that your distribution efforts are seen by your target market. Place determines where customers can buy or receive your products and services. For product companies, this refers to all of the locations a customer can find your merchandise, such as resellers' stores, the company's own stores, a catalogue, ecommerce Web site, or a reseller's Web site. For service companies, this P is often thought of in terms of convenience. How easy is it for a customer to buy services from you? For example, a dry cleaning service increased convenience by centrally locating its operations, offering a delivery and pick-up service, and partnering with several tailors in town.

Estella's Exotic Escapes specializes in high-end, hard-to-find vacation packages. However, half of the packages she offers include mega-chain hotels in places like Cancun and Kona. Her prices are geared toward a large budget and her ads are in publications that have a subscription base of senior citizens. Do you see the "marketing mix" chair falling over? The "legs" of the chair don't support each other. Clearly, this example is over exaggerated, but you always want to make sure that your marketing mix has a message that works together.

The cycle of (product) life

From a strategic perspective, looking at where your product or service is in its life cycle helps determine actions in each of the Four Ps related to your target customer groups (see the previous section for info on the Four Ps).

The four product-life cycle phases are

- **Introduction:** This phase provides a period of slow growth with nonexistent profits (because of the extensive promotional costs). Examples: Third-generation mobile phones, e-conferencing, iris-based personal identity cards.

- **Growth:** Growth is a period of rapid market acceptance and developing profits. Examples: MP3 players, e-mail, breathable synthetic fabrics, smart cards.

- **Maturity:** This phase is a period of slow growth, level profits, and increasing marketing expenditures to defend the product's position against competitors. Examples: Personal computers, faxes, cotton t-shirts, credit cards.

- **Decline:** Decline is a period of falling sales and profits. Examples: Handwritten letters, check books, CD players.

Figure 11-2 provides an example to help you develop actions for each of the Four Ps depending on where your product is in the product-life cycle. For each target customer group, follow these steps:

1. **Determine your marketing goal for the target customer group.**

   Flip to Chapter 12 for guidance on writing goals.

2. **Determine what phase of the product-life cycle your product or service is in.**

   Use information in the section above, "The cycle of (product) life," to determine where your product or service is in its life.

3. **Develop an action plan that addresses product, price, promotion, distribution.**

Use the information in Chapter 13 to develop an action plan that supports the goal you developed for this target customer group.

You may not need to take a specific action for each of the Four Ps. But write down what's happening so you can ensure the marketing mix works cohesively.

	Introduction	Growth	Maturity	Decline
Marketing objectives	Create product awareness & trial	Maximize market share	Maximize profits while defending market share	Reduce expenditure & "milk" brand
Product	Offer basic	Offer new features, extensions, service, & warranty	Diversify brand & models	Phase out weak items
Price	Usually high; use cost +	Maintain pricing	Match or lower than competitors	Cut price
Distribution	High expenses	Increase number of outlets	Intensify distribution	Very selective
Promotion	Build awareness among early adopters	Build awareness & interest in mass market	Stress brand differences & benefits	Reduce level to maintain loyal customers

Figure 11-2: Developing your marketing action plan.

Staying Market-Focused

The process of researching, segmenting, targeting, and reaching new customers doesn't need to be something you do only when you're focused on finding new customers. In fact, world class companies have made it a habit to be market-focused. Being market-focused means taking marketing activities out of just the marketing department and away from initiatives. In fact, world-class companies have made it a habit to be market-focused. It means making marketing part of everyone's job.

In the following sections, I explain how being market-focused works and give you tips on staying in the know.

Gathering relevant information

The key to being market-focused is continuously gathering relevant information about your customers and your market. Most likely, you already gather a significant amount of customer information in meetings and discussions with customers and distributors, from sales reports, through databases, and so on.

When you gather this info, you have to do something with it. Take these tips to heart about your info:

✔ Start collecting the info in a systematic fashion by making a group marketing storage unit such as a physical filing cabinet or a file on your company server.

✔ Scan the environment for information about government regulation and policies, technological changes, competitors and their activities, and future industry trends. Continual environmental scanning allows you to stay proactive, taking advantage of shifts as they happen, instead of being reactive, and scrambling to keep up.

Sources for info include trade publications, industry events, and your local network. Consider doing this scan quarterly or semi-annually.

Sharing what you know

When you get a bunch of information, what are your going to do with it? The information you gather should be regularly compiled in a usable form and then shared with employees in various ways. These sharing avenues can include

✔ Informal meetings

✔ Customer and market databases

✔ Staff meetings

✔ Company newsletters

✔ Brown-bag lunches

✔ Forums

✔ Internal message postings

✔ Company blogs

Intelligence needs to be communicated clearly, continuously, and appropriately so that your staff can strategically respond to the needs of the market.

Responding to what you've discovered

Responding to your market is critical to being market-focused. You can generate information and communicate it internally, but unless you respond to market needs, nothing gets accomplished. Your company should be driven by

- ✔ An understanding of what your customers want
- ✔ The knowledge of how to meet the customers' needs
- ✔ The delivery of the product or service customers want

Many of you reading this may already be doing most of these activities. Great job! If you aren't, it's okay. Take some action to formalize your process. Studies show that companies that link these activities together achieve greater levels of performance when compared to their competitors. A company that increases its market focus by ten percent can see a growth of between 17 and 20 percent in overall performance.

Want to evaluate how market-focused your firm is? Check out this free, online assessment tool: www.m3planning.com/survey.

Putting It All Together: Organizing Customer Information

Businesses that succeed do so by creating and keeping customers. Because marketing plays the key role of making that happen, it has a large part in setting the strategic direction of the organization. But unlike the other sections of your plan, the marketing section starts with a target customer group instead of a goal. Figure 11-3 is an example of how to organize your customer profile information.

You can use the marketing portion of your strategic plan to develop a complete marketing plan, which would include more detail about your markets and your action plans to reach them. However, smaller organizations often choose to just have one plan, a strategic plan, that covers your intended marketing actions.

> **Example Company:** Hallelujah Acres of Shelby, NC offers products, counseling, workshops, and conferences to help people attain and maintain optimal health while eliminating sickness and disease, and to influence them to adopt a healthier lifestyle based on Biblical principles.

Customer Group:	People with cancer
Strategy:	Market development
Segmentation Base:	Need, motivation, and desire to find an alternative cure to cancer because none of the traditional methods are working
Customer Profile:	*Needs*: Hope, encouragement, education (information), wellness plan, support, accountability to someone *Primary benefit sought*: A non-traditional cure for cancer or relief from pain *Demographics*: All types of non-terminal cancer, any demographic *Geographic*: Located in the Southeast region of the United States *Lifestyle*: Survivors, involved in cancer activist and support groups, SAD, misinformed, deceived, bought into the medical establishment, no energy, no hope, depressed, overweight, clogged up, overfed and undernourished, toxic and starving *Personality*: Highly motivated, will do anything it takes to get better *Usage*: Very loyal, repeat usage until cured
Segment Attractiveness:	*Segment Size*: 19,200 *Growth Rate*: 12 percent annually *Profitability*: 960 new customers (5% of market) * $1,200 = $1,152,000 *Accessibility*: Reach through doctors, support groups, associations *Differentiation*: This segment is self-identified. The company is not serving any other group similar to this one.
Position Statement:	When this group thinks of Hallelujah Acres, we want them to think we are the only healthy, alternative solution to cancer that really works.
Marketing Objective:	Reach 5 percent of the Southeast cancer patient market with the Hallelujah Acres message by 2007.
Stage of Product-Life Cycle:	Growth
Product/Services:	Develop a Hallelujah Acres' cancer-curing kit, complete with cancer-specific books, Hallelujah Acres' Diet products, and DVD movie featuring cured patients. Open Hallelujah Acres' Cancer Clinic in partnership with Oasis Hope Hospital.
Pricing:	Maintain current product pricing. Segment is not cost conscience.
Promotion:	Partner with state cancer associations to provide newsletter content, speakers, special promotional offerings to their members. Develop a specific section on the Hallelujah Acres' Web site for cancer information. Direct mail Hallelujah Acres' brochure with cancer-specific testimonials to target market.
Distribution:	Sell cancer-specific products on Web site, through distribution locations. Direct mail product catalogue to target market.

Figure 11-3: Target customer group profile, goals, and action plan.

Chapter 12

Establishing Your Strategic Priorities

Congratulations! If you've been working through this book from beginning to end, you've made it halfway through the strategic planning process. Right about now, it's common to feel like the process is a little out of control. This occurs primarily because you have collected so much information, input, and feedback that sorting through it all seems impossible. It can feel disorienting. So step back and review what you're doing. Strategic planning answers where you are now, where you're going, and how you're getting there.

Visualize a famous bridge such as the Golden Gate Bridge, Brooklyn Bridge, or Tower Bridge. All bridges have two primary support pillars and span in between the two, allowing one part of land to be connected with another. One of these pillars explains where you are now — your mission, your values, your strengths, weaknesses, opportunities, and threats. The pillar on the far side represents where you are going — your vision. And how you get there is the span or the road in between — your strategic objectives, goals, and action plans.

Now because the span between the two pillars is quite long, in order to bridge the gap, you need long-term strategic objectives and short-term goals. How you build the bridge is your strategy. You can have a different strategy for each section of the bridge. You can have a consistent strategy for the whole thing, it doesn't matter. But think about the strategy as the *how,* and the goals and strategic objectives as the *what.*

The critical part of this analogy is that in order for the bridge to function properly, every element has to support the other or it collapses. So as you look at the ideas you generated in the previous chapters, some of them help connect the two pillars and some of them are probably outliers.

Use the following process to develop your road, which connects your mission to your vision:

✔ Evaluate all the strategic priorities generated by assessing your strategic position.

✔ Develop a "short list" of internal and external strategic priorities.

✔ Create strategic objectives (three to five years).

✔ Create short-term goals (one year).

✔ Develop action plans based on the goals (next 90 days).

✔ Establish who's responsible for carrying out the goals.

✔ Agree on how and when to measure progress.

In this chapter, you're going to evaluate your strategic opportunities, priorities, and goals. I use the words *opportunity, choice, alternative, ideas, possibilities, thoughts,* and *actions* to mean anything that you're considering acting on and including in your strategic plan. So keep that in mind as you read.

Evaluating All Your Opportunities

Being strategic is about making choices. Strategic choice is about making subjective decisions based on goal information. To do so, you first generate a list of all feasible alternatives. That means *everything*. Don't be shy — put down all your thoughts about potential opportunities for your organization.

In Chapters 7 through 11, you cast your net out wide to determine the actions to take based on your current strategic position. In fact, it probably feels a little messy right now. If you worked through each of the previous chapters, more than likely you have pages of notes that list ideas, possible goals, suggested actions, to-dos, and some short-term and some long-term strategic objectives. (A long list of ideas and actions isn't necessary.)

Identifying opportunities from your SWOT analysis

The snapshot of your strategic position is captured in your SWOT analysis (from Chapter 9). By itself, a SWOT isn't actionable. By matching up factors from one quadrant with factors in another quadrant, you can start to identify potential actions based on the SWOT analysis.

The point of matching up internal factors with external factors is to identify a fit between organizational strengths and market opportunities. In other words, what opportunities can you take advantage of, based on what you've already got to work with? Also, by matching weaknesses up with opportunities or threats, you may see some compelling pairs that are worth pursuing.

In this exercise, get creative! Put all your ideas down, even if they seem ridiculous. Allow yourself and your team to brainstorm. You can pull it back down to Earth at the end of the exercise. See Figure 12-1 for a visual.

	Strengths-S *List Strengths*	**Weaknesses-W** *List Weaknesses*
Opportunities-O *List Opportunities*	**SO Alternatives** *Use strengths to take advantage of opportunities*	**WO Alternatives** *Overcome weaknesses by taking advantage of opportunities*
Threats-T *List Threats*	**ST Alternatives** *Use strengths to avoid threats*	**WT Alternatives** *Minimize weaknesses and avoid threats*

Figure 12-1: Making your SWOT actionable.

To develop a variety of choices, work through these steps with yourself or your team:

1. **Pull out your SWOT analysis from Chapter 9 (if you've completed that already).**

   No SWOT? Then pull one together for this exercise or jump to the next section.

2. **On a white board or a big piece of paper, draw a matrix similar to Figure 12-1.**

   If you have a lot of strengths, weaknesses, opportunities, or threats, you don't have to rewrite them all in the matrix boxes, just work from a handout.

3. **In the box labeled SO Alternatives, match internal strengths with external opportunities.**

4. **In the box labeled WO Alternatives, match internal weaknesses with external opportunities.**

5. **In the box labeled ST Alternatives, match internal strengths with external threats.**

6. **In the box labeled WT Alternatives, match internal weaknesses with external threats.**

7. **Review all four quadrants and highlight the choices that look the most promising.**

8. **Use the items you highlighted as a source of potential actions when developing your priorities in the section, "Creating a short list of priorities."**

Here are some generic examples of how this exercise works:

- ✔ Strong reputation (strength) + Market growth in a neighboring community (opportunity) = Expanded operations in new market

- ✔ High cost structure in a specific product line (weakness) + Arrival of new technology that would reduce supply chain overhead (opportunity) = Improved operations through technology investment

- ✔ Cost advantages through proprietary knowledge (strength) + Primary industry is in decline (threat) = Entering new industry that leverages cost advantages

- ✔ Poor employee morale (weakness) + Tight labor market (threat) = Development of an improved employee benefits package

Sorting through your other opportunities

In addition to your SWOT analysis, throughout the strategic planning process, you've kept ideas and notes (I hope) about possible actions to include in your strategic plan. But in case your ideas aren't all in one place, use the following list to gather your thoughts about your current strategic position:

✔ Last year's incomplete goals and actions (Chapter 4)

✔ Improvements, modifications, enhancements to current products and services (Chapter 4)

✔ Improvements to operational process (Chapter 7)

✔ Enhancements to capabilities and resources (Chapter 7)

✔ Action to eliminate cash drains and improve cash creators (Chapter 7)

✔ Ideas to improve current customer value, retention, and loyalty (Chapter 8)

✔ Opportunities and threats in the environment, industry, and market (Chapter 9)

✔ Entering new markets and serving new customer groups (Chapter 11)

Look at these different lists and eliminate anything that's unrealistic, unimportant, and excessive. Create a list of choices that are truly important to your organization right now. As with the previous exercise, use this list as a source of potential actions in the section "Create a short list of priorities."

Choosing the Best Opportunities

This section brings you to the scary part of strategic planning. Why? Because people are terrified of making the wrong choice. If you worked through the previous section, you have some lists of choices, but you can't do everything, so it's elimination time. Know that every other business owner, executive director, and department manager has come to the same place as you are right now. Although there are never guarantees in business, this section helps you develop your own guidelines to assure that you make the right choices. But at the end of the day, you have to make a decision.

First off, know that there are four reasons people put off making decisions:

✔ They don't have enough data.

✔ They may have too much data to decipher.

✔ They don't know that a decision is required.

✔ People are afraid of losing their job.

The one concept that most business owners, executives, and managers forget is that the lack of a decision results in more derailments of the mission than any other cause.

Developing your own rules

In my work, clients often ask for a tried and true method to evaluate all the strategic choices that are in front of them. Unfortunately, in my experience, I haven't found such a fail-safe method. What does work is establishing a set of parameters or rules that are specific and unique to your operating environment. Use these rules to judge any and all strategic choices that come up.

Clearly in the strategic planning process, you seek out options and choices. But such decisions occur regularly outside of strategic planning. By establishing a set of rules, you can quickly evaluate whether an opportunity is really an opportunity or a distraction. Develop a set of rules and use it as a litmus test. If the opportunity doesn't pass the test, it's out.

Here are some categories of rules:

- ✔ **Priority rule:** With this rule, you prioritize some opportunities over others based on their connection to reaching your vision. Set a rule to require that all opportunities must help you reach your vision.

- ✔ **Timing rule:** This financial rule helps you prioritize opportunities based on how much money you want to see returned within what time period. Pull in your finance or accounting people to help you establish this one.

- ✔ **Boundary rule:** This rule says that every opportunity is evaluated based on whether it's within your mission. Set a rule to require that the opportunity aligns with the organization's core mission and values.

- ✔ **How-to rule:** Develop a rule that requires you to sketch out how to implement the opportunity if you took advantage of it before jumping in. If you can't clearly define an action plan for the opportunity, you know that trying to execute it will go poorly.

Sorting out internal and external priorities

Grouping priorities helps you compare like things when making trade-offs. For example, choosing between investing in new technology or hiring a new person are both expense decisions with similar outcomes, whereas choosing between entering a new market or implementing a succession plan aren't directly related. So at this point, you want to divide your choices into two groups — those that have internal implications and those that have external implications.

How do you decide what's internal and what's external?

> ✔ **Internal priorities** include everything related to productivity improvement such as employees, training, operations, technology, efficiencies, research and development, and anything else that deals with the internal operations of your organization.
>
> ✔ **External priorities** include everything that's related to revenue generation such as entering new target markets, developing new products, and partnering with other organizations.

The quickest and easiest way to sort through your list is to highlight internal priorities one color and external priorities another color.

Creating a short list of priorities

Creating a short list is the last part of synthesizing all your options down to the select few for your strategic plan. Ideally, you want to have between three and five internal and external priorities. If you have too many, you may lose focus and your plan may become too big. More than likely, your lists contain a dozen or so priorities, so it's time to eliminate some more.

After you've sorted out your internal and external opportunities (see the previous section), start comparing your priorities to figure out which to take off first. Remember to compare only opportunities that are directly competing (external to external and internal to internal). You make this comparison because you need to make some trade-offs. Making equitable trade-offs requires comparing apples to apples. Internal priorities are competing with other internal priorities, and external priorities are competing against other external priorities.

If you have a hard time limiting your priorities, make a someday list. This list contains priorities that are important and that you'll get to some day. If there are still too many options, use the paired comparison analysis that follows.

The paired comparison analysis helps you limit or prioritize your opportunities. (You can see how to set up this tool in Figures 12-2 and 12-3.) This analysis helps you set priorities when there are multiple demands on the same resources — your time and money. The paired comparison analysis isolates choices and removes some subjectivity.

Use the tool to compare each option with each other option — one at a time. Here's the step-by-step guide to use this tool:

1. **Use your pared-down list of opportunities, and draw up a grid with each option in both a row and a column header.**

   Assign a letter to each option.

2. **Block out cells on the table where you're going to be comparing an option with itself.**

   There is never a difference in these cells. Normally you block out the diagonal running from the top left to the bottom right.

3. **Block out cells on where you'll duplicate a comparison.**

   These cells are below the diagonal. See Figure 12-2 and copy the layout.

4. **Within the remaining cells, compare the option in the row with the one in the column.**

   For each cell, decide which of the two options is more important. Write down the letter of the more important option in the cell, and score the difference in importance from 0 (equal importance) to 3 (much more important).

5. **Consolidate the results by adding up the total of all the values for each of the options.**

   Convert these values into a percentage of the total score to determine rank of importance.

	Opportunity #1 (A)	Opportunity #2 (B)	Opportunity #3 (C)	Opportunity #4 (D)
Opportunity #1 (A)	Blocked Out			
Opportunity #2 (B)	Blocked Out	Blocked Out		
Opportunity #3 (C)	Blocked Out	Blocked Out	Blocked Out	
Opportunity #4 (D)	Blocked Out	Blocked Out	Blocked Out	Blocked Out

Figure 12-2: Setting up your paired comparison analysis.

Chad's Chimps, a small, local construction company, is looking at a variety of expansion options described in Figure 12-3. With limited resources and bonding capacity, the company can only pursue one opportunity at a time. The opportunities include the following:

✔ Expanding into new markets by opening satellite offices

✔ Buying a concrete company

✔ Establishing an exclusive partnership with a civil engineering company

✔ Expanding service line to include custom homes and remodels

	Expanding into new market (A)	Buying a concrete company (B)	Partnering with an engineering firm (C)	Expanding service line (D)
Expanding into new market (A)		A, 2	A, 3	A, 1
Buying a concrete company (B)			C, 3	D, 2
Partnering with an engineering firm (C)				D, 2
Exapanding service line (D)				

Figure 12-3: Using the paired comparison analysis.

Company executives compare the opportunities. First they write down the letter of the most important option, and then they score their difference in importance. For example, when comparing expanding into a new market (A) with buying a concrete company (B), the executives chose A over B. Then they decided that expanding into a new market was two times more important than buying a concrete company. Therefore, in that cell they wrote in A,2. They went through the same process for each comparison, then added up the A, B, C, and D values and converted each into a percentage as follows:

✔ A = 6 (46 percent)

✔ B = 0 (0 percent)

✔ C = 3 (23 percent)

✔ D = 4 (31 percent)

Expanding into a new market is the most important opportunity (A), followed by expanding the current service line (D). Buying a concrete company is the least important and may come up when the other opportunities have been realized. You can see how the comparison allows each opportunity to be evaluated against the others as well as show the difference in importance between each one.

Balancing Out Your Strategic Priorities

Often, business owners and executives fall prey to the allure of setting too many financial goals. Or, their goals are exclusively financial. This detracts from the other reasons you're in business, such as employing people, contributing to their communities, or providing a needed product or service. Enter the Balanced Scorecard.

The Balanced Scorecard (BSC) is an excellent management tool that ensures you have a holistic and balanced strategy as well as a way to track performance over time to assess if goals are being met. I introduce the Balanced Scorecard in this chapter to help you write goals in the four key areas that all organizations must excel in to succeed. Then if you head to Chapter 14, you develop the rest of your scorecard — specifically, how to track your measures and targets.

To have a balanced and holistic strategy, organizations must have goals that feed off each other. These perspectives are described below:

- **Financial or mission:** When you provide value to your customers, you achieve your financial or mission goals.

- **Customer:** If you want to generate additional revenue, you need to provide value to your customers.

- **Internal and operational process:** In order to provide value to your customers, you must have internal business process to create that value.

- **Employee (centering on learning and innovation):** And in order for your business processes to function, you need people who are skilled and knowledgeable.

Tammy's Tantalizing Tacos top line financial goal is to increase the revenue by 10 percent annually. How will she achieve her financial goal? Sell more tacos. In order to sell more tacos, she must provide great customer service. And what does she need to do to deliver great customer service? Have efficient processes that deliver food quickly. To excel at quick food delivery, she has to have well-trained employees.

The scorecard of success

The BSC was introduced by Robert Kaplan, a Harvard Business School professor, and David Norton, the founder and president of Balanced Scorecard Collaborative, Inc., in the early 1990s as a new way to work with business strategy. Today, over half of the Fortune 1,000 companies in North America are using the Balanced Scorecard, which has become the hallmark of a well-run organization. Many organizations say the scorecard is the foundation of their measurement and management systems.

For each perspective, develop at least one long-term strategic objective but no more than five. If you develop too many at the beginning, your plan may become unwieldy. Look at your short-list of external and internal priorities you developed in the previous section. Note which priorities fall where. If you're short in any area, consider developing additional priorities to have a balanced strategy.

Financial priorities: If we succeed, how will we look to our shareholders?

Goals in the financial area come in two flavors: revenue generation and productivity improvement. A solid strategic plan has one goal in each of these activities. The financial perspective contains priorities that explain how your company looks to shareholders, which are usually owners and investors. By serving your customer well, you increase your revenue generation. By improving your internal business process, you enhance productivity improvement. Your financial goals may include the following:

✔ **Revenue generation**

- To increase revenue by 10 percent annually

- To increase gross profit by 10 percent annually

- To increase sales by 10 percent annually

✔ **Productivity improvement**

- To decrease expenses by 5 percent

- To increase net profit by 10 percent

- To improve overall efficiency as measured by output over a period of time

- To improve overall productivity (doing more with what you have)

Customer priorities: How do we provide value to our customers?

Customer priorities support the financial goals. These goals focus on meeting the needs of the customer through products and services. All of your external goals fall into this category. Crafting new customer and current customer goals is a good way to structure this section. Some important long-term strategic objectives for valuing your customers include

✔ **New customer goals**

- Introduce existing products into a new market.
- Introduce new products to new and existing markets.
- Anticipate future customer needs through customer feedback.
- Expand sales to the global marketplace.

✔ **Current customer goals**

- Expand sales to existing customers.
- Increase customer retention.
- Increase customer loyalty.
- Cross sell existing products/services to current clients.
- Achieve and maintain outstanding customer service.
- Develop and use a customer database.
- Anticipate future customer needs through customer feedback.

Internal priorities: To satisfy our customers, in what processes must we excel?

Internal business process goals serve several purposes: Support the customer and financial goals; focus on administrative processes that have an impact on creating customer value and satisfaction; and focus on internal management activities and operational functions needed to support the products and services. Look at your list of internal priorities for this section. In Chapter 7, you find all the areas of organization you must look at in order to succeed. You may glean some additional ideas from that chapter. Here are some long-term strategic objectives to prioritize your internal goals:

✔ Acquire enhanced CRM data mining capabilities.

✔ Improve internal processes.

✔ Increase efficiencies through the use of wireless or virtual technology.

✔ Increase community outreach.

✔ Develop and implement a promotional plan to drive increased business.

✔ Establish one new strategic alliance annually.

✔ Improve internal communications.

✔ Redirect or restructure available resources.

✔ Improve distributor and supplier relationships.

✔ Improve marketing, advertising, and public relations.

✔ Capitalize on physical facilities (location, capacity, and so on).

✔ Improve organizational structure.

Employee priorities: How must our organization grow and improve?

Employee priorities drive everything else in your plan. Without your team, you don't have an organization. These goals focus on developing people, increasing the company's knowledge base, improving through innovation, and discovering best practices. Check out Chapter 7 for additional information on employee priorities. Work on these long-term strategic objectives with your employees:

✔ Continually discover and adopt current best practices.

✔ Align incentives and rewards with employee performance.

✔ Employ professionals who create success for customers.

✔ Develop a broad set of skills useful for customer support.

✔ Develop a team who understands strategy.

✔ Transfer knowledge from your leading-edge clients.

✔ Continually develop a set of best practices in your industry and your clients' industries.

✔ Improve labor relations, human resource development, and training.

Turning Priorities into Strategies, Objectives, and Goals

This area is probably the most widely debated part of strategic planning. Having goals, objectives, and strategies are great, but knowing how they all work together (if in fact they do) and if you need them all is another story. I suggest ignoring the semantics and focusing on establishing a time frame. What matters is having a combination of long-term and short-term markers to keep your organization moving in the right direction. Think of the following hierarchy to demystify the terms of your priorities:

✔ **Core Values:** Your guiding principles that *rarely* change and that you to stick to no matter what vision you're pursuing

✔ **Mission:** The underlying reason why you're in business in the first place

✔ **Vision:** The big, hairy, bold goal you're headed for, and the thing concept that everything your company does is focused on

✔ **Strategy:** The guiding statement that explains how you get to your vision

✔ **Three-year strategic objectives:** Intermediate goals that are broad and continuous, that you achieve on the way to your vision, and that explain the activities you need to be in to achieve your vision

✔ **One-year goals:** One-year markers that support your long-term strategic objectives

✔ **Action items:** Items that explain who and the when

Figure 12-4 illustrates how to use the four balanced scorecard perspectives as well as how strategies, goals, and objectives fit together.

Overall strategy: Leverage current resources to gain market share.

3-year goals	1-year goals	Measures	Targets	Person Responsible
Financial				
To establish a financially stable and profitable company.	1. Increase our billable hours by 10% over the next 12 months.	# of billable hours	1.2% increase each month	
	2. Achieve sales growth of 10% per year.	Monthly sales	1.2% increase each month	
Customer				
Introduce current products to two new markets.	1. Realize 10% of the company's annual sales from the small business market by end of next year.	# of small business clients	100 clients	Marketing department
Internal Business Processes				
To achieve order fulfillment excellence through on-line process improvement.	1. Reduce the time lapse between order data and delivery from 6 days to 4 days by this June.	# of days to process each order	4 days	Shipping department
	2. Reduce the number of returns due to shipping errors from 3% to 2%.	# of returns due to shipping errors	2%	Shipping department
Employee & Learning				
To provide employee with challenging and rewarding work.	1. Reduce turnover among sales managers by 10% by the end of the year.	Employee turnover	10%	Sales department
	2. Hire and train a human relations director by the end of the year.	Director hired	Director hired	CEO

Figure 12-4: Putting together your goals and strategies.

Strategizing how to reach your vision

Your strategies are the general methods you intend to use to reach your vision. Although strategies are embedded in all elements of your strategic plans, consider listing the top one to two strategies or long-term activities your company needs to pursue in order to achieve its vision.

A strategy is like an umbrella. It's a general statement(s) that guides and covers a set of activities. You can develop strategies for your whole organization, a department, a specific set of activities, or a guiding statement for a year. No matter what the level, strategies answer the question of how you do something.

To write strategies, answer the following questions:

- ✔ What initiatives do we need to pursue?
- ✔ How will we achieve our vision?

Here are a few sample strategies:

- ✔ Starbucks' strategy is to build the brand one cup at a time, based on three key ingredients: the quality of the coffee, their retail stores, and selective brand extensions.
- ✔ Erlach Computer Consulting's strategy for 2008 is to lay the foundation for growth.
- ✔ The Economic Development Authority of Western Nevada's strategy is to move toward economic development and to increase the base of companies contributing to the region's measurable quality of life to ensure long-term vitality of the community.

Writing your long-term strategic objectives

Strategic objectives are the general areas in which your effort is directed to drive your mission and vision. With strategic objectives, the company moves from motive to action. They define what an organization is intending to accomplish both programmatically and organizationally. Strategic objectives are broad categories — non-measurable and continuous.

To help you write your strategic objectives, think about your answers to the following questions:

- ✔ What areas do you need to be involved in to accomplish your mission?
- ✔ In what areas will you continue being actively involved in for the next five years?

Making your short-term goals SMART

Realistic goals ought to serve as a tool for stretching a company to reach its full potential; this means setting them high enough to be challenging to energize the company and its strategy. Short-term goals are immediate mileposts on your way to your vision. Think about achieving them in a one-year timeframe. With goals, the company converts the mission, vision, and long-term strategic objectives into performance targets.

For effective goals to function as yardsticks for tracking a company's performance and progress, they must state how much of what kind of performance and by when it is to be accomplished. They must be relevant, aggressive yet achievable, and be stated in measurable or quantifiable terms. Think SMART when you create your goals:

- ✔ **Specific:** Goals need to be specific. Try to answer the questions of *How much* and *What kind* with each goal you write.

- ✔ **Measurable:** Goals must be stated in quantifiable terms, or otherwise they're only good intentions. Measurable goals facilitate management planning, implementation, and control. (See the section below for more on measuring your goals.)

- ✔ **Attainable:** Goals must provide a stretch that inspires people to aim higher. Goals must be achievable, or they're a set-up for failure. Set goals you know you, your company, and employees can realistically reach.

- ✔ **Responsible person:** Goals must be assigned to a person or a department. But just because a person is assigned to a goal doesn't mean that she's solely responsible for its achievement. See Chapter 14 for ideas on how to hold your team accountable for goal achievement.

- ✔ **Time specific:** With reference to time, your goals must include a timeline of when your goals should be accomplished.

Pegging Your Measures

Goals are desired outcomes. The progress toward attaining an goal is gauged by one or more measures. There are causal relationships between goals — one action causes another outcome. Because you have established SMART goals, it is easier to pull out or delineate the measures you need to track.

Measures are the indicators of how a business is performing relative to its goals. For every goal, you should track one, maybe two, measures that tell you how you're progressing toward achieving the desired outcome. Measures are quantifiable performance statements, and they must follow certain guidelines:

✔ Relevant to the goal and strategy

✔ Placed in context of a target to be reached in an identified time frame

✔ Capable of being tracked period after period

✔ Owned by the person who's responsible for the goal

Sometimes the measures are obvious, like number of new customers. Other times, they can be very hard to come up with. If you're stumped, ask yourself some of the following questions:

✔ What causes this goal to occur?

✔ What causes increased sales?

✔ What causes operations to improve?

✔ What causes an increase in market share?

✔ What causes customer satisfaction?

✔ What causes employee satisfaction?

See Figure 12-5 for a list of possible measures.

Figure 12-5:
A long list of possible measures.

Financial	Customer	Internal Business Processes	Employee and Learning
Net sales (dollar growth and percent increase)	Improving image/reputation	Percentage operating costs	Employee retention
Gross profit margin	Number of customer complaints	Billable efficiency	Employee satisfaction
Pretax earnings (dollar growth and percent increase)	Percentage market share	Quality of product/service	Number of quality resumes on hand
Operating expenses (SGA) as a percent of sales	Number of customers retained	Defects ratio	Employee turnover
Receivables turnover	Customer satisfaction	New product success rate	Number of ideas in the pipeline
Inventory turnover	Dollars per account	Cycle time to deliver	Number of employee suggestions
Debt-to-equity ratio	Time spent with customer	Project turnaround time	% of employee who are systems efficient
Total equity ratio	Revenue per customer	Number of defects or returns	Average sales per employee
Operating cash flow	Number of transactions per unit time	Delivery times	Number of net new positions
Investing cash flow	Average sales dollars per transaction	Delivery response time to customer	Number of relevant trainings attended
Financing cash flow	Customer satisfaction index	Number of test market trails	
Ending cash	Number of customers	Relative product quality	
Earnings per share	Number of new customers	Number of new products produced	
ROI, ROE, ROA	Ratio of new to existing customers	Average cost per product	
	Average sales per customer	Number of products sold	

By creating good solid measures, you've established the first step in developing your scorecard (see Chapter 14 for more scorecard info). Your corporate scorecard is a tool to help you monitor the progress of your business and your strategic plan. A scorecard consists of two pieces for every goal:

✔ **Measures:** This measurement is an explanation (word text) of what you want to achieve. These indicate whether the overall strategy has been accomplished. This is an end point.

✔ **Targets:** These quantify (numeric) the outcome measures. Target measures are the specific numbers you need to hit in order to achieve your goal and can be expressed in weekly, monthly, or annual figures.

Determining measures can be tough work. Don't agonize over finding the best measure. Start with the most obvious and easiest to collect. As you work with your plan over the next several years, you can refine your measures.

Part V

Creating and Making the Most of Your Plan

The 5th Wave   By Rich Tennant

STRATEGIC
PLANNING
SEMINAR

2:00
BOOTH 701

In this part . . .

This part is the heart of the work on your strategic plan. You put your plan together in a cohesive, clear document, and then you move to executing the plan. You read about everything from how to empower your employees to holding effective strategy meetings. I also cover contingency planning — what to do if your plan fails and you need to head to Plan B. If you run a governmental agency, nonprofit organization, small business, or a department, this is the part for you.

Chapter 13

Putting Your Plan Together

*Y*ou've arrived! If you're at this chapter in sequence, you've reached the point where you can actually put your strategic plan together and give your plan life. You've developed your business strategy and you have a clear roadmap designed to reach your vision. You've identified what you're best at (Chapter 5), refined your mission, vision, and values (Chapter 6), sized up your internal and external environment (Chapters 7, 8, and 9), determined your growth strategies (Chapter 10), selected new markets to reach (Chapter 11), and established your strategic objectives and goals (Chapter 12). The next step (this chapter) is to put all these elements together and put your plan in action.

Before your plan is complete, you develop action plans and complete a financial assessment. Also in this chapter, you create a strategy map, which really is your roadmap to your vision!

Assembling Your Strategic Plan

With all the work you've done up to this point, it's time to put it together in one comprehensive document. This may seem tedious, but I guarantee there's someone on your staff who loves this type of detail work. Seek that person out to collate everything you have done to date. If you don't have such a person, brew up a big pot of coffee and get to work!

Here's why this part of the job is so important:

- ✔ **The strategic direction becomes clear.** Without bringing everything together in one document, your plan is just a bunch of different parts. When the parts become whole, you clearly see how you can reach your vision.

- ✔ **Ideas become action.** Up until now, you've developed and collected a bunch of great ideas. By formalizing them into a plan, you can develop action plans and assess the financial viability of your choices.

- ✔ **Gaps are identified.** With everything in one place, stand back and evaluate your plan. Does it make sense? Are your goals supporting one another? Have you missed anything?

If you've kept your notes in your strategy notebook (explained in the Introduction), bringing everything together should go quickly. Don't forget to bring together the ideas and input from your team that you've been soliciting throughout the planning process. If you didn't use a strategy notebook, here are the main topics to reference:

- ✔ Competitive advantage: Chapter 5

- ✔ Mission, vision, values: Chapter 6

- ✔ Long-term strategies: Chapter 12

- ✔ Strategic objectives: Chapter 12

- ✔ SWOT analysis: Chapters 7, 8, 9

- ✔ Customer profiles: Chapter 11

- ✔ Three-year and one-year goals: Chapters 10, 11, 12

- ✔ Action plan: Chapter 13

- ✔ Financial projections: Chapter 13

Please note that a strategic plan isn't like a business plan because the strategic plan document is primarily for your internal use. It's not a sales piece for outside critique (except in the case of seeking financing), so you don't need any extra verbiage or fluff. Just make sure that the text looks nice and is easy to read. Consider adding your logo to the header or footer and formatting it so it looks professional.

More than likely you have some ideas, goals, and considerations that aren't part of this plan, but you don't want to lose them. Create a "Someday List" or file. Put all your extra information in this file for your next strategic planning session.

In addition to using the chapters referenced in the preceding list, tailor your strategic plan to your business by incorporating the ideas in Chapters 17 and 18, depending on your business type.

To see a sample strategic plan, check out my Web site, www.mystrategicplan.com/dummies/plan.

Getting Down to Business and Taking Action

By the time company managers get to the action planning part of strategic planning, many are tired and worn out from all the work leading up to this point. But don't stop yet! Setting action items and to-dos for each short-term goal is essential, and now it's time to connect those goals with people, deadlines, and costs.

You are developing an action plan for each goal. An *action plan* explains who's going to do what, by when, and in what order for the organization to reach its goals. The design and implementation of the action planning depend on the nature and needs of the organization.

Although this may seem like a monumental task, here are a few ways to simplify the process:

- **List the concrete steps or to-dos that you need to accomplish in order to achieve your goals.** You don't need to list every single action item for each goal — that might take all year.

- **Focus on identifying large to-dos that warrant discussion at a team level.** Stay away from big items that are so big that you don't know where to start.

- **Identify all the actions that need to occur in the next 90 days.** Continue this same process every 90 days until the goal is achieved.

To develop your action plan, take a look at these approaches:

- **The group approach:** With your strategic planning team or a group of staff members who are impacted by the goal, you can identify the next actions for each short-term goal. The benefit of working in a group is the ability to generate a lot of ideas about how best to achieve the goal. The drawback is action planning in a group setting can take a long time.

- **The individual approach:** Because every short-term goal is assigned to a person or department, you can have each party develop action items for the goal he or she is responsible for. Then reconvene as a group and discuss each action plan. The benefit to this approach is speed and personal buy-in. The drawback is you may miss out on group ideas.

For every short-term goal, identify the following items. These items are listed in logical order and flow to make it easy to develop each one:

- ✔ **Action item or to-do:** Start the sentence with a verb to show the action that's being done. After all the action items are listed, order them based on priority.

- ✔ **Person or department responsible:** If there's shared responsibility, make one person the lead.

- ✔ **Start and end dates:** Start dates are important because they allow you to see the duration of an action. Without the start date, you won't know if you are behind schedule until the end date passes. When establishing an end date, commit to the deadline.

- ✔ **Expense:** Identify an estimated expense if applicable.

- ✔ **Progress or current status:** Use this gauge to indicate what percentage of the action item is complete or to explain what's happening with the action item right now. Update this field regularly for reporting and tracking purposes.

See Figure 13-1 for visual representation. Also see Figure 12-4 in Chapter 12 for an expanded version of this figure.

Figure 13-1:
Pulling
together
your action
plan for
each short-
term goal.

Action Plan						
Priority	Action Item	Person Responsible	Start Date	End Date	Progress	Expense
Goal: Realize 10% of the company's annual sales from the small business market by end of next year.						
1	Gather secondary market research.	Susie	1/1/06	2/1/06	50% complete	None
1	Hold 3 focus groups.	Beth	2/1/06	3/1/06	25% complete	$10,000
2	Develop a marketing plan.	Beth	3/1/06	4/1/06	Not started	None
3	Execute marketing plan.	Beth	4/1/06	12/31/06	Not started	~ $100,000

Don't worry about writing action items for your financial goals. All your financial goals are achieved through the rest of the goals in your plan. For example, increasing sales by 10 percent is a function of marketing and sales reaching new customers or selling more to existing customers.

Ensuring Your Plan Makes Cents

After you've completed your goals and actions, assess the financial viability of your strategic plan. While your action items and goals are fresh in your mind, estimate the costs associated with the implementation of each item.

All the best-laid strategic plans are subject to time and money. In this section, you look at the estimated expenses and the potential revenue. This review helps you make decisions about when to implement certain action items and whether your cash outlay generates the required revenue to meet your financial goals. As with every business, budgets are never big enough to do everything you want to do.

A business can be considered a financial success when it

- ✔ Stays in the black and turns a profit
- ✔ Has a healthy balance sheet (See Chapter 4 on ratios)
- ✔ Generates good cash flow
- ✔ Produces a good return on investment (ROI) for its shareholders

Attaining financial success, starts with a financial assessment that's based on historical record and future projections. By looking at the past to help plan and predict the future, you can gain much better control over your company's financial performance. A good financial plan gives you a detailed picture of the financial health of your business and the viability of your strategic plan. It also helps you know if you're getting off track during implementation so you can take action before anything serious occurs — like running out of cash.

To conduct a financial assessment of your strategic plan, take the following steps:

1. **Estimate revenue and expenses.**

2. **Conduct a contribution analysis to determine if your strategies positively contribute to the bottom line.**

3. **Combine all your numbers in a one-year and three-year financial projection.**

The cold reality is you're in business to make money. If you're not making a return on your investment, at some point, you don't have a business; you have an expensive hobby. Ouch! That hurts, I know, but it's the truth. If you don't believe this, skip this section. But if you do, your financial assessment concludes with an analysis on your ROI. After all, there's no sense in implementing a plan if it won't yield the desired return.

As an owner, you're either investing in or drawing out of your business. If you're investing for growth, you ought to have a clearly defined payback period and strategic plan to get you through it as fast as possible. Your payback period needs to match up with your owner's vision (see Chapter 6 for more info). Business owners often plan for growth without considering how long it takes to get a payback or developing the action plans to get there.

By looking at how quickly you'll get paid back for your investment, it forces you to answer the question if you're comfortable with the time period. If it is too long and too big of an investment, don't invest. Revise your strategic plan by removing some goals and action items until you develop a plan you can live with. Remember, the plan works for you — you don't work for the plan.

Estimating revenue and expenses

Expense and revenue estimating is an imperfect science. However, it's meant to give you an idea of the additional cash outlay required to implement each area of your plan and the revenue you can expect to generate. In the previous exercises, you identified potential expenses for action items as well as potential revenue for each target market group in Chapter 11. Here you combine that information with your current operations to get a complete financial picture. It's important to identify large expenses that might prohibit implementation.

Revenue

An easy approach for estimating potential revenue is by each target customer group (see Chapter 11 for information on finding new customers). Ideally, your market research gives you a rough idea of how much you can anticipate generating. Use the following formula to determine estimated revenue.

> Multiply the number of customers by the average sale per customer by the number of sales per customer per year. That equals your estimated revenue per year.

Expenses

List expenses associated with any goal or action in the plan that aren't part of your normal operating expenses. Additionally, estimate your current operating expenses by forecasting each item based on how it increases to accommodate for the expected growth.

Contributing to the bottom line

Just because a market looks attractive, doesn't always mean that you can serve it profitably. Before your creative folks start churning out cool ads, do a quick contribution analysis. A *contribution analysis* determines whether a particular target customer group contributes to the overall financial well-being of the company. In other words, is this customer group profitable?

This analysis provides you with a projection of whether your strategy generates revenues in excess of expenses. If the contribution analysis determines that the dollar investment in the strategy required to reach this target customer group can't be justified, rethink and adjust customer goals and financial goals. Use Figure 13-2 as a guide to conduct this analysis for each of your target customer groups. Eliminate the groups that don't positively contribute to the bottom line. Those that do are used in your financial projections in the next step, covered in the next section.

	Example
Estimated Revenue (Number of customers x average sale per customer x number of sales per customer per year)	100 x $1,899 x 2 = $379,800
Minus Cost of Goods Sold (Cost of goods sold = Unit cost x number of sales per customer per year. If you are a service company, there may not be a cost of goods sold.)	$50 x $100 x 2 = $10,000
Gross Profit (Subtract cost of goods sold from estimated revenue)	$379,800 – $10,000 = $369,800
Minus Action Item Expenses (Expenses from action items associated directly with this target customer group.)	$10,000 + $100,000 = $110,000
Minus Other Direct Expenses (You may have other action item expenses required to reach this customer group.)	One additional staff member @ $50,000
Contribution to Bottom Line	$369,800 – $110,000 – $50,000 = $209,800

Figure 13-2: Contributing to your financial well-being.

Projecting out your financial future

By putting all your revenue and expense numbers together and projecting them out over three years, you can see in black and white how successful your business can be. Projecting also allows you to grow the business without running out of cash. Growth in sales always incurs additional cash requirements to generate and support the additional revenues. When used properly, financial projections help you determine what additional assets are needed to support your increased sales and what impact that has on your balance sheet. In other words, the plan indicates how much additional debt or equity you need to stay afloat.

All commonly-used financial and accounting system packages come with functions to create financial projections. Use these tools to create your financial projections by plugging in assumptions based on your strategic plan. If your system doesn't allow for projections, create an Excel document similar to Figure 13-3 and Figure 13-4.

Your financial projections include forecasting out all three of your financial statements. Produce projections by month for year one and then by year for the next two years. Follow these steps:

1. **Project the income statement.**

   Use the estimated revenue for each target market group that you determined in the section "Estimating Revenue and Expenses." Plug in the expenses and operating expenses as well, and use all three figures to determine your net profit (hopefully) or loss. See Figure 13-3.

2. **Project the balance sheet.**

   As sales go up, so do other areas of the business — variable assets (accounts receivable, inventory and equipment), variable liabilities (accounts payable and accrued expenses) and (hopefully) net income. If your net income plus the increase in variable liabilities equals or exceeds the increase in variable assets, the company has the resources to finance itself. If not, you must bring in additional debt or equity. Use your current balance sheet to determine the various asset and liability accounts in your business.

3. **Project cash flows.**

   Using the information in Steps 1 and 2, project how these numbers impact your cash flow, paying special attention to how much new debt or equity you need to inject into the business and when to inject it. See Figure 13-4.

Like much of the work you've done up until now, creating financial projections isn't an easy task. But don't skip this exercise or you miss an important part of developing a sound strategy.

Undoubtedly, one of your financial goals is to increase your sales and profitability. After you've completed your projections, even if they're rough, double-check to make sure that your goals match up with your numbers. The financials tell you what goals to keep and what to cut. Keep the goals with a positive story. Revised the ones with a negative ending.

Account	Description	Year One Month 1 ... 12	Year Two	Year Three
Revenue				
	Target customer group 1			
	Target customer group 2			
	Target customer group 3			
	Etc.			
	TOTAL SALES REVENUE	$ –	$ –	$ –
Cost of Goods Sold				
	Unit costs, product/service 1			
	Unit costs, product/service 2			
	Unit costs, product/service 3			
	TOTAL COST OF GOODS SOLD	$ –	$ –	$ –
	GROSS PROFIT	$ –	$ –	$ –
Expenses				
Action Items				
	Expenses for goals			
Variable				
	Payroll			
	Sales commissions			
	Freight			
	Travel & entertainment			
	Sales tax			
Semi-variable				
	Advertising & promotion			
	FICA/payroll taxes			
	Supplies			
	Telephone			
	Auto & transport			
	Postage			
	Payroll			
	Interest			
	Insurance			
Fixed				
	Dues & subscriptions			
	Bank charges			
	Rent			
	Utilities			
	Office expenses			
	TOTAL EXPENSES	$ –	$ –	$ –
	PROFIT BEFORE DEPRECIATION & INCOME TAX	$ –	$ –	$ –
	(DEPRECIATION)			
	NET PROFIT BEFORE INCOME TAXES	$ –	$ –	$ –

Figure 13-3:
Projecting
your income
statement.

Account	Description	Year One Month 1 ... 12	Year Two	Year Three
	Beginning Cash Balance			
Cash flows (income):				
	Accts. Rec. Collections			
	Loan Proceeds			
	Sales & Receipts			
	Other:			
	Total Cash inflows	$ –	$ –	$ –
	AVAILABLE CASH BALANCE	$ –	$ –	$ –
Cash outflows (expenses):				
	Total Expenses			
Other cash outflows:				
	Capital Purchases			
	Loan Principal			
	Owner's Draw			
	Other:			
	Total Cash outflows	$ –	$ –	$ –
	ENDING CASH BALANCE	$ –	$ –	$ –

Figure 13-4: Projecting your cash situation.

Securing Funds for Your Strategic Plan

Did your financial assessment determine that you need outside investing to finance your strategic plan and your resulting growth? Before you dash off to the bank, review the tips in the following sections.

Find the correct financing product

When most business people think about financing, they immediately go to bankers or venture capitalists. But in today's capital markets, there's a wide variety of lending alternatives. You want to get the right financing product for your specific capital needs. In order to meet your capital needs, first follow these important steps:

- ✔ **Do your research.** Take the time to discover the many different types of financing available in today's capital markets. Identify the type of lender that fits your industry, company, and financing needs, and then focus your efforts in that area. Identify about 100 lenders and work your way down to a final short list.

- ✔ **Be 100 percent certain about your financing needs.** Make sure that your financial projections are accurate and not a wild guess. You want to know the exact framework of your financing needs before approaching the capital markets for financial assistance.

> ✔ **Get outside help.** The money spent to hire an experienced professional who can help craft your financial projections and find the right type of financing pays for itself. If you want to go it alone, have someone else review your finances and challenge your assumptions.

Minimize your risk

Growth carries enough risk on its own. Don't add to it by jumping into the wrong type of financing. You want to minimize risk through several different avenues:

> ✔ **Look for lenders willing to structure flexible agreements.** Normally, you won't find major banks that are willing to structure flexible agreements. Typically, state or local banks are going to be more willing to work with you because they are smaller and are more relationship-oriented. Because of their local emphasis, they are more likely to work with you to structure a flexible deal. But be aware that you have to knock on a lot of doors to find the agreement that works for you. Don't be disheartened by the first no.

> ✔ **Avoid agreements filled with restrictive covenants.** Covenants are additional causes in the contract to protect the bank and limit the business and some of its activities. For example, if your strategic plan has to do with launching a new product line and you are seeking financing to get it off the ground, the bank may restrict the loan to just the launch, which means you can't use the money for anything else. If another opportunity comes along, you might be stuck. Some covenants are also written to require that you maintain the same staff or personal for the life of the loan. Clearly, this could be a problem with staff turnover and other life changes.

> ✔ **Build in a cushion in case things go wrong.** A cushion is a compensating balance, which is borrowing slightly more than you need and keeping it in a rainy day account. A compensating balance is a good business practice and can protect you from seasonality, economic swings, and other changes to the business climate.

> ✔ **Don't take out a second lien on your house, give any kind of personal guarantee, or give up control of your company.** Many financing transactions require you to give up some equity in exchange for the money. Some equity is okay, but if you have to give up majority control to grow your company, don't do the deal. Obviously, if you give up control, you are no longer the owner of your business. The best way to avoid giving up control is to create competition for your deal, meaning find more than one financing opportunity.

✔ **Never give away opportunities to protect yourself.** Try to ensure that whatever collateral is securing the loan is all the bank gets to satisfy the loan in case of a default. You don't want to find yourself in a situation where the bank is taking other assets to satisfy the lending agreement.

✔ **Make sure your strategic plan is bulletproof.** Put together a strategic plan that describes everything you'll do in the next five years. Make it clear and compelling so lenders can understand it, react to it in a short period of time, and make a proposal to you. Additionally, everything in your plan has to add up. Your projected increase in sales, for example, needs to be supported by good market research and an action plan supporting that assumption.

Adjust your lending agreement

When lending institutions create loan packages, they typically discount your performance projections and increase their compensation through additional fees or equity. In most cases, you can't avoid this discounting because lenders need some way to protect themselves. However, you can negotiate a performance clause that adjusts the terms should you achieve your objectives in the agreement.

When you first walk in to the bank, you have no track record and no standing. However, after several months or years, you establish a solid track record proving you're a good risk. You want the opportunity to adjust your lending agreement after you've proven yourself because you want to decrease the cost of the loan as the perceived risk level decreases. If your lender refuses to consider this option, shop around for a different lender.

Think big

Plan your borrowing based on your company's potential, not on your current capital position. Project how much you need to grow the company to its full potential and strive to get the best financing with the least risk, the least dilution, and fairest transaction terms.

A few great resources to locate additional information about the complicated world of financing include www.businessfinance.com and www.vfinance.com.

Evaluating Your Strategic Plan

Now that your plan is all together in one place, it's time to step back and evaluate. Did you create the strategy you intended to create? More than likely, you and your team have put a lot of time into the document you now have in front of you. Put it away for a week and don't look at it. No peeking! After working on this document for months, it's easy to get so close to the plan that you miss obvious flaws (called the not-seeing-the-forest-for-the-trees syndrome).

When you pick your plan back up, reread it and answer these questions:

- ✔ **Does your plan connect your mission to your vision?** Make sure all of your goals and strategies align with your vision and supporting your mission. If there are outliers, modify or delete them. You want all of your energy focused on reaching your vision.

- ✔ **Is your plan realistic?** Overplanning is a common problem. Consider pushing some deadlines out further than you originally anticipated.

- ✔ **Is your plan integrated?** Make sure that all the elements of your plan support each other. (See "Visualizing your plan with a strategy map," later in this chapter for information on developing a strategy map to help answer this question.)

- ✔ **Is your plan balanced?** You developed your plan using the Balanced Scorecard Framework introduced in Chapter 12. Make sure that you have a good balance between financial, customer, internal business process, and employee and learning goals.

- ✔ **Is the plan complete?** Identify any holes in your plan or potential activities that are unsupported.

- ✔ **Is the document clear?** It's easy to write down an action item or a goal that makes sense in the moment, but making sure that the action makes sense in six months is crucial. Make sure every statement is explicit so everyone knows what's intended.

Visualizing your plan with a strategy map

Seeing your whole strategic plan — the relationships and dependencies — can be difficult, but it's necessary to make sure that your company sees the big picture. Unlike financial plans, with income statements, balance sheets, and cash flow statements, there are no common or uniform elements for describing a company's strategic plan. That's where a strategy map may come in handy.

The creators of the Balanced Scorecard created the idea of a strategy map. Strategy maps aren't tools for creating strategy; they only describe strategies. A *strategy map* has several purposes:

- ✔ To evaluate and make visually explicit the organization's perspectives, strategic objectives, and goals
- ✔ To visualize the fundamental relationships between each goal
- ✔ To connect employee learning and internal processes to customer value and financial goals

A benefit of strategy maps is everyone from the top of the ranks to the bottom can see how they fit into the company. In fact, you can color code the different goals by the department that's responsible to show how each department fits into the overall direction. See Figure 13-5 for an example of a strategy map and how to read it and evaluate your strategy. You're looking for linkages and interdependences. If you have an unsupported goal, it won't be achieved. You should be able to draw at least one arrow between one goal and the next.

Look at Figure 13-5 as you read the example below. This company can establish the link between high profits and improved sales training as follows:

- ✔ If we improve our technical and service skills by sending our staff to continued education classes at least once a year, our staff continues to be highly trained.
- ✔ If our staff is highly trained, they become problem solvers instead of order takers.
- ✔ If they're problem solvers, we're increasing the perceived value for services provided by regularly adding value to our customers.
- ✔ If we continue to add value to the services we provide, revenue increases through improved sales.

Every goal doesn't need to link to every other goal. But you do need to make sure that there are no outliers. For example, if your goal is to increase overall efficiencies, but you don't list a goal for time management or productivity training or improving your internal process, you won't increase efficiency. Naturally, just stating something doesn't mean that it happens.

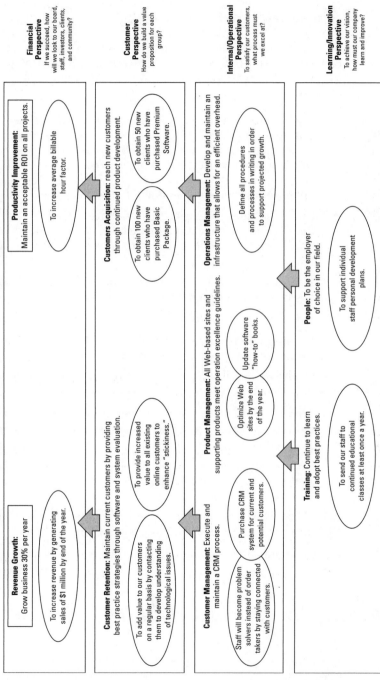

Figure 13-5: Mapping your strategy.

Sierra Technology Software

Vision: To be known as the technology experts and resource center for small to medium-size organizations.

Financial Perspective
If we succeed, how will we look to our board, staff, investors, clients, and community?

Revenue Growth: Grow business 30% per year

To increase revenue by generating sales of $1 million by end of the year.

Productivity Improvement: Maintain an acceptable ROI on all projects.

To increase average billable hour factor.

Customer Perspective
How do we build a value proposition for each group?

Customer Retention: Maintain current customers by providing best practice strategies through software and system evaluation.

To add value to our customers on a regular basis by contacting them to develop understanding of technological issues.

To provide increased value to all existing online customers to enhance "stickiness."

Customers Acquisition: reach new customers through continued product development.

To obtain 100 new clients who have purchased Basic Package.

To obtain 50 new clients who have purchased Premium Software.

Internal/Operational Perspective
To satisfy our customers, what process must we excel at?

Customer Management: Execute and maintain a CRM process.

Staff will become problem solvers instead of order takers by staying connected with customers.

Purchase CRM system for current and potential customers.

Product Management: All Web-based sites and supporting products meet operation excellence guidelines.

Optimize Web sites by the end of the year.

Update software "how-to" books.

Operations Management: Develop and maintain an infrastructure that allows for an efficient overhead.

Define all procedures and processes in writing in order to support projected growth.

Learning/Innovation Perspective
To achieve our vision, how must our company learn and improve?

Training: Continue to learn and adopt best practices.

To send our staff to continued educational classes at least once a year.

People: To be the employer of choice in our field.

To support individual staff personal development plans.

Mapping your strategy

Creating a strategy map is more art than science. Of course, strategies are as individual as companies, so you can modify the guidelines to map *your* strategy. As you try to map your strategy, check out Figure 13-5 — it provides a great framework.

Create your strategy map on a piece of paper and sticky notes first, and then transferring the notes into a Word document, using the draw toolbar or a graphic layout program. Use the steps below as a guide to create your map, but don't feel you have to follow them exactly.

1. **Write your vision statement at the top of the page.**

2. **Draw four horizontal rectangles — one for each of the four perspectives of your organization: financial, customer, internal business processes, and employee learning — stacked on top of each other underneath your vision.**

3. **Place your three-year goals in the top area of each perspective the objective is associated with.**

   Space the goals out so you have enough room for the next step.

4. **Put your one-year goals on individual sticky notes or in circles underneath each associated three-year goal.**

   Make sure that the one-year goal supports the three-year goal that it's under. If not, move it to where it does fit.

5. **After all the goals are on your map, draw arrows between the goals to indicate the cause and effect relationship between them.**

   A great way to start this is to look at your financial goal and ask what causes the goal to happen. Go through this type of questioning for each goal except in the area of employee learning because everything stems from your employees.

6. **Take a hard look at your strategy map to make sure that there are no unsupported goals and that they are all integrated.**

   Congratulations! You now have a strategy map for your organization.

Making Your Plan a Living Document

The bane of any and all strategic plans is that they sit on a shelf and collect dust. Don't entomb your outstanding business strategy in a three-ring binder. Make your plan a living document by using parts of the plan for different audiences. Your audiences may include, but aren't limited to, your board, management team, employees, and banks. You also have different functions in your organization that need different pieces to the plan. For example, a department only needs the goals and action plans assigned to it. The same is true for individuals. Here is a list of different ways to break up your plan to make it a living document:

- **The complete version:** This document has everything and anything you developed in your strategic planning process. (Yes, the kitchen sink too!) This includes all the parts listed in the section "Assembling Your Strategic Plan," plus all the support material you collected such as market research, employee assessments, customer surveys, and so on. Keep all information in one centralized location so you can pull from it in your next planning sessions.

- **The board version:** The board version is best suited for boards and includes just the high-level stuff such as the mission, vision, values, strategic objectives, and goals. Exclude the measures, responsible persons, action plans, and so on.

- **The bank version:** Banks want a complete strategic plan as well as a narrative description and hard numbers. This version should include

    - A complete set of financial projections

    - A one-page executive summary

    - Bios of key management and staff

    - A list of key customers or accounts

    - An explanation of financing needs with supporting assumptions

- **The management version:** A management version of your strategic plan should be your scorecard. Your scorecard periodically tracks the key performance indicators. As the key performance indicators are tied to goals, your management knows whether you're on strategy. Use those tracking numbers to produce charts and graphs that quickly provide executives with a dashboard of your performance.

- **The communication version:** Strategic planning is as much about articulating a strategic direction as it is getting your staff pulling in the same direction. Communicate your strategic plan through your strategy map. Post the map in the breakroom or another common area so people are continually reminded of the corporate direction.

- **The department version:** For department managers to implement their portion of the strategic plan, the corporate plan needs to be translated to a department plan. See Chapter 14 for more information.

- **The individual version:** Like with the department mangers, individuals need to know exactly what they're responsible for so they can act accordingly. Creating an individual action sheet, which lists an employee's goals and action items, is a great implementation tool. You can use the same sheet as a reporting tool for employees to keep managers informed on their progress.

You probably don't need all these versions, and you may have some special versions based on your company's needs. Either way, you can see how much easier implementing your plan is when employees have the information they need to execute. By creating these different versions, you won't see your plan collecting dust!

As you make use of various sections of the document, make sure that you don't end up with a set of independent strategic plans. Always make sure that all versions point back to the master document. MyStrategicPlan.com was created by my company to avoid just the issue of versioning and to make it easier to implement a plan by giving people in your organization the parts of the plan they are responsible for.

How to avoid going broke

A recent survey found that 54 percent of all companies filing for bankruptcy are experiencing record sales levels in the days and weeks before closing their doors. In most cases, these companies are on a positive growth curve in all areas of their business: hiring new people, generating new business, and ramping up with suppliers. What happened? They ran out of cash.

Take the Tour de Nez, a small local cycling race. It was started 13 years ago by Tim Healion, owner of Reno's first coffeehouse Deux Gros Nez, to celebrate the restaurant's anniversary. Over the years, the event has grown from a bunch of revelers riding bikes to a pro cycling event with eight different races. With the growth also came the pre-event expenses. Although Tim was experiencing national recognition and wild success, the financial viability of the race became more and more dire. For a while, the coffeehouse profits were used to finance cash shortfalls. But eventually, the event's cash demands became even too much to finance internally. The result? Tim narrowly avoiding going broke this year through some big sponsorship sales. But next year presents the same issues again. His accounts payables continually outpace his accounts receivable, no matter how successful the event is.

How do you avoid growing broke? Protect your balance sheet at all costs. Most businesses owners get caught up in the income statement showing growth in sales. But it's easy to overlook how this growth impacts the balance sheet. Most of the cash in the business is actually generated and consumed on the balance sheet (by buying inventory, carrying receivables, paying off creditors, and buying fixed assets). Therefore, any time sales go up, it has an immediate and direct impact on both cash flow and the balance sheet. Understanding these relationships holds the key to surviving rapid sales growth.

Chapter 14

Putting Your Plan to Work

- -

In This Chapter

▶ Establishing a solid process to execute your strategic plan

▶ Determining how you roll out and communicate your plan across the organization

▶ Using accountability to help achieve your goals

▶ Monitoring your plan and assessing changes as needed

- -

*I*mplementation is the process that turns strategies and plans into actions in order to accomplish strategic objectives and goals. Implementing your strategic plan is as important, or even more important, than your strategy. The critical actions move a strategic plan from a document that sits on the shelf to actions that drive business growth. Sadly, the majority of companies who have strategic plans fail to implement them. According to a *Fortune* cover story in 1999, nine out of ten organizations fail to implement their strategic plan for many reasons:

✔ 60 percent of organizations don't link strategy to budgeting

✔ 75 percent of organizations don't link employee incentives to strategy

✔ 86 percent of business owners and managers spend less than one hour per month discussing strategy

✔ 95 percent of a typical workforce doesn't understand their organization's strategy.

A strategic plan provides a business with the roadmap it needs to pursue a specific strategic direction and set of performance goals, deliver customer value, and be successful. However, this is just a plan; it doesn't guarantee that the desired performance is reached any more than having a roadmap guarantees the traveler arrives at the desired destination.

In this chapter, you look at how to set up successful implementation, hold your team accountable, and create a process to monitor and adapt your plan.

Getting Ready for Implementation

For those businesses that have a plan in place, wasting time and energy on the planning process and then not implementing the plan is very discouraging. Although the topic of implementation may not be the most exciting thing to talk about, it's a fundamental business practice that's critical for any strategy to take hold. The strategic plan addresses the *what* and *why* of activities, but implementation addresses the *who, where, when,* and *how.* The fact is that both are critical to success. In fact, companies can gain competitive advantage through implementation if done effectively.

In the following sections, you discover how to get support for your complete implementation plan and how to avoid some common mistakes.

Avoiding the pitfalls

In this section, I've provided you with a list of lessons I learned the hard way. Because you want your plan to succeed, heed the advice here and stay away from the pitfalls of implementing your strategic plan.

Here are the most common reasons strategic plans fail:

- **Lack of ownership:** The most common reason a plan fails is lack of ownership. If people don't have a stake and responsibility in the plan, it'll be business as usual for all but a frustrated few.

- **Lack of communication:** The plan doesn't get communicated to employees, and they don't understand how they contribute.

- **Getting mired in the day-to-day:** Owners and managers, consumed by daily operating problems, lose sight of long-term goals.

- **Out of the ordinary:** The plan is treated as something separate and removed from the management process.

- **An overwhelming plan:** The goals and actions generated in the strategic planning session are too numerous because the team failed to make tough choices to eliminate non-critical actions. Employees don't know where to begin.

- **A meaningless plan:** The vision, mission, and value statements are viewed as fluff and not supported by actions or don't have employee buy-in.

- **Annual strategy:** Strategy is only discussed at yearly weekend retreats.

- **Not considering implementation:** Implementation isn't discussed in the strategic planning process. The planning document is seen as an end in itself.

✔ **No progress report:** There's no method to track progress, and the plan only measures what's easy, not what's important. No one feels any forward momentum.

✔ **No accountability:** Accountability and high visibility help drive change. This means that each measure, objective, data source, and initiative must have an owner.

✔ **Lack of empowerment:** Although accountability may provide strong motivation for improving performance, employees must also have the authority, responsibility, and tools necessary to impact relevant measures. Otherwise, they may resist involvement and ownership.

It's easier to avoid pitfalls when they're clearly identified. Now that you know what they are, you're more likely to jump right over them!

Covering all your bases

As a business owner, executive, or department manager, your job entails making sure you're set up for a successful implementation. Before you start this process, evaluate your strategic plan and how you may implement it by answering a few questions to keep yourself in check. Take a moment to honestly answer the following questions:

✔ How committed are you to implementing the plan to move your company forward?

✔ How do you plan to communicate the plan throughout the company?

✔ Are there sufficient people who have a buy-in to drive the plan forward?

✔ How are you going to motivate your people?

✔ Have you identified internal processes that are key to driving the plan forward?

✔ Are you going to commit money, resources, and time to support the plan?

✔ What are the roadblocks to implementing and supporting the plan?

✔ How will you take available resources and achieve maximum results with them?

You don't need to have the perfect answers to all these questions right now, but just make sure that you've given all the questions equal consideration. You don't want to look back six months from now, and wish you had identified some big issues that are now threatening your success. If you've identified some red flags, assess if they're huge obstacles or small ones. If they're big, get them out of the way before you implement, even if it means pushing your timeline out for awhile.

Making sure you have the support

Often overlooked are the five key components necessary to support implementation: people, resources, structure, systems, and culture. All components must be in place in order to move from creating the plan to activating the plan.

All hands on deck: People

The first stage of implementing your plan is to make sure to have the right people on board. The right people include those folks with required competencies and skills that are needed to support the plan. In the months following the planning process, expand employee skills through training, recruitment, or new hires to include new competencies required by the strategic plan.

Show me the money: Resources

You need to have sufficient funds and enough time to support implementation. Often, true costs are underestimated or not identified. True costs can include a realistic time commitment from staff to achieve a goal, a clear identification of expenses associated with a tactic, or unexpected cost overruns by a vendor. Additionally, employees must have enough time to implement what may be additional activities that they aren't currently performing.

If you build it, they will come: Structure

Set your structure of management and appropriate lines of authority, and have clear, open lines of communication with your employees. A plan owner and regular strategy meetings are the two easiest ways to put a structure in place. Meetings to review the progress should be scheduled monthly or quarterly, depending on the level of activity and time frame of the plan.

Plug it in, turn it on: Systems

Both management and technology systems help track the progress of the plan and make it faster to adapt to changes. As part of the system, build milestones into the plan that must be achieved within a specific time frame. A scorecard is one tool used by many organizations that incorporates progress tracking and milestones. See the section "Keeping Score of Your Progress" later in this chapter for info on how to create a scorecard for your company.

Make yourself at home: Culture

Create an environment that connects employees to the organization's mission and that makes them feel comfortable. To reinforce the importance of focusing on strategy and vision, reward success. Develop some creative positive and negative consequences for achieving or not achieving the strategy. The rewards may be big or small, as long as they lift the strategy above the day-to-day so people make it a priority.

Determining your plan of attack

Implementing your plan includes several different pieces. Implementing a plan can sometimes feel like it needs another plan of its own. But you don't need to go to that extent because I've done it for you! Use the steps below as your base implementation plan. Modify it to make it your own timeline and fit your organization's culture and structure. What follows is a set of comprehensive implementation steps:

1. **Finalize your strategic plan after obtaining input from all invested parties.**

2. **Align your budget to annual goals based on your financial assessment, especially if you're funding the plan.**

3. **Produce the various versions of your plan for each group (see Chapter 13 for ideas on how to use different parts of your plan for employees, management, and your board).**

4. **Establish your scorecard system for tracking and monitoring your plan (see section "Keeping Score of Your Progress" later in this chapter).**

5. **Establish your performance management and reward system.**

6. **Roll out your plan to the whole organization (see "Rolling out the plan" below for roll-out ideas).**

7. **Build all department annual plans around the corporate plan (see Chapter 16 for more departmental information).**

8. **Set up monthly strategy meetings with established reporting to monitor your progress.**

9. **Set up annual strategic review dates, including new assessments and a large group meeting for an annual plan review.**

Communicate, Communicate, Communicate

Good communication unlocks many organizational mysteries, so it's not surprising that communicating your business strategy is critical to your success. When the owner, executives, and managers continually demonstrate the link between strategy and specific business decisions, staff members are encouraged to think strategically as well. After the initial goal setting process is complete, devise a plan for communicating those goals. Your communication plan falls into these three categories, which are explained in the sections below:

✔ **Don't wait until the plan is close to completion to start talking about it.** Obtain feedback and get buy-in from employees early on in the process. By facilitating upfront communication, you head off any resistance later on.

✔ **Roll out the plan when you feel it is as close as it'll be to completion.** Consistently communicate the plan to everyone in the organization.

✔ **Continue to communicate how the execution of your plan is going.** This keeps the plan top of mind and everyone committed to achieving the goals.

In a recent budgeting process in Washoe County, Nevada, one of the county commissioners required that every budget request support the organization's strategic priorities. Now that's top level commitment! All the departments quickly figured out to match their initiatives up with the strategy.

Making sure everyone buys in

Don't assume that individuals will automatically buy in to your plan. What may seem clear to the planning team may not be clear to those not as involved in the strategy development. Give employees an opportunity to get involved on the back end of the process by setting up a feedback mechanism such as a brown-bag lunch, a suggestion box, or one-on-one meetings, so they have a chance to respond as well.

By gathering and responding to feedback, you facilitate employee buy-in and build a broader understanding of the organization's goals and objectives. If you don't get people to buy into the plan, the plan may ultimately fail. You can also take it a step further and share the strategic plan with other stakeholders like investors, customers, alliance partners, vendors, and so on. An open approach can generate more helpful ideas and suggestions about the future of your business.

Rolling out the plan

Rolling out your plan can range anywhere from a big high-profile campaign to a low-key announcement. Whatever you decide to do, make sure that everyone in your organization is informed. Certain groups of stakeholders may get complete copies of the plan, including background material in appendixes, whereas other groups may receive only the body of the plan without its appendixes.

Here are a few tips for involving people in your plan and having a successful rollout:

- ✔ Consider an annual state of the union message where the finalized plan and vision are rolled out to the entire organization.
- ✔ Make the announcement exciting and get everyone engaged!
- ✔ Every board member and executive needs a full copy of the plan.
- ✔ Distribute all of the plan, or at the very least the highlights, to everyone in the organization.
- ✔ Post your one-page plan or strategy map in a break area or another common area.
- ✔ Consider giving each employee a card with the mission, vision, and values statements printed on it.
- ✔ Incorporate your strategic plan into the orientation process for new board members and employees.
- ✔ Include portions of the plan in policies and procedures, including the employee manual.
- ✔ Provide copies of the plan for key partners such as funders/investors, business coaches, vendors/suppliers, and so on.

Continuing communication

Launching goals with a major rollout isn't enough. Goals must be visible, and repeated, to keep the commitment alive. Why not have some fun with your ongoing communication? There are plenty of creative ways to keep your employees up to speed on the status of the plan. Taking it one step further, you can reinforce goals without coming across as a nag by adding humor, inspiring quotes, and customized encouragement to the messages. You can't say "thank you" enough: Keep that in mind when goals are attained.

Here are just a few ways to ensure ongoing communication:

- ✔ In monthly e-mail messages
- ✔ At "surprise" coffee breaks
- ✔ On computers as screen savers
- ✔ In envelopes with paychecks
- ✔ In company newsletters or e-letters

- ✔ On the bulletin board in a common area
- ✔ Through your company blog
- ✔ Through your intranet

One client of mine dedicates a whole room to ongoing communication, dubbed *the war room*. The room includes anything and everything about the company's strategy. On one wall is a timeline with sticky notes that display all the different goals and their deadlines. Another wall contains charts and graphs of the company's key performance indicators from the scorecard. And yet another wall contains space for brainstorming and contributing to key strategic issues at hand. The wall also contains an area for capturing items that are hard to measure such as innovative ideas, customer complaints and compliments, and employee training schedules. The room is updated monthly, and anyone in the organization can walk in and see what's happening with the business.

Holding People Accountable (Including Yourself)

Accountability is key to successful implementation — hands down. If you and your team don't have to report to anyone on your progress, the plan may find itself further and further down your to-do list or at the bottom of your stacks of paper. You don't need an elaborate accountability system, but you do need something.

One of the most important pieces to successful implementation is you. In addition to your strategic plan manager (covered in the next section), find someone to hold you accountable — a business coach, an executive group, a colleague, an outside consultant, or anyone else who's outside of your business who advises you.

Don't forget to discuss the consequences for non-performance with your team. Just like rewards, consequences are critical in any action plan. Often, the consequences are removal from the team that's working on the goals. Peer pressure creates such an intense expectation of performance that it causes action, so hold monthly strategy meetings where everyone has to publicly report on their progress. If you had to give a report in front of your peers, you'd have your act together, right? Just the thought of humiliating yourself in front of the team for non-performance may make you sick to your stomach.

In the next few sections, you find out about appointing a strategic plan manager, paying for performance, and coaching for success. All of these ideas have been tested, and they really work.

Appointing a strategic plan manager

Charge a key staff member with the responsibility of overseeing implementation of most aspects of the strategic plan. This person is the *strategic plan manager* or *engineer*. This individual makes sure that processes are running on schedule and monitors other staff who are responsible for meeting specific goals. He is also responsible for providing monthly reports and facilitating your strategy meetings. In my experience, without a manager, all the good ideas in the world won't go anywhere.

Feel like you need to find a taskmaster? You've got it! A strategic plan manager's job description should read like this:

- ✔ The individual needs to have enough respect in the organization to keep you and everyone else on top of their responsibilities.

- ✔ The manager understands the strategic planning process and the strategic plan itself.

- ✔ The manager has a good understanding of the business or organization. Ideally, this person has the ability to get along with everyone.

- ✔ This person has good attention to detail and is deadline-oriented.

Oh, and by the way, the manager can't be you — the business owner or executive. You have enough other stuff to worry about.

Paying for performance

A common trend in compensation plans is to pay for performance. No doubt about it; people pay attention when it comes to their own pocket books. Linking performance to short-term goals and action items in your strategic plan is a natural connection. Performance-based compensation is a huge way to structure performance plans. Check out Inc. Magazine's compensation guide at www.inc.com/guides/hr for ideas on compensation.

Although linking pay to performance is a good way to ensure your plan gets implemented, it's not the only factor. For additional ideas, check out the sidebar at the end of this chapter, "Creating a strategy-focused organization."

Here are some best practices to make your incentive plan as successful as possible:

- ✔ Tie incentives to corporate results, team results, and individual performance, where appropriate.
- ✔ Fit the compensation plan in with your core values and culture.
- ✔ Simplify a complicated plan so everyone, regardless of education level, can understand it.
- ✔ Communicate your incentive plan as much as possible.
- ✔ Involve employees in the process by sending out an employee survey before you structure your plan to see what they're looking for.
- ✔ Shell out incentives in the form of cash, time off, company perks, group outings, and so on. Don't be tightfisted: Outstanding results can come from a history of outstanding rewards.
- ✔ Get your employees energized about the incentive plan by making the plan exciting and motivational.
- ✔ Share financial and business plans with employees and provide education if they don't understand financial issues.
- ✔ Don't expect attitudes and behaviors to change overnight: Implementing an incentive program involves a long-term process, not a one-time event.

Remember the purpose of incentive plans is to change behavior and move your whole organization as a team toward your vision. Make sure that your incentive plans clearly link performance to business goals. That link exists to ensure that you reward only those behaviors that lead to accomplishing your business goals.

Coaching for achievement

Think about your favorite Olympic athlete. Do you think the athlete's goal is foremost on her mind every day? You bet it is. That's why it's your job and your manager's job to act as a coach to get Olympic-level performances out of all your people.

In addition to focusing on the goal, Olympic athletes are incredibly disciplined. Implementing goals that were set months ago is no different. It requires that same level of commitment and discipline.

This is where you and your managers need to lead rather than fight fires and do detail work. By acting as a coach, use the strategic plan as your framework to guide your team to high performance. What do coaches do?

- **Encourage:** Everyone needs to feel like they're doing a good job and are appreciated for their hard work. Coaches say encouraging words to their team to keep them motivated and engaged.

- **Support:** Without the right skills and resources for the job, no amount of prodding and pushing will get it done. Coaches support their teams by making sure they have the training, knowledge, and ability to complete the task.

- **Yell at the right time:** Just like athletic coaches know when to yell, managers need to know when to "push" their team when they need it. A good coach knows when performance is lagging and when to turn on the pressure.

- **Bring out the best:** Seeing the strengths and weaknesses of your team allows you to bring out the best in your staff. Coaches know how to make you the best you can be.

- **Monitor performance:** Keeping track of how everyone is performing is another trait of a good coach. With your SMART goals (covered in Chapter 12), you can assist your employee in creating an action plan if it isn't already established and keep them on the path toward achieving it. Meet with the employee regularly to discuss the status of goal accomplishment.

Coach your team when there are setbacks or roadblocks. Coach your team for success by recognizing and rewarding employees for achievements.

Keeping Score of Your Progress

To help monitor your strategic plan, one of the best tools around is the Balanced Scorecard (introduced in Chapter 12). Keep in mind that the scorecard is to be used as both a measurement and management tool to assist in fulfilling your company's vision. Think of it as an instrument panel guiding your company toward achieving an integrated single strategy. With it, you can actively track progress toward your goals. You can use it to make your company more strategy-focused and deliver demonstrable performance that is aligned with your vision and mission. Note that the scorecard uses the term *measures* to refer to numbers that you track regularly. These are also known as key performance indicators and metrics.

Building your scorecard

Although scorecards are very effective, they can also be daunting. For your first crack at this, consider just building your scorecard for high-priority goals. Identify the top seven to ten goals and associated measures that are most important to your company this year. Then follow these steps to build your scorecard. In the following years, consider building a scorecard that monitors all of your goals:

1. **Identify the right measures.**

   Most of your short-term goals should have measures associated with each one. You build your scorecard off of these measures. But just because you picked a measure to track a goal doesn't mean that it's a good measure. Work with the measures for several months. If you see that some are meaningless or to hard to track, dump them and find new ones. See Chapter 12 for examples.

2. **Establish increments that mesh with the targets.**

   In addition to getting the right measures, make sure to get the right time frame and size of measures. For example, if you're target is a ten percent increase in sales over the year, break the target down to a monthly number. For ease of tracking, try to use the same increments for all your measures. If you're reporting monthly, use monthly measures.

3. **Identify the data source.**

   Clearly identify where the monthly number is coming from and who's responsible for reporting on it. Without easy access to numbers, you find yourself doing a ton of extra busy work. If you can't get access to a data source or there's no data source, find a new measure.

4. **Input numbers monthly.**

   Enter numbers every month for each measure. Use the *Year to Date* column to track your running progress. This column should add up or average all the months entered to date.

5. **See the big picture.**

   The primary purpose of key indicators is to give you a big-picture look at the business with a relatively small amount of information. If you aren't seeing the big picture, change the measures. A great way to get a visual is to produce a chart or graph for each measure.

6. **Take action.**

   Taking action means doing it in a timely manner. The whole point of using a scorecard is to make adjustments to the business now and on time, before it's too late. Your strategy meetings should easily facilitate this process.

The easiest way to build your scorecard is to use the framework from Figure 14-1 in an Excel spreadsheet. Make it part of the strategic plan manager's job to provide a monthly scorecard report. See the next section, "Using a scorecard to measure progress," for a streamlined reporting process.

Goals	Measures	Targets	YTD	Jan.	Feb.	Mar.
Increase number of new paying customers by 50%	Conversion of new contacts within 2 months	50% conversion rate	37%	39%	41%	30%
Increase number of former paying customers by 25%	Renewing of previous relationships that were inactive	25% return of former customers	16%	10%	12%	25%
Improve inventory turns	# of inventory turns per year	4 - 6 turns per year	2.0	1.0	–	1.0

Figure 14-1: Your strategy scorecard.

Using a scorecard to measure progress

Using your scorecard should be a step-by-step process in your organization. The following list provides steps in the process for using your card (If you don't have multiple departments, ignore the department references):

1. **Provide each department or individual with their respective scorecards.**

2. **On a monthly basis, have each individual or department collect its data based on the specific measurement for each goal.**

3. **Have each department or individual summarize the data collected for each measurement on their department or corporate scorecard.**

4. **Direct any questions to the strategic plan manager.**

5. **Have each department or individual submit individual scorecards to the strategic plan manager for the month.**

6. **Have the strategic plan manager update the overall organizational scorecard with the numbers from the department or individual scorecards.**

7. **Have each strategic plan manager report the status of the overall organizational and department scorecards at the monthly strategy meeting, or have each department head report the status on his own.**

Holding effective strategy meetings

A monthly strategy staff meeting is critical to making the numbers and achieving company strategic goals. The meeting gives the company the ability to manage the activities that drive future results and to hold people accountable for making sure those activities happen. By using the key measurements, you can make key course corrections each month. And if top management attends the meeting each week, their presence creates visibility and recognition for the people getting things done. They also know that senior management is regularly paying attention to their actions.

So you're holding these meetings and they need to be effective, but how do you make your meetings more effective? Check out the following tips:

- ✔ Schedule the monthly strategy meetings on the same day and at the same time each month.
- ✔ Invite individuals or heads of each department.
- ✔ Make the meeting mandatory — no exceptions.
- ✔ The meeting should last no more than 30 minutes.
- ✔ Start and end on time and stay on task with an agenda.

Your meetings are designed for individuals and department heads to give a quick report on where they stand in regards to the measurements identified on their scorecard. Restrict the meeting to reporting on measurements and nothing else, so you can stay on task and remain within the 30-minute time limit. By following this process, everyone on the management team knows exactly where the company stands in terms of key measurements.

If problems arise, convene a separate task force team meeting immediately afterwards. Task force team meetings should last no more than 30 minutes, too, and include only those people who are directly responsible for the measurements or those who can contribute to resolving the problem. The primary purpose of this meeting is to brainstorm ideas and give the appropriate department heads some fresh thinking on how to approach the problem. Everyone puts their best ideas on the table and the manager in charge goes back and decides which ideas to implement. The following month the department head reports back to the task force team on the actions they took to resolve the issue.

How 'bout some reports to go with that scorecard?

For the past two years, a large manufacturing company has used a process whereby each department head turns in a one-page monthly summary linked to the comprehensive corporate strategy. These summaries include the department scorecard and reports of performance on strategy. The reports also explain how well the company's progressing with the defined action plans, what obstacles exist, and what can be improved.

At a monthly meeting, the company starts by defining a series of actionable items based on the monthly reports. From there, action plans are developed and reported back on the one-page summary reports.

The CEO feels the benefits are usually quite substantial. After all, when action items are consistently elevated, department heads know they're responsible for implementing the items as efficiently as possible (that's called work peer pressure). The department heads appreciate this process because it raises the bar for everyone and keeps their staff focused on the right things.

Keeping Your Plan Working for You

A strategic plan needs to be adaptive to survive changing or unanticipated conditions. A business that develops and executes a strategic plan gains significantly from the experience, and starting with a working model and achieving a tangible plan can be more successful for your business than having no plan at all.

Over the life of a strategic plan, a company's vision and mission often remain the same, but its goals and objectives probably need to be revised. Depending on the industry, some businesses can maintain a strategic plan for a year or longer, whereas others have to respond to market changes more frequently. Move ahead with the plan as established, but be prepared to let go and switch strategies as necessary. Corrective actions need to be taken quickly to compensate for the dynamic business environment most businesses operate within. In today's ever-changing business environment, who has the time to stop and figure things out? No one. You adapt on the fly and so should your plan.

Change: The only constant

Two caterpillars are conversing and a beautiful butterfly floats by.

One caterpillar turns and says to the other,

"You'll never get me up on one of those butterfly things."

What a powerful, and fun, parable about change. Change, even though we often resist it, is inevitable. In fact, your strategic planning process may trigger changes in your own organization, either in terms of the work done or in the internal structuring of the work. No matter how you present it, people struggle with change. They may need help accepting and adapting positively to the changes, though. That's where you come in.

Determining which changes require action and which require monitoring is the responsibility of you and your management team. When change is needed, take the following steps:

1. **Make sure everyone understands the change and why it's necessary.**

   Even if people have been part of the strategic planning process, they may need the implications of decisions explained to them afterwards.

2. **Respond to people's ideas and feelings.**

   Let them express their concerns and respond to them. If you can't agree, at least be sympathetic about the feelings that are generated by change.

3. **Develop a planned process of change.**

   Share the process with everyone in the organization or project, so people know what to expect and when to expect it.

Need more information and ideas? Check out the Change Management Learning Center online at `www.change-management.com`.

Adapting your plan as necessary

Never lose sight of the fact that strategic plans are guidelines not rules. It's fine to deviate from your plan, but you need to understand why you make a course correction. Figure 14-2 gives a visual decision map to help you determine whether you need to adapt your plan.

Every three months or so, evaluate the plan implementation by asking these key questions:

✔ Will the goals be achieved within the time frame of the plan? If not, why?

✔ Should the deadlines be modified? (Before you modify deadlines, figure out why you're behind schedule.)

✔ Are the goals and action items still realistic?

✔ Should the company's focus be changed to put more focus on achieving the goals?

✔ Should the goals be changed? (Be careful about making these changes —
know why efforts aren't achieving the goals before changing the goals.)

✔ What can be gathered from this adaptation to improve future planning
activities?

Adapt your plan according. Always keep copies of past plans and include an
updated date in the footer of the document.

Remember that implementation is the most difficult part of the planning
process. No one factor listed above makes or breaks the successful implementation of the strategic plan. However, when these areas are considered
and acted on, the chances for successful implementation are greatly
improved. Most importantly, a business that has a strategic plan and imple-
ments it is ahead of 90 percent of the companies who have no plan at all.

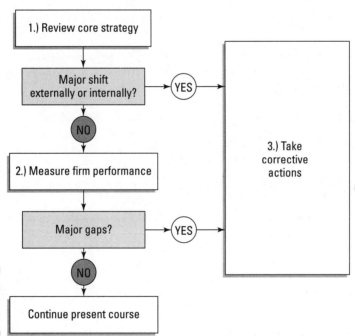

Figure 14-2:
To adapt or
not to adapt.

Creating a strategy-focused organization

Organizations that are strategy-focused are more effective with their resources, have higher employee retention, and make more money because they serve their markets better than their counterparts. And they stay in business longer because they proactively respond to the environment around them. Want to create a culture that's strategy-focused? Here's a hit list of ideas gathered from a bunch of different organizations to help create the organization:

- Be a strategic leader. Lead by example and prioritize your strategic plan over everything else. Stay committed.

- Cut out the jargon. Make sure everyone in your organization really understands the plan.

- Hang your one-page strategic plan in the break room or another central location.

- Involve your staff in the final development of the plan. Ask for and use employee ideas.

- Create a "champion" or owner for every goal and action. Make strategy everyone's job.

- Ask your employees to create the action items to support their assigned goals.

- Review the plan with management or the group.

- Align the organization with the strategy.

- Use a scorecard to monitor progress monthly.

- Schedule regular updates. Hold a monthly meeting, one-on-one with the team leaders, where you only discuss strategy. Hold a quarterly full staff strategy meeting to report on the progress.

- Challenge underlying assumptions. Revisit and refine the strategic plan three months from now.

- Hold yourself accountable through a mentor, personal coach, or business organization.

- Link strategy to performance.

- Continually scan your environment to identify changes that may impact your strategy.

- Reward success! Throw a party when significant goals are reached.

Chapter 15

Contingency Planning: Your Plan B

· ·

In This Chapter

▶ Identifying potential risks and threats facing your business

▶ Planning for business continuity

▶ Stepping into the future with scenario planning

· ·

*Y*ou're surrounded by circumstances and choices every day, and you need to be ready. Readiness isn't just about disaster preparedness; it's about being ready for opportunity, as well as adversity. Readiness is a lifestyle, and any organization needs to prepare for all those little things that can go wrong and that seem to add up when the time is right.

The first step to getting ready is focusing on what you want and then creating a mental picture of what fulfills that desire. But a real barrier is procrastination. People often feel overwhelmed by trying to think of everything. Stop. Take a breath. If you're procrastinating, understand that *worry* is the source. So ask yourself, "What is it about this task that concerns me?" and then make a list.

All the strategic planning in the world isn't enough unless you have contingencies in place. This chapter helps you identify what to prepare for when business doesn't go as planned. You're not only preparing for unexpected threats but also trying to foresee unanticipated opportunities. In the following sections, you look at the risks of doing business and two types of contingency planning — continuity planning and scenario planning — that help you minimize your risks.

Facing Up to Real Business Risks

Conducting business in today's world almost always involves some type of risk. Consumer trends and habits change; new competitors enter the market; external factors can create obstacles. In your planning, risk is best defined as how you perceive the likelihood of suffering a loss. The perception of the impact of a particular risk varies from person to person: A particular risk may seem trivial to one person but catastrophic to another.

As you plan for your future, risk analysis and risk management can help you make plans to better maneuver around obstacles. Assessing risks in advance allows you to determine the most cost-effective strategies to handle each type of risk.

Although this section may seem doomsdayish, don't shy away from it. You've put a lot of time, energy, and money into your business. Keeping it out of harm's way is just another step in the process.

Identifying common risks and threats you might face

The first stage of a risk analysis is identifying threats facing you in your internal and external environments that can interrupt business as usual.

I the next two sections, you identify potential threats to your company. Review the lists and mark the threats that apply to your business. Get others involved in your risk assessment; they may have a different perspective: You can never have too many people looking out for the health of your business.

Potential threats to your business

Potential threats include, but aren't limited to, the following:

- ✔ **Economic woes:** A downturn in the economy or cycles in consumer spending threaten business as usual depending on how sensitive your business is to changes in economic conditions.

- ✔ **Financial issues:** These issues can include business failure, poor budgeting, or unexpected expenses, which are all internal financial risks. Additionally, external financial risks include the state of the stock market, interest rates, and unemployment and are more difficult to control, but can have a huge impact on the financial state of an organization.

- ✔ **Lack of processes:** Internal processes and systems pose a risk from failures of accountability and controls, organization, and fraud. Consumer fraud and employee fraud are two of the biggest risks to businesses.

- ✔ **Legal or regulatory action:** Changes in the political environment affect businesses through tax policies, public opinion, consumer confidence, government policies, and foreign relations. Any of these changes may result in unforeseen legal action.

✔ **People issues:** Losing key people due to illness, resignation, maternity leave, and death are common threats to businesses. Anyone who's lost a key employee can relate to the difficulty of recovering from the loss of the knowledge that leaves with that employee.

✔ **Tarnished reputation:** Your image in the market is important to create a solid customer base. Unfortunately, confidence in a company can be hurt by the loss of a business partner or employee confidence or damage to one's reputation in the market. A tarnished reputation can be a risk that takes years and years of undoing and unraveling.

✔ **Telecommunication, computer, or key equipment failure:** Disruption of daily tasks can be caused by an electrical outage, a shortage of supplies, slow operational processes, loss of access to essential assets like your digital files, and failures in distribution.

A small, but busy, independent travel agency found out the hard way what can happen when standard telecommunications systems go out. During the month of January, which is the high season for this industry, the systems failed due to cut power lines. Road crews were resurfacing a street and cut a supply cable, which shut down the power for three days. The company relies on these systems to confirm prices, check availability of hotels and flights, and complete currency exchange transactions for its customers. As a result, the travel agency lost a considerable amount of business to competitor agencies, including one key business contract. Customer loyalty and repeat business are very important in what is now an extremely competitive business. The company suffered from negative customer experiences and lost its most profitable customer. If the travel agency was able to set up its office remotely, the company would've been up and running again with only a short delay. Instead, this outage cost the company thousands of dollars.

In another example, a small local optometry clinic was defrauded when an employee was buying designer sunglasses and reselling them on eBay. The employee was ordering sunglasses on company purchase orders that weren't recorded and then stealing the shipments before anyone saw them. The lack of an internal purchasing system with the proper controls allowed this employee to defraud the clinic of $50,000.

Disaster planning

Disasters are another form of risk all businesses need to pay close attention to. Events like Hurricanes Katrina and Rita, the terrorist attacks of 9/11, and other global disasters make you assess how such unexpected events affect your business.

The following adversities are just a few of the misfortunes that can occur, from some of the biggest to the smallest:

- **Natural disasters:** Hurricanes, earthquakes, tornados, or fires can all bring your thriving business to a halt. Even if you're not in a hurricane-, earthquake-, tornado-, or fire-prone area, don't underestimate the power of storms. Summer storms can cause flooding and wind and hail damage, and winter storms may cause pipes to burst from freezing conditions.

- **Terrorist attacks:** As much as you hate to think about this, those businesses located in big cities realize that terrorists are a real threat. Although most small businesses aren't concerned with being directly targeted by terrorists, it's important to consider how a terrorist attack affects operations.

- **Theft or vandalism:** If someone deliberately crashes your computer systems or steals CD-ROMs with vital client information, the criminal activity not only affects the cost of the equipment but also the information stored on its hard drive and the time you spent collecting those records.

- **Fire:** Different from natural disaster fires, office fires are a real risk that can leave your business paralyzed from the loss of equipment and business records and digital files at the very least.

- **Loss of power:** Many businesses rely on power. Think about how you use electricity. Are there ways your business can continue to function without power? What primary functions do you want to maintain during a power outage?

- **IT system failure:** Businesses are increasingly dependent on computers. Consider the potential effects of computer viruses, attacks by hackers, or system failures on productivity.

- **Outbreak of disease or infection:** Depending on your type of business, an outbreak of an infectious disease among your staff, in your premises, or among your livestock can present serious health and safety risks.

Assessing the impact of your risks

Now that you've identified the potential threats to your business (see "Identifying common risks and threats you might face" in the previous section), it's time to determine how big those threats really are. Ask yourself three questions:

- What are the odds that each particular threat may occur?
- How frequently can each threat pose a problem?
- How may the threat impact my business?

Follow the steps below to assess your risks and to get started thinking about how to manage those risks:

1. **List all the potential risks to your business you identified in the previous section.**

   Your organization may face some unique risks that you don't want to overlook. If you're stumped, ask your employees as well as other colleagues in your industry.

2. **Rate the probability of each particular threat occurring on a scale from high to low.**

   By rating them, you eliminate the ones that are unlikely. For example, you may decide to do nothing about a low-probability disaster for your area, like an earthquake if you live in Indiana. You know its effects can be disastrous, but given the fact that it's unlikely to occur, it's better to focus your efforts on other threats.

3. **Look at the risks that you rated highest or the most likely to occur.**

   Determine the possible impact of one of these disasters on your business and assign a monetary value. For example, how much would it cost you if your computer equipment was stolen or damaged? If a key employee left, how would that impact your business?

4. **Review the list of risks with monetary values assigned to them.**

   Select the three that have the biggest impact on your businesses.

Taking action to manage the real risks

After you've evaluated the risks you may encounter, and they've been prioritized (see the previous two sections), you can start to look at ways to manage them. As you evaluate potential solutions, consider a cost-benefit analysis. You may find in some cases it's better to play the odds than to incur the cost of managing the risk. There are numerous ways of managing risks:

- ✔ **Utilize your current assets:** Find ways to use existing resources to offset risk. These methods could be as simple as improving existing methods and systems, reallocating responsibilities, or improving accountability and internal controls.

- ✔ **Invest in new assets:** You may have identified some risks that can be managed through the purchase of new assets. For example, if the cost of an electrical outage to your business is substantial, you could store files off-site where employees can access them through home computers. If a natural disaster, such as a flood, is a big threat, you could move your offices to higher ground. Naturally these actions may not be simple, but you may find that diminishing the risk is better than the liability.

✔ **Develop continuity planning:** You may decide to accept a risk, but choose to develop a plan to minimize its effects if this happens. A good continuity plan allows you to take action immediately if you find yourself in a crisis management situation. Check out "Keeping Your Business Humming Along No Matter What: Continuity Planning" in the next section.

For further reading, check out *Disaster Planning and Recovery: A Guide for Facility Professionals* (Wiley) by Alan M. Levitt.

Keeping Your Business Humming Along No Matter What: Continuity Planning

Whew! You might be worn out by all the planning, planning, and more planning discussed earlier in this chapter. But don't worry. *Business continuity planning* just brings it all together. It's about making sure that your business doesn't stop running and minimizing the impact for your employees, customers, and your reputation if it does. I've given you the basics to ensure that your business keeps on humming.

Your continuity plan can be a one-page section at the end of your strategic plan or it can stand on its own. It's nice to incorporate continuity planning into your strategic planning process because a good continuity plan should change as rapidly as your environment changes. Revising it at least once a year is a good idea. Being prepared with a plan helps you better navigate your business through a variety of circumstances.

Throughout history, companies have failed simply because they've failed to plan for the bad times. When FTD's computer system failed just before Mother's Day several years ago, the flower distribution company didn't have a backup plan. Management was surprised by the disruption and lost a ton of orders. In another instance, when the electricity failed just before the high-profile Preakness horse race, all-important last-minute bets couldn't be entered into the computer system.

You don't want disaster to strike your business. So continuity planning is a great way to prepare your business for an unpredictable future. And trust me — you'll sleep better at night knowing that you have a backup plan in place for the unknown.

Just the basics, ensuring you're covered

Don't get overwhelmed by your continuity plan by diving too deep into the details. Keep it simple and follow the basics. As shown in Figure 15-1, your continuity plan can be a checklist for each of the sections below. Indicate how often and who's responsible for the tasks in each area. The following sections are the absolute necessities your plan must cover to avoid panic in the presence of a threat.

	What is the next update?	Who is responsible?
☐ Data is backed up		
☐ Current contact information is available in a hard copy format		
☐ List of alternative suppliers and buyers is available		
☐ Premises are secure		
☐ Equipment and machinery is fully maintained		
☐ Employees are cross trained		
☐ All insurance plans are current		
☐ Employees know about the plan		
☐ Employees are able to work offsite		

Figure 15-1: Checking off your business continuity plan.

Back up your data

Always have a backup when handling records and data. There's nothing worse than informing a client you were careless enough to lose his personal information. Here are a few tips to take care of your info:

- ✔ **Establish an off-site server to store records.** Select a remote location with a replica of your primary computer system with all the important programs, updates, and documentation. It's absolutely essential that this system be checked at least every quarter to ensure that the backup of all important company information actually runs on the off-site system.

- ✔ **Install anti-virus software.** Although everyone knows this is important, we rarely associate anti-virus software with ensuring the longevity of our data. Running anti-virus software is just as important as storing your records off site.

✔ **Ensure that the right maintenance agreements are in place.** You want to make sure that your off-site server is being maintained correctly. A good maintenance agreement protects you, ensures daily backups, and provides regular software updates and patches.

Many IT companies provide service packages, which include regularly backing up your data off site on a secure server.

Keep a hard copy of current contact information

Make sure that you update your contact information (including e-mail and fax numbers) quarterly and that you have a copy of that info for the following groups of folks:

✔ All customers

✔ All employees

✔ All suppliers and vendors

✔ Insurance agents, including copies of policies and policy numbers

Know your alternative suppliers and buyers

Consider how dependent you are on your suppliers and buyers. What are your alternative options if something in your supply chain goes down? For example, if you're in a distribution business, do you have an alternative way to ship your products? What would you do if you still had the ability to ship but no access to your office? Think about cultivating relationships with other suppliers and buyers out of your area and theirs. Additionally, keep an off-site list in case you need to contact them and you can't access your premises.

Secure your premises

Keep up regular maintenance on fire and burglar alarm systems and review safety guidelines for electricity and gas use. Think about an alternate location to call home base in the event of an emergency. For example, you may suggest an arrangement with another local business to share premises temporarily if a disaster affected either of you. You can also use a business continuity supplier, which can make alternative premises available on short notice. You can find a supplier online in bigger metros. Businesses in smaller markets most likely don't have this option available.

Business continuity suppliers can be expensive. By planning in advance, you give yourself the opportunity to evaluate more cost-effective options.

The flu brings down a company

A medium-sized management consulting firm discovered how important it is to have a continuity plan that details how to react when key employees are unavailable. One of its directors came down with a rare, but horrible, strain of the flu. Unfortunately, before he was diagnosed, he came into work feeling ill. As soon as the doctor diagnosed him, the director was advised to immediately inform anyone with whom he'd been in contact with over the past three days of the infection. Due to the nature of this particular strain of the flu, the CEO of the company was forced to quarantine and send home key team members who'd been in contact with the director.

Temporary employees were bought in to cover essential work requirements, but they weren't trained to access the key systems needed to keep various important projects moving forward. Consequently, many projects were delayed and the company missed several key deadlines. Cross-training or systems manuals could've eliminated some elements of this crisis.

Maintain your equipment or machinery

If your business requires particular equipment in order to function, look into available maintenance plans to ensure the quickest service. You know what machinery is vital to your operation. Do all that you can to avoid downtime for any piece of equipment that makes or breaks your production.

Cross train employees on important tasks

Because a fully-functioning staff is critical to most everyone's business in times of emergency, don't depend on only a select few. If the knowledge of a skill or process is in the head of one or two people, what do you do in a time of emergency or even if they both go on vacation at the same time? Provide cross-training for employees on various tasks and processes. If cross-training feels too overwhelming, invest in training temporary cover from a recruitment agency.

Stay current with your insurance

Insurance is a necessity in any effective risk-management strategy. Go through all the potential threats your business could face and consider what types of insurance might be offered to offset some of the risk. If you have a major loss, your insurance coverage is there to back you up and help rebuild your company.

Communicate the plan to key employees

Compile a list of everyone who knows where the continuity information is located and make sure that the site is accessible to other employees. Think about how you're going to get your employees to the remote location in the event of an emergency and how you can communicate instructions to them. Do you need walkie talkies, two-way radios, or cell phones for emergency purposes only?

Have a way for employees to work from home

Coming into the office isn't always practical or safe if your business is in a state of emergency. A great way to ensure that your business keeps running is to step up your office for remote access. That way, your employees can keep working from home, and everyone feels safe, sound, and productive.

Getting more specific

If you're ready to move beyond the basic continuity plan, follow the steps below to be better prepared. Knock off the items that pertain to you and get to the rest when you have time:

- ✓ **Create a detailed plan for the immediate actions to be taken and collect the resources you need to implement that plan.** The first hour following an emergency is often the most critical. Being prepared for that first hour can minimize the impact of a disaster.

- ✓ **Ensure that all employees are aware of what they have to do and where to find the resources they need to perform their jobs.** Can additional staff training be beneficial in an emergency?

- ✓ **Create checklists arranged around the plan to ensure all steps are followed.** In an emergency situation, some people lose focus; a checklist can help your staff be more thorough and calm.

- ✓ **Compile a list of contacts you're likely to have to notify in an emergency.** Your list can include emergency services, insurance providers, local authorities, legal counsel, customers, suppliers, utility companies, and neighboring businesses. It's also worth including details of service providers such as glaziers, locksmiths, plumbers, electricians, and IT specialists. Having contact information ready can save time and makes certain you remember to call everyone.

- ✓ **Include maps of your premises to help emergency services.** These maps show fire escapes, sprinklers, and other safety equipment.

- ✔ **Determine who the company spokesperson is to handle questions from the media.** Ideally, you would identify your CEO or another person in a leadership position who's always the media contact, no matter what. Ask yourself who's best equipped to handle questions and maintain a positive outlook. Appoint that person as well as a back-up person. Inform stakeholders such as staff, customers, and suppliers that they should direct media questions to the appointed person.

- ✔ **Make sure that you have hard copies of your business continuity plan.** Store these copies safely at your home, with your bank, and with other key members of the staff.

- ✔ **Update your plan regularly.** As changes occur, take a moment to make a note in your plan. For example, moving locations may necessitate reevaluating your entire plan immediately.

- ✔ **Schedule regular tests of your plan.** Testing can make a difference in an actual emergency and may give you peace of mind that everything can run smoothly in times of emergency.

The U.S. government provides even more detailed information about continuity planning for businesses at www.ready.gov. You have access to additional detailed emergency planning information and checklists.

Scenario Planning: What If . . . ?

Scenario planning is a way of simplifying a complex future by providing you the opportunity to ask the "what if" questions and to rehearse how you may respond should a certain event or trend happen in the future. Scenario planning is a subset of strategic planning. Basic strategic planning tends to address the incidents of the day, such as the decision to increase staff because of a projected influx in sales. But scenario planning looks at what might happen tomorrow. It's focused on understanding what the future looks like.

Scenario planning was first developed and used by the U.S. Air Force during World War II. The planning method gained acknowledgement in the business world when Shell Oil utilized scenario planning techniques to predict the oil crisis of the 1970s.

For organizations, scenario planning provides an invaluable opportunity to have a strategic discussion around key drivers and critical uncertainties in your operating environment. With scenario planning, you're imagining not just one, but a variety of future possibilities.

The scenarios you develop serve two purposes:

- ✔ **To manage risks where you can "test" your strategies' possible futures:** By understanding how the strategies perform in each of the scenarios, you can make modifications to resolve potential weaknesses or highlight the need for contingency plans.

- ✔ **To generate creativity and spark new ideas:** The scenarios often highlight ideas previously thought too outlandish or combine things in ways that lead to new conclusions. Scenarios can provide an organization with an invaluable insight for new directions.

You don't always have time to do scenario planning in your traditional strategic planning process. But for those of you who are just tuning up your plan, consider doing a scenario analysis to push the bounds of your thinking. You never know what you might come up with!

Through scenario analysis you develop several different paths your company can take given a variety of environmental changes. You can look at small environmental changes or big ones. The following sections guide you through doing either one.

Considering the smaller what ifs . . .

Although driving forces may present an array of opportunities and threats, there are a number of smaller scenarios that hit closer to home — the *what ifs*. Calling these *smaller* scenarios is a bit of a misnomer because when they happen, they can happen quickly and with devastating consequences, so they don't seem too small. When you run through your potential scenarios — in the next section — make sure to include at least one or two of the following variables in your mix:

- ✔ What if sales are flat this year or if sales decline by 20 or 30 percent?
- ✔ What if sales increase rapidly, such as 25 percent or more?
- ✔ What if accounts receivable collections slow by 30 days?
- ✔ What if banks increase interest rates by several percentage points?
- ✔ What if our biggest customer goes out of business or if we lose our biggest client?
- ✔ What if our competitors actively pursue our accounts?

✔ What if we have a major public relations crisis such as a bad product or a lawsuit?

✔ What if we find out that important information from our company found its way into the hands of our competitors?

Thinking about the big what ifs . . .

The most significant trends likely to affect the larger world are those forces that are the big what ifs — the driving forces. These cases tend to push your thinking and are usually classified as the big unknowns. The forces generally come in four flavors:

✔ **Social dynamics:** This area includes specific demographic issues such as how influential youth might be in ten years; and softer issues of values, lifestyle, demand, or political energy, such as people getting bored with online chatting.

✔ **Economic issues:** Macroeconomic trends and forces shape the economy as a whole. How does the price of crude oil impact the cost of running your business? Microeconomic dynamics are also a factor — what might your competitors do? How does the very structure of the industry change? And within the company itself, will you be able to find the skilled employees you need?

✔ **Political issues:** You may need to handle electoral concerns such as who's going to be the next president. Legislative changes can affect tax policies, and regulatory issues can include figuring out what to do if Microsoft were to go under.

✔ **Technological issues:** In this category, you deal with direct access such as how high-bandwidth wireless affects land-line telephones; enabling technologies such as nanotechnology bringing in the next chip revolution; and indirect technology, such as biotech evolving past medicine into mainstream full-body entertainment.

Identifying which of the big what ifs might impact your firm is the key to scenario planning for these forces. Some of these may seem farfetched, whereas others are quite a bit more likely.

The goal in scenario planning isn't to create one specific future. Instead, by drawing attention to key drivers and exploring how they push the future in different directions, planners create an array of possibilities resulting in the ability to make crucial decisions today.

Stepping into your future

Ready to step into your future? Below is a guide to run scenarios with your team. But first, how many scenarios should you develop? Ideally, you develop scenarios for the situations that you're most likely to face. Three to five is a good number to push you and your team's limits.

Unfortunately, developing a few plans can be expensive, complex, and time-consuming. But don't get bogged down in the number. Decide to run a handful and have fun!

Here are the steps to running your own scenario planning:

1. **Define a timeframe for each scenario.**

   Some events may occur in 20 years, some in two. But you can't work with indefinite, open-ended scenarios.

2. **Establish the primary variable in your scenarios.**

   Use the questions listed in the previous sections to determine your variables. Alternatively, you can use current and future trends outside of the company. Assess ways in which these trends may present opportunities or threats to your business. Check out Chapter 9 for a list of current and future trends.

3. **Clearly articulate the scenario with a problem statement.**

   On a white board, write down "What if ____?" and fill in the blank. For example — what if we lose our biggest client, resulting in a 50 percent decrease in revenue? Or what if a public relations scandal ruins our reputation or brand image?

4. **Create a compelling headline or working title for the scenario.**

   Something like "ABC Company Takes Its Production In-House" or "Partner in Company X Sued Over Malpractice" can work.

5. **Flesh out the details of the scenario.**

   Clarify exactly the situation your company would be in.

6. **Develop options for action if the scenario in Step 5 should occur.**

   These options make up what are called *robust strategies,* which are designed to work regardless of how the future turns out.

If you run several scenarios, a range of choices that identify potential threats and opportunities may come up. Many of these choices otherwise go unnoticed if you focus obsessively on your organization's present-day situation.

Create your doomsday kit

Only you know what types of threats or disasters your business faces. Define your doomsday and think about what you can do to lessen the impact. Gather the supplies you may need in one place to save yourself valuable time during an emergency. Here's a list of items to consider for your doomsday kit:

- A copy of your continuity plan — remember to store copies in multiple locations

- Contact numbers (which should be in your continuity plan)

- Map of the premises with detailed information about fuse boxes, gas lines, water pipes, and so on

- Extra keys

- Flashlights

- Battery powered radio

- Extra batteries (replace every six months)

- Supplies to operate without a functional computer such as a laptop with a spare battery, battery powered calculator, carbon copy receipts, sales tax chart, and credit card imprinting machine

- Supplies for stranded employees such as water, non-perishable food, and blankets

- Backup personal items, especially medications (have employees keep them in their desks or handbag)

- First aid kit

Chapter 16

Planning Considerations for Entrepreneurs and Department Managers

In This Chapter

▶ Establishing an exit strategy for business owners

▶ Discovering how to cascade goals throughout an organization

▶ Watching out for departmental planning pitfalls

*O*ne size doesn't fit all when it comes to strategic planning. You can easily pick and choose the pieces of strategic planning that apply to your company (as presented in the previous chapters). However, there are a few cases that deserve special attention: entrepreneurs and department/division/group managers.

Business owners have the unique responsibility of determining the strategic direction of an organization based on their personal *endgame* — the final result they want out of their business. An endgame can be anything from continual cash flow, to a business sale, to more time off. Whatever it is, the endgame is the personal vision of the business owner (see Chapter 6). Multi-department or multi-tiered organizations must drive the strategic direction down to every level of the company. This process is easy when there are only a handful of employees. But when you have many departments or divisions or numerous locations, planning becomes more complicated.

This chapter is intended to be an addendum to rest of the book. Although everything presented in the previous chapters is completely applicable, this chapter takes planning one step future for entrepreneurs and department managers.

In this chapter, you determine the value of your company and how to plan for your company's survival after you leave. You also discover how to cascade goals throughout your organization, whether you have one level or ten.

Planning Issues for Entrepreneurs

Although publicly-traded companies get all the media limelight, roughly 90 percent of the businesses in the United States are privately held. As a business owner, you have some special considerations in your planning efforts:

✔ How will your business continue when you exit stage left?

✔ How do you establish the value or projected value of your business?

Although you may not want to think about some of these topics today, each of these topics influences the strategic direction of your company. Many owners have a difficult time thinking about life after their company. However, your endgame is arguably the most important part of your strategic planning effort. Although you may not share your ideas with your staff, you want to have a clear plan for your departure.

Take a few moments to consider the legacy you want your business to leave. Will it continue on indefinitely or pass to your children or employees? Do you plan on cashing out or will it just cease to exist? Many entrepreneurs aren't clear about what their businesses look like without them, so they leave their exit strategy to chance instead of intention. Bottom line: The ownership of the business will be transferred at some point with or without you. Your death or other unforeseen life changes may force the transfer, but through careful planning, you can leave a legacy of how you want to business to run.

The upcoming sections help you put the finishing touches on your strategic plan in the case of your absence. Take the self-assessment in Figure 16-1 to see where you are with your exit planning.

Ensuring your business continues after you

The fact that you'll leave your business at some point is a given. If you've been ignoring this point, you're not alone. People start and run businesses for numerous reasons, and so much energy goes into that process that most owners never really consider how it may end. Of course, the reason most business owners avoid this entire discussion is because it's not the most inspiring topic. Nevertheless, setting a clear exit strategy is imperative to ensure that your years of hard work pay off in the end.

Planning an exit strategy shouldn't begin when you decide to sell your company. Knowing your options and a few best practices can make this task seem less intimidating. Check out the following sections on how to make the important transition.

Planning for transition

The best time to start planning the exit strategy is when your venture is launched or purchased. Any number of front-end decisions and strategies can have long-term impact on the operations.

Self-Assessment for Exit Planning

Rate your exit planning activities against best practices. Remember to be completely honest in this assessment because the beneficiary of good planning is you. Use the following scoring of 1 to 5, where: 1 = serious problem area; 2 = area needs major improvement; 3 = acceptable but could use some improvement; 4 = only needs minimal attention; 5 = solid effort, well done.

Action	Score
I have determined when I want to exit my business or I know how to determine the appropriate time.	
I have a written exit/succession plan.	
I understand there are two major considerations in exit planning – personal interests in regards to management activities and financial interests as an owner.	
I have assembled a group of valued consultants/professionals to advise me in this planning process.	
I know the current value of my business.	
I have determined what the value needs to be at the point of transfer to achieve my financial goals.	
If I have decided to transfer the business rather than sell it, appropriate successor(s) have been identified.	
I have a plan in place to appropriately train and equip my successor(s).	
I have identified a board of advisors and written a "management letter" for my spouse in the event of my untimely demise.	
I have determined my purpose in life beyond the business in anticipation of having a fulfilled life in retirement.	
I include my spouse in exit planning and purpose planning.	

Figure 16-1:
An exit planning assessment.

If you average less than threes on the eleven questions, you have a significant amount of work to accomplish *today*.

The end is inevitable

Studies show that a majority of business owners are in denial or just postponing the inevitable. Here are a few reasons why you don't want to be part of the majority:

✔ Only about a quarter of businesses with less than $200 million in sales have a formal exit/succession plan.

✔ A study of more than 5,000 franchised businesses showed that only 24 percent were sold and 76 percent essentially closed their doors with some possibly being liquidated.

✔ A survey of thousands of business owners concluded that most misjudged the value of their business by 50 percent or more. In some cases, this amounted to a difference of a million dollars.

✔ Without a reasonable plan developed, the owner will undoubtedly receive a much smaller financial return than anticipated.

✔ A strategic buyer generally pays a higher price than a financial buyer. Seeking a strategic buyer can require research and extra time.

✔ Most family businesses need to increase profits or grow by at least 15 percent to cover the cost of transition.

The first phase of your transition is called *exit planning* — directing how to transfer the business when you leave. Exit planning is a key part of your organization's strategic direction because it dictates how you set up your business for the long run. Of the four different ways to exit your business, each one requires a unique strategy. The second phase is *succession planning*, which involves determining who runs the business when you depart.

There are basically four ways to exit your business:

✔ Transfer ownership to a family member

✔ Sell to employees or other owners

✔ Sell to a third party

✔ Liquidate

Consider drafting your own personal vision statement for your business, which includes your exit strategy. This doesn't need to be shared with your staff, but it can guide the strategic growth of your organization.

Considerations for exiting your business

No matter whether you're considering an outright sale or deciding to groom another person to lead the business, you have some critical considerations to ponder to start developing your exit strategy:

✔ **Timing:** When is the right time? Timing has an impact on the quantity and quality of buyers. You need to decide when the right time is based on your business life cycle. Ideally you'll exit when you're on the top, not on the downward slide.

✔ **Value:** What is an objective sale value or price for your company? Business owners are often unpleasantly surprised at the low value an outside entity places on their business. Get an outside valuation so you won't be surprised when you're ready to exit.

✔ **Succession or sale:** What is the appropriate selection process or training sequence to prepare for a smooth transition? The next section, "Preparing for a smooth exit," discusses the elements of finding the right person to take over.

✔ **Income tax considerations:** Uncle Sam's cut can play a bigger role that you might like. Maximizing value requires reducing income taxes as much as possible. Talk to your CPA about the best way to do this.

✔ **Separate self (management) from the investment:** How will you separate yourself from the value of the business? You want the investment to stand alone, without your involvement. To do all these things, you need to slowly pass clients, relationships, and responsibility to other employees in your firm. Often, businesses have branded their last name into the business name. It's important to figure out if you can eliminate that tie.

✔ **Purpose beyond business:** What are you going to do after the transfer? Don't wait until after the sale or exit to answer this question. Have a plan for what you'll do without your current daily activities. For some of you, this may be very easy; for others, it may not. Take care of yourself just as you're taking care of your employees during this time of transition.

Preparing for a smooth exit

After you've determined how you can exit the business, succession planning helps you determine who runs your business after its transfer. (This is relevant for all exit strategies except liquidation.) While you still have ownership and control, this time is crucial to add your input. No one knows the business better than you, so take advantage of your current situation and aid a successful succession.

To make sure the succession goes smoothly, update or establish your strategic plan so it can be used as the guide for the person who takes over. This guide helps maintain financial stability and future growth of the company. You want your successor to flourish because undoubtedly your financial future is intertwined with your business's future success. Therefore, take adequate time to develop a complete strategic plan so your successors have a steering wheel to guide the business safely through the competitive marketplace. Follow these steps to help you develop a succession plan:

1. **Write a job description for your successor(s).**

   You know the requirements of the position that you'll be vacating better than anyone. Make a list of everything that you do with details. Then ask your direct reports to comment and add to it.

2. **Develop a training program for your successors(s).**

   You know the needed skills and knowledge to be competent in your current position. Consider having your successor shadow you in your job, make an assistant CEO/leadership position, or create a management training program. All of these options or combinations of them achieve the goal of giving your successors the tools they need to do your job.

3. **Formalize and communicate the plan to all interested parties.**

   No matter who you appoint to take over or whoever your successor is, someone may get hurt feelings. There may be disgruntled family members or employees. If you communicate your plan with detailed explanations, people may better understand why you made the decisions that you did. Time can resolve sensitive issues. Make sure to also create all necessary legal documents to protect your business decisions.

4. **Create a management letter for your spouse (or significant other).**

   In the event of an untimely transfer, your spouse (if you have one) needs to know how you want to handle the situation, what your current goals are, who can be trusted and relied on in the current management team, and who can compose a dependable board of advisors. Write out a statement including all these factors.

   If you don't have a spouse, you should still craft a management letter because you need to explain how you want your to transfer your business.

   In either situation, provide a copy of your management letter to your spouse or most trusted confidant as well as your corporate attorney. Consider putting this letter in a safe deposit box as well. The most important point of this letter is to ensure that your intentions are upheld in case you aren't there to oversee the transfer.

Gathering additional resources

You should assemble a group of trusted advisors to help protect your assets and future desires. When taking all considerations to heart, developing sufficient responses and eventually setting a solid strategy can be easier with outside expertise and resources.

Inspired by success

In case you don't think selling your business is likely or even possible, here are examples of some entrepreneurial companies who've sold their businesses (I hope you're inspired by their success):

✔ **Catalytica Pharmaceuticals:** A 1,700-employee, Mountain View, California-based pharmaceutical outsourcer that made the world's supply of such drugs as AZT and Wellbutrin. The company was founded in 1993 and was sold to DSM of Holland for $800 million in 2000.

✔ **MLMReporter.com:** Founded in 2000, this company, which sells online marketing programs and systems, was sold two years later to KMT Media for just under $250,000 in April 2002.

✔ **PayPal:** An online payment service based in San Jose was sold to eBay three years after it was founded for $1.5 billion in stock in June 2002.

✔ **MySpace:** A social networking Web site (the fourth most popular English language Web site as of May 2006), was sold to media giant News Corp for $580 million in 2006 three years after it was founded.

The people to seek guidance from include the following:

✔ A CPA with estate planning experience

✔ An estate attorney

✔ A valuation expert

✔ A financial planner or money manager

✔ A life insurance specialist

A few free, online resources are also available to help you start your transition process:

✔ www.cashing-out.com

✔ www.buysellbiz.com

✔ www.thebizseller.com

Valuing your business

Few business owners are fortunate enough to sell their company when its value is at an all-time high. Even fewer owners who've sold their companies will ever know how or whether they could've achieved a higher price.

Check out the following sections for information on how to determine your business's value.

Establishing a value

Many factors can pique a buyer's interest — strong management, quality products, proven processes — but earnings will always be key. Historical, verifiable, and sustainable earnings that increase year-over-year are most attractive to perspective buyers. With that in mind, understanding how your business achieves the highest possible earnings becomes the roadmap to your strategic planning process.

The process begins by measuring how well your business is currently managed in comparison with other similar businesses that have recently sold. For example, when comparing two recently sold companies in your industry with similar revenue, you might find that Company A sold for a multiple of 3.5 times earnings while Company B sold for a multiple of 4.9 times earnings. Further analysis might uncover major differences in such factors as ratio of earnings, salaries, or cost of goods sold in relation to revenue.

More planning tips for business owners

In addition to valuing your business and thinking about an exit strategy, here are some additional planning tips for privately-held companies:

✔ **Engage all your employees.** Don't leave anyone out of the planning process because in a smaller organization you run the risk of alienating some people. Although you may not think it's appropriate to include everyone on staff, how will it look if everyone but two or three members aren't included? Find ways to engage everyone in the process.

✔ **Recognize your constraints.** As the owner, you probably have grand ideas and big plans. But remember not to overwhelm your staff by thinking too big or grandiose. Recognize your constraints and create a realistic strategic plan.

✔ **Have a clear vision.** Being crystal clear about what the owners want to achieve is critical to the success of any privately-held business. Do you want to grow or stay small? If you want to grow, by how much (see the preceding valuation discussion)? What future do you want to create for your business? It's really important for you to be clear about your owner's vision. Because if you're fuzzy on your vision, it will never materialize.

✔ **Just do it!** I know this slogan can be overused, but it fits perfectly here. It seems like setting aside time for planning in smaller organizations is hard because you don't have a person who can dedicate their time to strategic planning. Take the time to make strategy part of your culture. After the effects of executing your strategic plan are felt, you'll realize that you didn't have time *not* to do it. I promise!

Determining your value

The comprehensive approach to determining your value is to conduct a business valuation that includes market comparisons. First determine what your revenue or net profit needs to be to make your organization worth selling. Then have an analyst or valuation specialist research the market.

Several major databases exist via subscription: Done Deals, Biz Comps, IBA Market Data. Business owners can also get valuations from accounting, consulting, and investment banking firms.

The quick, less scientific way to determine your value is to look up sales of similar companies online. Inc.com's Web site provides a free valuation service: www.inc.com/valuation. Any angle you choose, make sure to include in your owner's vision the dollar value for which you're shooting to sell your business. (See Chapter 6 for more information on an owner's vision.)

Armed with the valuation results, identify areas you need to fine-tune and improve to create increased earnings and, ultimately, a higher price when selling your business.

Planning Concerns for Department Heads

Organizations that execute with excellence focus on a handful of clear goals and align the focus of every department and employee to those few goals. Take FranklinCovey Co. and Harris Interactive as examples. They conducted a study to test the gap between goal setting and the actual achievement of those goals in various companies. With more than 11,000 respondents, the results shed some light on issues around planning for organizations with multiple levels and departments. Here's what the study found:

- **Lack of clarity:** Only one in six workers think their organization sets clear goals and fewer than half say they understand what their companies are trying to achieve. Flip back to Chapter 14 for solutions to this issue.

- **Wasting time on non-critical tasks:** By their own account, respondents spend only 49 percent of their time on crucial organizational goals. One hour out of three is spent on urgent but irrelevant tasks, such as checking e-mail. One hour in five is wasted dealing with pointless bureaucracy issues such as politicking and attending unproductive meetings. By having a strategic plan that everyone buys into and understands, you can increase time spent on the crucial aspects of your organization.

✔ **No accountability:** Only about 50 percent of all respondents said that they feel accountable for performance. They're rarely, if ever, called on to report progress. Chapter 14 also addresses this problem.

✔ **No line of sight between organizational goals and work:** Only 20 percent of people has clearly defined work goals and 10 percent clearly understands how work relates to the organization's top priorities.

The next section addresses how to get alignment throughout an organization, no matter what the size.

Cascading corporate goals to department goals

Cascading goals means breaking down the corporate goals into a set of smaller goals that are relevant to each department. A simple way to think about this process is to think about goals spilling over a cliff like a waterfall. Goals must spread throughout an entire organization in order to be executed, as Figure 16-2 shows.

The department goals describe what each unit needs to achieve. These goals are then broken down further until individuals in the unit have their own performance goals. In this way, progress throughout the organization is measurable.

Cascading goals isn't an easy or fast process. Be prepared to meet resistance in getting people to get on board. Some may need specific training because they don't know how to develop goals and others may need coaching to enhance their performance.

Figure 16-2: How cascading goals work.

Reduce waste by 10% across the company by end of 2008.

Manufacturing Dept.: Reduce scrap by 5% from widget production by end of 2007.

Shipping Dept.: Reduce returns resulting from mis-picks by 5% by August 2008.

Administration Dept.: Institute a paper recycling program to reuse scrap paper for in-house printing by end of 2008.

Follow these steps to cascade goals in your organization:

1. **Select a person to be in charge of managing the cascading process.**

   If you've appointed a strategic plan manager, he's the ideal person for the job.

2. **Create a grid like Figure 16-3.**

   The grid lists all the corporate goals on the left-hand side and all departments horizontally across the top.

3. **Identify which departments are responsible for each goal.**

   Some goals may require two or more departments.

4. **Ask each department head or manager to develop department specific goals to support the corporate goals they've been assigned.**

   See Figure 16-4 for an example. Managers should ask these questions: What must we, as a team, do to support that the corporate goals? What must I do to support my team's goals?

5. **Repeat Steps 2 through 4.**

   This process cascades the goals down to as many levels as you choose, including individual players.

The planning team should ensure that the department level goals achieve the corporate goal after all department goals are completed. Review Chapter 14 for information on communication goals, holding everyone accountable, and tips on execution.

Corporate Goals	Departments			
	Manufacturing	IT	Marketing	HR
1. Improve net income by 10% by 12/31/07.	X		X	
2. Improve customer loyalty by increasing retention by 15% by 12/31/07.	X	X	X	X
3. Increase employee retention by reducing turnover by 5% by 9/31/07.		X		X
4. Improve operational efficiency through the implementation of an ERP system by 6/30/07.		X		

Figure 16-3: Spreading goals to different departments.

When goals cascade successfully, the results can be dramatic because you get alignment across the entire organization. All the executives at the same level need to agree on how they support the CEO's vision and what they can do to minimize conflict. Cascading goals creates constancy of focus, which gets everybody thinking about their contribution and how they are the foundation for the corporate goals.

Corporate Goals	IT Goals
1. Improve net income by 10% by 12/31/07.	N/A
2. Improve customer loyalty by increasing retention by 15% by 12/31/07.	2.1 Train all employees on the new CRM system by 9/31/07 to increase system utilization and reduce customer complaints.
3. Increase employee retention by reducing turnover by 5% by 9/31/07.	3.1 Reduce employee frustration by responding to IT requests within 24 hours. 3.2 Provide remote desktop access to all employees by 7/31/07 to allow employees to work from home.
4. Improve operational efficiency through the implementation of an ERP system by 6/30/08.	4.1 Install Phase One modules of the ERP system by 12/31/07. 4.2 Establish a regular training schedule by 10/31/07 for employees to learn the new system and provide feedback for Phase Two.

Figure 16-4: Translating corporate goals to be meaningful for each department.

Avoiding landmines in departmental planning

Some organizations are more political, departmentalized, controversial, or dysfunctional than others. And it's helpful to know if you're headed into a minefield before you take your first step. But don't despair! Your planning efforts can still be wildly successful.

In the next sections, I cover potential barriers to your planning, so avoiding these pitfalls (if you can) prevents your planning efforts from blowing up.

Limited budget and resources

If you lead a department, often there are externally imposed resource and operational constraints that severely hinder your ability to plan and act autonomously. For example, your budget may be so constrained because you're a cost center that even lining up training for your people to develop staff may not be possible. You're allowed to budget for operational overhead only, and you're only allowed to go off what was done in the past.

Cascading goals at Giant Eagle

Schuster-Zingheim and Associates, Inc. (www.schuster-zingheim.com) is a consulting firm that works with hundreds of clients to align corporate goals with employee performance. The company customizes pay and total rewards programs to engage the workforce and make them stakeholders in creating organizational success. Here's an example of how cascading goals worked for one of their clients:

Giant Eagle is a market-dominant East Coast grocery chain that employs 30,000 mostly-unionized retail grocery workers. Jack Flanagan (then executive vice president, Retail Operations) believed that for the company to improve on key dimensions, including customer satisfaction, the unionized workforce had to become stakeholders in the success of the stores in which they worked — they had to share in the financial performance of the store as measured in terms of customer satisfaction, store sales performance, and controllable cost.

Giant Eagle's chairman and president joined Flanagan and other executives to develop an incentive strategy with the goal of aligning unionized employees with key measures of success at the store level. Measures of customer satisfaction, sales, and cost were selected as paramount. In the past, differences in store performance hadn't impacted how store employees were paid — they weren't stakeholders in the success of the store, and their rewards weren't tied to how an individual store or the Giant Eagle company as a whole performed. The strategy called for the design of an incentive plan that focused performance on key goals. Although Giant Eagle is able to measure nearly all aspects of store performance, a commitment was made to add measurement tools if they were needed to make the incentive plan more viable.

The design team devised a way to more effectively gather and apply customer input at the individual store level and developed operational measures to ensure a positive cost/benefit relationship between dollars expended on incentives and value added to the store. When the incentive paid off, both employees and the store gained measurably.

The result was an incentive plan based on individual store goals or key performance measures. Measures and goals were communicated throughout the stores, and a monthly check was paid based on goal achievement.

If this is your situation, get creative. Be a change agent. Rework your departmental budget, buddy up with other departments, develop a non-expense option to implement your plan, or start your political positioning to get around your roadblocks.

Technology seems to always be a resource constraint and roadblock. For example, the shipping department may not be able to explain why they need $3 million for a new shipping system, while the legacy system continues to age and create operational drag. The current system still seems to work and job gets done. The fact that a new system is needed has to be defended early and often. For many groups, getting something like this is a multi-year political battle.

Alliances and coalitions

Because of resource constraints (see previous section), you must often ally with other groups and departments to get anything long-term done. You may not think that group work is a barrier, but it is because your goals may not align with the other department's goals.

To create buy-in, there's often compromise or a co-mingling of goals and resources. Think of it like going on vacation alone, versus going on vacation with another family. The competing expectations and agendas often muddy the water and you end up having a different trip, which often happens to departments that are forced to work together because they can't act alone.

Conflicting missions

Department missions often clash with other department missions. At the operational level, planning happens in individual groups, whereas organization-wide strategic planning often happens only at an executive level and rarely at an operational level. So there's a huge gap between the folks on the top and the people near the work. Within a system, these groups do whatever they want, and they do it without awareness of the larger whole. The exact opposite happens at the executive level. They plan at a 100,000 foot level, but have no idea how to actually execute anything or track progress. Successful organizational leaders have to live in that demilitarized zone between.

People handling

People are the most important resource in the plan. People add a tremendous amount of value to the equation, but they can also be the biggest obstacle to achieving your goals.

You'll never be able to do anything alone, so you have to think about others, cater to others, and so on. So sharpen your people handling skills in all aspects in order to prosper strategically. See Chapter 14 about coaching for achievement.

Departmental identity

You must be able to know your department's value and identify it for your stakeholders. It may be different depending on the audience. In the organizational environment, it is the little things that matter. Letting another group use your conference room, or your color printer, or your laminator, or your trucks with a lift-gate result in the right words being whispered in the right ears at meetings you're not invited to. Know what you have to trade and offer.

Also, know what you have that someone else may find valuable. They can go directly to your chain of command and ask for something that causes you a panic and a loss of resources as you struggle to fulfill a last minute request. Anticipate their need and desire and incorporate it into your plan. You simply must understand what outsiders find valuable about you and your organization, or you become a leaf in the wind.

Metrics, metrics, metrics

When you're always asking and pitching for everything you want on a strategic level, you must build in the time, resources, and processes to track everything. Measurements can be an extremely crucial tool to getting you what you want. You must be able to prove worth or protection from something that can get you off track at all times. That means you have the data and the fancy reports on tap. You can say, "Gee, boss, we'd like to help you, but we're already overcommitted by 23 percent. In fact, I'd like more people. So if you can get me the staffing I need, maybe I can take this extra thing on." Hand over a fact sheet that explains it in black and white.

Chapter 17

Planning for the Social Sectors

. . . .

In This Chapter

▶ Shifting from a profit focus to a resource focus

▶ Involving your board in strategic planning

▶ Understanding governmental planning

▶ Thinking about competition in nonprofits

. . . .

Strategic planning in social sectors, specifically defined as the government and nonprofit organizations, is becoming more and more common for several reasons:

✔ The communities in which we live and work are increasingly complex.

✔ Social issues are more difficult, more interrelated, and more critical to solve.

✔ Community leaders and executive directors are being asked to be more accountable for the performance of their organizations and communities.

✔ As change accelerates, managers need proven management approaches, often borrowed from the private sector, to help them be more effective with their resources.

That said, many not-for-profit and governmental organizations have been crafting strategic plans far longer than the business community. Best practices from this field have been adopted by private organizations and visa versa. Many of you may not be running a nonprofit or governmental entity, but you may sit on several boards or committees. This chapter can help you be a better board member by understanding your role in strategic planning.

This chapter is intended to be a supplement to rest of the book. Although the majority of ideas and concepts presented in the previous chapters are applicable, a few modifications are necessary for effective social sector strategic planning.

Moving from Profit to Sustainability

Clearly the big difference between for-profits and nonprofits and governments is that pesky little word *profit*. Social-sector organizations are mission-driven, not profit-driven. So instead of the bottom line being strictly money — although that's necessary to keep the doors open — the real reason for these organization's existence is public service.

Jim Collins, author of *Good to Great,* just published a supplement to his book that talks about how social sector organizations should think about their economic engine not in terms of profit but in terms of resources. Collins says, "The critical question isn't 'How much money do we make?' but 'How can we develop a sustainable resource engine to deliver superior performance relative to our mission?'"

Based on Collins's research of hundreds of social sector companies, the resource engine has three components, which can be developed into goals in the Balanced Scorecard areas in Chapter 12:

- ✔ **Time:** How well does your organization attract staff and volunteers to contribute their efforts at normally lower than market wages? Think about developing goals in areas of *people* and *learning.*

- ✔ **Money:** How stable and sustainable is your cash flow? In the Balanced Scorecard areas, this is covered in the *customer* perspective. Do you have solid programs that deliver to keep your cash flowing?

- ✔ **Brand:** How effective are you at developing relationships and emotionally connecting with potential supporters? Managing your brand is part of the *operational* area.

With these components, you can develop revenue goals to create an effective resource engine. (See Chapter 12 on goal writing.) And these types of goals make more sense to your staff and board, instead of talking about profit.

Getting Your Board on Board the Planning Effort

Your organization's governing or policy board plays an important part in your strategic planning efforts. The degree of influence boards have varies from nonprofit to government organizations. But in some form or fashion, these appointed or elected members are responsible for defining the organization's purpose and mission, articulating the strategic priorities for the planning year, and monitoring the execution of the plan.

The role of the policy board

So just what is the role of the policy board, board of directors, board of county commissioners, the city council, and so on, then?

Effective policy board members should do the following:

- ✔ Focus their attention on their policy-making role and stay out of the day-to-day

- ✔ Establish a clear set of priorities for the organization

- ✔ Hold the staff accountable for achieving the established priorities through regular meetings and tying budget requests to the strategic plan

- ✔ Listen and acknowledge staff recommendations regarding the execution of the plan

- ✔ Concentrate their resources on being more effective at policy making

Being tight on the ends and loose on the means

Being *tight on the ends* involves building a strong commitment and understanding of objectives and goals of your organization and its board. Although the objectives and goals are written in ink, create the action items in pencil. Allow those who are responsible for the goals — that is, your board — to develop their own methods to best achieve the goals. Hence, *loose on the means.*

Many strategic planning experts have recognized the importance of flexibility and authority in the implementation of a strategic plan. Those people involved in the implementation process need to have enough flexibility and authority to be creative and responsive to new developments — without having to reconstruct an entire strategic plan. Flexibility is important as adjustments are necessary when planning for an uncertain future. An organization's objectives and goals are much less likely and far more difficult to change than the programs and activities planned to achieve them.

An organization's goal is to increase new customers by ten percent this month. In order to achieve this goal, corporate headquarters created a sales promotion as an action item. The local employees realized there was a major conflicting event in their community that would hinder the success of their promotion. Clearly those responsible for implementing the promotion needed to adjust the program plan without changing the original goal. Among their options are an extended promotion or a new date altogether.

Planning for Governmental Entities

Governmental planning reaches further than business planning because most plans — whether community cultural plans, regional tourism plans, county plans, or neighborhood development plans — exist outside the realm of any single agency. Therefore, successful planning requires enough authority and resources to assure the plans' intentions are fulfilled. Basically, the majority of for-profit planning takes a single entity approach instead of a community or regional scale approach. When you're planning for a single organization, boundaries, authority, and responsibilities are well defined. When the planning scale is expanded beyond individual organizations to include a community, different methods are required.

The next section highlights the key areas where planning for the governmental entities is different than private sector planning.

Recognizing how governmental planning works

Because governmental entities operate as monopolies in most cases, have elected boards that change every four to six years, and provide services that are legislated instead of based on market demand, these organizations must recognize how these factors affect their planning. The following sections contain my advice for how to accommodate some factors that affect governmental strategic planning.

Leadership

Leaders must win internal and external support for strategic planning. Often the agency that initiates a plan deliberately seeks community leaders outside its own organization to head the planning. This strategy helps demonstrate that the planning is intended to benefit the whole community. Cross-agency cooperation requires leadership and dedication to get the plan completed and executed.

Governing board

A broadly representative steering committee of between 10 and 15 members should be created to oversee the planning. This committee is your governing board. In governmental planning, it's common for a few initiators to identify a larger group of community leaders to form a temporary steering committee. This brings more authority and resources to the planning table. Additionally, you can form cross-agency or departmental task forces around key priorities or goals to help facilitate the implementation. Both the steering committee and the task forces help cut across agency and departmental lines.

Power and politics

Power and political conflict can be volatile enough to derail planning from its course. Here are a few examples:

- A regional cultural tourism plan can run up against agencies with competing interests.
- Culture-war based political agendas can erupt in public planning.
- Public-sector initiatives too closely associated with one mayor or county commission can be dismantled by their successors.
- Even an uncontroversial issue like arts education can evoke conflict when competitive grants for implementation are at stake.

There are no simple remedies for these conflicts except to be alert for power issues and try to sidestep the politics before getting embroiled in it. Wise planners don't assume that all people have the same interests. Proactive planners identify potential political power bases and get buy-in at the beginning of the process by recognizing the different interests.

Values and culture

An organization's culture tends to be more homogeneous than not. Members of an organization, although potentially diverse, have much in common arising from their voluntary association with the group. They share many values, and if they didn't, they wouldn't join and stay as staff or volunteers.

Cities, counties, and communities, on the other hand, are more diverse than most private or nonprofit organizations. A plan for a varied community must respectfully accommodate those differences if the resulting recommendations are to be taken seriously. Use assessments that reach people in neighborhoods, job sites, and churches, which represent a community more authentically than one where consensus depends on those who speak up at a public hearing in city hall. Be genuinely inclusive.

Administrative systems

Community-wide planners may need to create the administrative systems that sustain their work. Often the absence of a dependable means of communication or a system for monitoring the development and execution of a strategic plan can derail the process. Setup good, clear administrative systems that keep everyone appraised of the process as well as the results from their hard work.

Community involvement

Successful governmental plans consider the community to be the constituents on whose behalf the plans are made. Here are a few suggestions:

✔ Do a community-wide survey or assessment.

✔ Get your various citizen groups involved in developing your plan.

✔ Hold community-wide workshops.

✔ Provide numerous methods for community input such as an online forum, a discussion board, a primary point of contact, or hotline.

After all, governmental plans are undertaken to fulfill a community need.

Envisioning a bright future

The Minnesota Community Development Joint Powers Board conducted an extensive community survey that resulted in the 2000 Ely Area Visioning and Land Use Study. Every year, the board updates the visioning document and uses the goals from the study as the framework for its agenda each month.

According to board members, the visioning document set out the big picture of how people want change and development to happen in the region. After the visioning document was created, action items were established that groups can work together to accomplish. Those action items are the building blocks to help the area accomplish the larger goals set out in the visioning statement.

The Ely Area Vision 2000 document looked at several parts of the community, including educational, transportation, environmental, and economic development goals.

Here are just a few of the area successes:

✔ Achievement of resurfacing and better maintenance of area roads

✔ Secured federal funding for highway improvements

✔ Increase communication between the Ely Airport and joint powers board to share the costs of a local match for airport improvements

Additional resources for governmental entities

Tons of great resources exist for governmental strategic planning that can be very helpful in your planning efforts. Here are just a few recommendations:

✔ **International City/County Management Association:** This organization is the professional and educational organization for chief appointed managers, administrators, and assistants in cities, towns, counties, and regional entities throughout the world. On its Web site, you find a resource library with outstanding articles on numerous topics relevant to the public-sector, including strategic planning. Some articles are open whereas others require membership. Check out the site at www.icma.org.

✔ *Good to Great and the Social Sectors: Why Business Thinking Is Not the Answer.* This book was published in 2005 by Jim Collins as a supplement to his popular book *Good to Great.* You can also find free articles, podcasts, and exercises on his resource-rich Web site at www.jimcollins.com.

✔ **Internet searches:** If you want to see some examples of governmental strategic plans, simply use the search term *strategic plan* in Google or your favorite search engine. The search returns numerous agency strategic plans in the first several results pages.

Central control of implementation

Central control of a governmental entity plan's implementation can be quite difficult. Assuring action on the policy and program plans that characterize most governmental and community-based organizations can hit roadblocks if execution isn't centralized. Centralized control can be achieved by appointing one or two people within the organization to monitor the execution of the plan. Everyone in the organization needs to know who's acting in an oversight capacity to move the plan along. With central control, implementation is more consistent and smooth because problems can be addressed and solved more quickly.

Getting advice for governmental planning

Here are some tips to help planning in your agency or community:

✔ Identify specific agencies charged with implementation of clear outcomes. This only works if named agencies participate in the planning.

✔ Identify a single, coordinating entity charged with overseeing implementation. In some cases, the coordinating agency or group is created to implement the plan.

   ✔ Involve respected and representative community and business leaders
     in your process.

   ✔ Reconvene the planning steering committee periodically to monitor
     implementation progress. The expectation of a public accounting for
     results can be a powerful incentive to act.

   ✔ Plan for the municipality or county to commission a formal evaluation of
     the plan two to five years after publication.

   ✔ Widely distribute a well-designed plan. Describe goals in general terms
     and actively encourage individual groups and agencies to fulfill the plan
     as it serves their interests.

Planning for Nonprofit Organizations

Nonprofit staff are often uncomfortable discussing competitiveness or
resource allocation — not because they don't understand these ideas, but
because they like concentrating on the people they help through their work
instead of these concepts. Unlike for-profit businesses, which compete for
customers and whose very survival depends on providing services or products to satisfied, paying clients, many nonprofit organizations operate in a
non-market, or grants/memberships, economy — one in which services may
not be commercially viable.

Competition is now being introduced into the nonprofit sector. Lack of competition had left little incentive for nonprofit organizations to improve their
services or operations. There was no internal drive to assess whether the
needs of clients or member requests were being met, or to examine the cost-
effectiveness or quality of services being provided. Without the threat of
competition, nonprofit organizations did little to improve their business
processes. So with a growing number of nonprofit organizations offering similar services, stakeholders want to ensure that the organization is providing
optimal results for the resources they have been given.

Nonprofits are finding that success only increases the number of competitors
entering the field to compete for grants. Growing competition in the nonprofit
market has made grant money and membership contributions scarce, even
as need and demand increase.

Today nonprofit organizations find themselves competing for a small pool of
resources. In order to compete more effectively, today's executive directors are
required to understand their competitors, rethink their business processes,
create a sustainable competitive advantage, and to increase collaboration,
where appropriate.

Redefining competition with the Matrix (but without Keanu Reeves)

To maximize resources and funding, organizations need to focus on what they do best and outsource the rest. Easy to say, right? That concept is harder to do in practice. The *MacMillan Matrix,* a tool developed by Wharton School of Business professor Ian MacMillan, was specifically designed to tackle this task.

The Matrix can help you discover the program areas that are most needed in your community and that you're in the best position to provide. The Matrix is based on the following assumptions:

- ✔ Nonprofits should avoid duplicating services to ensure that limited resources are used well and quality of service is maximized.
- ✔ Nonprofits should focus on a limited number of high-quality services, instead of providing many mediocre services.
- ✔ Nonprofits should collaborate so that a continuum of service can be provided with each partner focusing on specific pieces.

The Matrix therefore helps organizations think about some very pragmatic questions:

- ✔ Are we the best organization to provide this service?
- ✔ Is competition good for our clients?
- ✔ Are we spreading ourselves too thin, without the capacity to sustain ourselves?
- ✔ Should we work cooperatively with another organization to provide services?

Here is the step-by-step process to apply this Matrix to your organization:

1. **Assess each of your programs in relation to the four criteria in the next four sections; each is placed in the MacMillan Matrix.**

   For example, a program that's a good fit is deemed attractive and strong competitively, but if there's a high alternative coverage, you would assign it to Aggressive Competition.

2. **Evaluate which programs are worth competing for aggressively and which ones should be divested.**

   Critically look at your programs to determine which ones to keep and which ones to eliminate.

3. Identify whether you have any programs that are a good fit with your mission.

These programs should have few competitive alternatives, and your organization's offering should be very strong. MacMillan refers to these programs as the *Soul of the Agency* and describes them as difficult business but essential to the members.

A detailed overview of the model can be downloaded at The Forbes Group Web site (`www.forbes.com`). The report is free although site registration is required.

Using the MacMillan Matrix is a fairly straightforward process of assessing each current (or prospective) program according to four criteria (covered in the next sections). See Figure 17-1.

		High Program Attractiveness: "Easy" Program		Low Program Attractiveness: "Difficult" Program	
		Alternative Coverage *High*	**Alternative Coverage** *Low*	**Alternative Coverage** *High*	**Alternative Coverage** *Low*
GOOD FIT	**Strong Competitive Position**	1. Aggressive Competition	2. Aggressive Growth	5. Build up the Best Competitor	6. "Soul of the Agency"
	Weak Competitive Position	3. Aggressive Divestment	4. Build Strength or Get Out	7. Orderly Divestment	8. "Foreign Aid" or Joint Venture
POOR FIT		9. Aggressive Divestment		10. Orderly Divestment	

Figure 17-1: The MacMillan Matrix.

#1: Alignment with mission

Services and programs that belong or fit within an organization are in alignment with the mission or a good fit. Criteria for a good fit include

- Supports the purpose and mission of the organization
- Draws on existing skills in the organization
- Shares resources and coordinate activities with programs

#2: Program attractiveness

Program attractiveness is the degree to which a program is attractive to the organization from an economic perspective, such as whether the program easily attracts resources. Here's a list of criteria that makes a program attractive:

- High appeal to groups capable of providing current and future support and stable funding
- Need from a large client base and low resistance to program
- Appeal to volunteers
- Measurable, reportable program results
- Able to discontinue with relative ease, if necessary
- Intended to promote the self-sufficiency or self-rehabilitation of client base

#3: Alternative coverage

Alternative coverage is the number of other organizations that deliver a similar program to similar constituents. If there are no other large, or very few small, comparable programs being provided in the same region, the program is classified as *low coverage*. Otherwise, the coverage is *high*.

#4: Competitive position

Competitive position is the degree to which the organization has a stronger capability and potential to deliver the program than other agencies. Most programs can't be classified as being in a strong competitive position unless they have some clear basis for declaring superiority over all competitors in that program category. Criteria for a strong competitive position include

- Good location and delivery system
- Large pool of loyal clients, communities, or support groups
- Past success of securing funding and ability to raise funds, particularly for this type of program
- Superior track record (or image) of service delivery
- Better quality service or service delivery than competitors with the most cost effective delivery of service
- Superiority of technical skills and organizational skills needed for the program
- Ability to conduct needed research into the program and properly monitor program performance

Additional resources for nonprofits

As all executive directors know, the nonprofit world shares information freely and openly. Here is a list of a few resources that help nonprofits with their strategic planning:

✔ *Strategic Planning for Nonprofit Organizations: A Practical Guide and Workbook:* This resource was written by Michael Allison and Jude Kaye and is outstanding for nonprofit planners because it provides a comprehensive set of worksheets for all aspects of nonprofit planning.

✔ **Compass Point's Nonprofit Genie:** This resource provides free information about

nonprofit topics including strategic planning. Check them out online at the following site: www.compasspoint.com/askgenie.

✔ **Alliance for Nonprofit Management:** This group is a professional association of individuals and organizations devoted to improving the management and governance capacity of nonprofits and to assist nonprofits in fulfilling their mission. The association's Web site has a host of free resources dedicated to nonprofit management. Visit www.allianceonline.org.

Five years ago, there was little funding for case management by AIDS Service Organizations. Unwilling to let clients fend for themselves in getting the help they needed, many organizations devoted staff time to this service. At the time, this was a *soul of the agency* program. These days, this program is more attractive (fundable), although there's also growing alternative coverage. Therefore, organizations in a strong position to serve the clients well, with cultural competence and program expertise, should aggressively compete. Those in a weak competitive position should get out of the business.

Specific strategies for nonprofits

Listed below are several strategies applicable to both the organizational and program levels, adapted from Philip Kotler's *Strategic Marketing for Nonprofit Organizations.* This list helps generate ideas and goals about how your organization can reach its vision. As you review this list, take note of what strategies you're employing or ones that you could be.

✔ **Surplus maximization:** An organization runs in a manner that increases the amount of resources on hand. Usually this strategy is adopted to accumulate resources for expansion or growth.

✔ **Revenue maximization:** An organization manages itself to generate the highest possible revenues, perhaps in an effort to establish a reputation or critical mass.

✔ **Usage maximization:** Organizations work to serve the highest number of users of their services. This strategy can be used to position the organization or program for funding or budgetary purposes.

✔ **Usage targeting:** An organization provides services in a manner that encourages serving a specific number or type of constituents. This strategy is used to address unmet needs of specific populations or to cover the costs associated with providing services.

✔ **Full cost recovery:** An organization manages its programs and services so that it financially breaks even, providing as much service as the finances allow. Many nonprofits adopt this strategy in an effort to provide services without entering fiscal crisis.

✔ **Partial cost recovery:** Organization operate with a chronic deficit every year, providing services that are critical and can't be provided at a breakeven level of costs (for example, mass transit or the post office). These organizations rely on public and private foundations, individuals, and governments to cover the annual deficit.

✔ **Budget maximization:** An organization maximizes the size of its staff, services, and operating expenditures regardless of revenue/cost levels. Organizations that are concerned with reputation and the impact of trimming services or infrastructure on that reputation employ this strategy.

✔ **Producer satisfaction maximization:** An organization operates toward a goal of satisfying the personal/professional needs of a founder, staff, or board of directors instead of the established needs of external clients and customers.

✔ **Fees for service:** An organization provides services to clients for a fee. The fee is typically below market rates and doesn't cover the full cost of providing the services.

✔ **Retrenchment strategies:** An organization emphasizes efforts to reduce internal costs to offset the potential or real loss of revenues or grant monies. Examples include increasing staff workloads, increasing use of part-time or volunteer staff, eliminating services or programs, or reducing non-fixed expenses such as training or supplies.

Whew! Is that it? I'm sure you'll have all of these in place by tomorrow! In all seriousness, pick one or two strategies that you think could be the most effective in your organization and use them to develop the basis of your strategic plan.

Scouting out the new future for girls

The Girl Scouts of America is in the throes of what's arguably one of the biggest transformations in a nonprofit organization ever and provides a great example of an approach to planning. Girl Scouts was founded in 1912, and although 2012 may seem far away, that's the organization's 100th anniversary. Because of this milestone, the leaders decided to scrutinize how they serve girls, how they recruit and use the dedicated service of volunteers, how they attract donors, and how they govern themselves. The executives keenly realized that the lives of girls are changing, and so the Girl Scouts too must change.

In June 2004, Girl Scout leadership enlisted the services of Willie Pietersen, a professor of the Practice of Management at Columbia Business School, to help the Girl Scouts develop a strategy to ensure their future success and growth. After identifying the Girls Scouts' strengths, challenges, and imperatives for success, they zeroed in on five strategic priorities that now represent the organization's focus:

✔ **Program Model and Pathways:** Building the best-integrated personal leadership development model that defines activities and outcomes, differentiated by age level, for girls 5-17, and offers flexible pathways for participation

✔ **Volunteerism:** Developing a nimble, state-of-the-art model of volunteerism that mobilizes a variety of volunteers committed to the Girl Scout mission

✔ **Brand:** Transforming the Girl Scout image with a compelling, contemporary brand

✔ **Funding:** Substantially increasing contributed income to fund a vibrant Girl Scout organization

✔ **Organizational Structure and Governance:** Creating an efficient and effective organizational structure and democratic governance system

With these strategic priorities in place, the next step was implementing this major shift. The solution was to form six Gap Teams comprised of a variety of Girl Scout members from all levels, functions, and geographic regions of the organization. The Gap Teams are charged with identifying the transformations needed to move Girl Scouts from the organization it is now to the organization it can become. This organizational transformation is expected to continue through 2008. The result is expected to be an improved organization to serve the changing needs of girls and provide a new direction for the future of the Girl Scouts.

Part VI
The Part of Tens

In this part . . .

*E*very *For Dummies* book has a Part of Tens. This part neatly sections off important things to know in groups of ten. In this part, you discover ten ways to keep your strategic plan off the shelf and dust free. You also uncover some pitfalls of strategic planning and ways to ruin your strategic planning meeting. Lastly, I give you ten shortcuts to getting your plan done.

Chapter 18

Ten Ways to Keep Your Strategic Plan from Hitting the Shelf

- -

In This Chapter

▶ Making your strategic plan a living document

▶ Avoiding a strategic plan that gathers dust

- -

More often than not, life and day-to-day operations take over a well-intentioned strategic plan implementation. If the strategic plan is one more thing everyone has to do, it begins to feel like a burden instead of being exciting. By embedding your strategic planning into daily operations, completing items on your strategic plan becomes natural instead of something extra or something you pull off the bookshelf and review only when you happen to remember it's there. This chapter covers ten quick ways to keep your strategic plan from landing on the shelf and collecting dust.

Getting Everyone Involved from the Start

Make your organization's plan everyone's plan. Start by involving everyone on your staff from the start of the plan. If you only look to the folks at the top of your company, you're making a recipe for failure, because employees at all levels aren't only a wealth of information, but also they're the implementers of your plan. You need them to feel part of the planning process, even if they don't have a seat at the table.

As you read the chapters in this book, you find references to group exercises and employee feedback. Use this info to help develop a strategic plan that everyone feels part of, and assign every staff member a goal or objective. Then everyone has direct responsibility for achieving a piece of the organization's strategy.

Deleting the Fluff

The sure death of a strategic plan is entombing it in hundreds of pages of text. Less is more. Delete the nonessential text that just clutters up the page. What are the essentials of your plan? See Chapter 1, which outlines the major pieces of your plan.

My Web site, `www.mystrategicplan.com`, provides a good example of a strategic plan that does not have any fluff.

Your strategic plan isn't a business plan. Your strategic plan is a guide and a roadmap that tells how to get from where you are to where you want to be. Every part of your plan has a role in clearly defining that journey. Unlike a business plan, you're not explaining your business to the reader. You, your staff, and board are the readers of the plan. It's not a sales piece. It's an action piece.

Appointing a Strategy Engineer

Appoint someone (other than yourself) to be the go-to person for the strategic plan. Anoint him or her as the strategy engineer who's responsible for

- Keeping track of your progress through the use of a scorecard (see Chapter 14)
- Getting updates from managers and staff on goals, objectives, and action plans
- Organizing meetings and communications about the strategic plan

Creating a Strategic Plan Poster

By putting your strategic plan on one huge page, you keep your strategic plan from even touching the shelf (unless, of course, you have a really big shelf). Yes, you need back-up documentation, which can be in that three-ring binder on a shelf, but put the key parts of your strategic plan on one page. Blow the page up at your local print shop and hang it in your breakroom or common area. The poster helps keep everyone focused on your organization's strategic direction.

Hooking Achievement into Incentives

Everyone likes to be rewarded for a job well done. Dangling a carrot out there for successfully implementing your strategic plan is a sure way to get some action. Incentives take all different shapes and colors. The green kind (ahem, money) is always welcome, but you can develop all sorts of creative perks. By paying for performance, you elevate the importance of your strategic plan. See Chapter 14 for additional considerations.

Using a KISS

When all else fails — Keep It Simple, Stupid. (Sorry, I don't like calling anyone stupid, but that's what the last S of KISS stands for.) For your strategic plan to be implemented, everyone in your organization has to understand it. Failing prey to big business lingo and confusing jargon diminishes the effectiveness of your plan. It's really easy to develop a confusing strategic plan, so resist the urge.

Holding a Monthly Strategy Meeting

Groan . . . another meeting? Well, yes and no. *Replace* one of your regularly scheduled staff meetings with a strategy meeting. Meetings about strategy can be exciting and people want to be involved. The purpose of the meeting is to discuss the status of your plan. Cross off what's been completed. Troubleshoot if something isn't happening. Make changes where needed.

If your meetings are boring, spice them up a bit. Ask each employee to report on one or two accomplishments. Limit everyone's report to one minute (have someone keep time). For people who are having an issue or problem where they need help, ask them to list it on the board. Spend 10 to 15 minutes as a group working to solve the issue. Remember, the issues need to be related to the strategic plan; otherwise, they should be discussed at another time. Don't let the meetings run over; keep them to a set time.

You may be surprised at the enthusiasm and effectiveness of this type of meeting. People like to talk about strategy. It's exciting! It's also exciting to accomplish important initiatives. See Chapter 14 for more info about how to hold effective strategy meetings.

Using a Scorecard

Keeping your plan alive requires constant communication, which can seem like too big of a task and may just fall to the wayside. But if your staff doesn't know where they stand, it's impossible to keep implementing your plan. Some people like to play ignorant and ignorance is bliss.

Use a scorecard to keep everyone in the loop. A scorecard provides a quick snapshot of who's contributing and who isn't. The scorecard allows you to track the progress of each goal by listing the status of the goal each month. Ideally, you've developed goals that are measurable. With measurable goals, you have numbers associated with the status of each goal every month.

Think about your scorecard as your one-page progress report of every goal in your plan. Turn the scorecard into charts and graphs, and you have a quick visual that communicates your progress and is fun to look at! The scorecard may also help with employees holding each other accountable for each other's part in meeting the strategic plan. Chapter 14 explains scorecards in detail.

Leading by Example

Be a purposeful leader and your people will follow. There's no better way to keep your plan alive than through your leadership. Your complete and total commitment is critical to the success of your plan. If you pull back, even just a little, it gives everyone a license to slack off. So talk about your organization's strategy regularly. Use it in conversations with clients, customers, and board members. Ask questions of your staff about its progress — is it working or not? When making budget decisions, point back to your plan. Does the budget fit into your plan?

Celebrating Your Success — Whenever You Feel Like It

Too often you're so focused on tomorrow's tasks that you forget to recognize today's successes. Don't wait until the end of the year to recognize achievement. Celebrate small successes along the way! Did you achieve a big goal? Have a pizza party. Take the staff to lunch. Give everyone the day off. Go on a fun outing. No matter how big or small, by celebrating success along the way you keep everyone excited, engaged, and motivated to keep working.

Chapter 19

Ten Ways to Ruin Your Strategic Planning Meeting

In This Chapter

▶ Improving the success of your planning meetings

▶ Avoiding typical pitfalls of strategic planning meetings

The three words *strategic planning retreat* provoke reactions anywhere from sheer exuberance to ducking for cover. In many organizations, retreats have a bad reputation because it's easy to step into one of the many planning pitfalls. Holding effective meetings can be tough, and if you add a lot of brainpower mixed with personal agendas, and you can have a recipe for disaster. That's why so many strategic planning meetings are unsuccessful. The sections in this chapter focus on the ten guaranteed ways to ruin your next meeting.

Refusing to Use a Facilitator

If you were having a party for 100 of your closest friends, assuming money was no object, would you cook for all of them or hire a caterer? More than likely, you'd hire a caterer. Not because you're incapable of whipping up potato salad, burgers, and homemade fries, but because it's more fun to sit back, relax, and enjoy the party. Besides, a caterer is trained and paid to make sure that everything goes smoothly. Why take on the extra stress?

A strategic planning meeting is no different. You or someone else in your organization are more than capable of running the meeting, but it's not the best approach. By hiring a facilitator, you can be fully engaged in the strategy and planning and leave meeting process and structure to someone else. Furthermore, hiring a facilitator is better because he or she can remain totally impartial.

Make sure to find a facilitator who understands and runs strategic planning meetings regularly. You want someone who can keep the meeting on task and guide the process so you achieve the desired outcome of a strategic plan. Outline the process:

- Sit down with the facilitator prior to the meeting.
- Make sure he fully understands what success looks like to you.
- Clearly explain your desired outcome, what business you are in, the strategic issues you're facing, and the dynamics of your team.

The best way to find a facilitator is through referrals. Tap into your business associates or your business networks for their contacts. Check out Chapter 3 for a list of what to look for in a good facilitator.

Neglecting to Conduct Any Research Before the Meeting

Picture this: You pick a date or series of dates for your strategic planning meetings, and the next thing you know, it's tomorrow. You get so caught up in the day-to-day operations that you don't have time to think strategically about your business. And it's necessary to think strategically in order to set up your strategic planning meeting effectively.

If you neglect to conduct research before the meeting, you get into your session and realize you don't have the information you need in order to make sound strategic decisions. The only way to have a solid strategic plan is to incorporate information about your external environment and your internal operations. The chapters in Part III help you identify the types of data and information you need to research for your strategic planning effort.

Some research is better than none. So if you find yourself in a pinch the day before or the day of the meeting, do what you can to get data about your customers' needs, your competitors' actions, and your employees' opinions.

Inviting Everyone

The old cliché that too many cooks spoil the broth couldn't be closer to the truth. Although it's imperative that key employees have a voice in planning, not everyone has to literally be at the meeting table. Too many people in the room can lead to chaos and confusion, resulting in a strategic plan by committee instead of through educated decisions and leadership.

If you have a lot of people who want to participate in the process, include them in a couple of different ways:

- ✓ **Collect employees' thoughts and opinions via an employee survey.** Check out Chapter 5 for an example of an employee survey used for strategic planning. Also in that chapter, you find a set of actions to take with the information you collected.

- ✓ **Hold a series of meetings.** Perhaps the first and last meetings are with your senior management team and a couple meetings in between are with key employees and staff. In either case, you've collected ideas and opinions that are valuable to developing your plan, but you've reserved the right to make the final decisions about what actions you take.

Groups of between 10 to 15 are the ideal size for strategic planning meetings. If you have more people than that, you can always break up into small teams.

Holding an Annual Retreat

Huh? Isn't this section about holding strategic planning retreats? Yes, it is. But one common thought process in strategic planning is that you have to hold a retreat. Setting aside a couple of days in an off-site location where everyone gathers in their sweatshirt and jeans drinking cocoa is a typical vision of a strategic planning meeting. Oftentimes a retreat is an annual event and all strategic decision making is reserved for that occasion.

Strategic planning should be a *habit,* not an event. Hold your strategy meetings regularly (more than once a year) to realize enhanced performance. With that said, annual retreats are okay, but make sure that they aren't your only meetings of the year. See Chapter 14 for more discussion on this topic.

Getting through the Agenda No Matter What

Strategic planning is hard work. It takes a lot of mental energy to pull all the pieces of the puzzle together, see the future, make strategic decisions, and organize the plan usefully. At every strategic planning meeting I've facilitated, people are mentally exhausted by the end. Getting through the agenda is usually what it takes to have a completed plan. However, sometimes it's just not possible to get it all done.

Have an agenda so everyone knows the structure of the day, but don't be so rigid that you stick to it no matter what. Remember to loosen up, have some fun, and take breaks. If you don't get through everything, plan another meeting or assign tasks for the outstanding items.

Forgetting to Explain the Process

A good facilitator makes sure to explain the strategic planning process and the expected outcome of the meeting from the get-go. Most people think they know how to develop a strategic plan, but that doesn't mean that they truly can do it. Naturally you don't want to insult anyone's intelligence, but do take the time to review the different terms used in strategic planning and each step of the process. By making sure that everyone starts on the same page, you eliminate any confusion that may derail your meeting.

Assuming Everyone Thinks Like You

Of course, everyone thinks like you do, right? As a good leader, you know that's not the case. Unfortunately sometimes you forget what's obvious and end up structuring a meeting based on your own preferences. In reality, it's pretty hard to step into other people's shoes and ways of thinking. But in strategic planning, you want everyone in the room engaged.

To get everyone engaged, make sure to secure a comfortable environment. People feel the most comfortable when they're operating in their own thinking preference. Do you see any of your team members in the following descriptions?

- Some people enjoy big picture thinking. These people get fired up talking about the mission, vision, and long-term strategies of the organization.

- Some people find big picture discussions frustrating. They'd rather get down to business. This group wants to know what you're going to do this year, who's going to do it, and when it's going to be done. These people are your goal setters and action planners.

✔ Another group wants to analyze all possible options before making a decision. This group wants to feel completely comfortable with the direction selected. These analyzers are great at synthesizing data from the SWOT and developing your SWOT. To some people, this tactic may feel like the discussion is going in circles.

✔ The last group of people want to make sure that all opinions are included. They're the ones who don't want to move on until everyone in the room has voiced their ideas. This group is your meeting minders. They make sure everyone is buying into the plan that's being developed.

You may not have all thinking types in your planning session, but by acknowledging that not everyone is going to be comfortable in all aspects of the planning process, you can structure the meeting and manage the discussion accordingly. To do so, first ask your employees which of the four thinking types they *most closely* identify with. Then explain which part of your agenda addresses each thinking type. In the preceding list, I indicate a part of the planning process where each type can shine.

Ignoring the Elephant in the Room

Would you like to see a strategic planning meeting go down in flames? Forge ahead, even though you know you have some staff issues. If any key staff member is upset or has an outstanding problem, your strategic planning meeting may be disrupted. That person may sit in the meeting like a brooding elephant and finally blow his top and get the meeting off course.

The best way to handle staff concerns is to have a one-on-one discussion with every person who will be attending the strategic planning session. Give your employee the opportunity to voice issues or concerns privately. Make sure that you clarify that your intent is to clear up any problems that may inhibit full participation during the strategy session.

Ending on a Low Note

You did it! You successfully made it all the way through your strategic planning meeting. You accomplished everything you intended. You have the key pieces of your strategic plan in place. You're feeling great. Everyone is slowly packing up their stuff and heading out the door, but you sense a feeling of exhaustion and maybe a little anxiety. You're wondering why.

What just happened is that you unintentionally ended your strategic planning meeting on a low note. In most cases, you have more to cover in your meeting than you have time for. You end up rushing the last part of the meeting to get it all done. I recommend, no matter where you are in your agenda, structuring the last half-hour of the meeting to end on a high note by getting everyone excited about the new strategic direction.

The best way to get people jazzed about the plan is to have them visualize success. What does success look like? Help your team feel successful by living the future today. Ask your team to draw a picture of what the company may look like if you achieve your strategic plan. How many employees? What is the office like? Where are you located? Who are your customers? What's the media saying? And so on. Then have them explain their vision to the group. After the drawings and explanations are over, tell your staff members to hang their creations at their desks to remind them of the plan and their part in it. That way, everyone leaves the planning session feeling successful instead of overworked.

Overlooking Life After the Meeting

The absolute worst thing you can do is continue business as usual, as if there never was a strategic planning meeting. Not only have you wasted everyone's time and your money, but also getting people to participate in the future is next to impossible.

Committing time and resources to implementing the plan is almost more important than the plan itself. Don't underestimate how much effort it takes to get the plan moving. Here are a few tips:

- ✔ Within a week after your strategic planning meeting, send out a timeline that contains the next steps and deadlines for completing the plan. Make sure to communicate this timeline to everyone in your organization so your employees know what's happening with the process.

- ✔ Do not, under any circumstance, cancel the next meeting in your planning or implementation process. As the leader, you're responsible for setting the example that the strategic plan is important. Canceling a meeting signifies it isn't important.

- ✔ Send out the strategic plan on the deadline you set, regardless if it's complete. You reinforce the importance of the plan.

- ✔ Post a visible result of the planning session in a common area. Items to post include your mission, vision, and values statements or a poster of your strategic plan.

Flip back to Chapter 14 for more ideas on how to implement your plan.

Chapter 20

Ten Shortcuts to Getting Your Plan Done

In This Chapter

▶ Moving your plan to completion

▶ Steering clear of common roadblocks

Completing your strategic plan is on your to-do list, right? But is it slipping lower and lower down the list? I know that feeling. And don't worry, you're not alone! In fact, I would wager that everyone reading this book is struggling with the same problem. Completing your strategic plan is arguably one of the most important things you have to do, so this chapter has a list of shortcuts to help you scratch your plan off your list. Some of these shortcuts work together, whereas others contradict one another. Use the ones that work for you and ignore the rest.

Focus on Your Top Five

Identify the top five strategic issues facing your organization right now. Write these down, along with what you need to do in the next 90 days to start achieving each one.

Although it's important to have a written strategic plan that includes your mission, vision, values, strategic objectives, goals, and actions, sometimes that's just too big of a mountain to climb. By identifying the five most important things you want to accomplish over the next few years, you bring focus and direction to your organization. You start taking baby steps toward your goal instead of waiting until you have a full plan together to start acting.

Remember That Something Is Better than Nothing

If you've made it partially through your plan, but can't seem to complete it, remember that something is better than nothing. Instead of beating yourself up for not having a plan that's 100 percent complete, just work with what you have. The majority of organizations don't even have a written plan, so the fact that you have a partially completed one puts you a step above the rest.

Each year your plan can grow and change:

- ✔ The first year: You embark on strategic planning, and the resulting plan is sufficient, but not as robust as you like. Why? Primarily because you end up spending a fair bit of time developing your mission, vision, values, and competitive advantage. By the time you get to strategic objectives, goals, and action plans, you're ready to be done planning. Write down a few objectives, goals, and actions. Make them more robust in year two.

- ✔ The second year: The plan is substantially better than the previous one because you're clear on where you are and where you're headed. This year you can spend the majority of your effort on objectives, goals, and action plans.

- ✔ The third year: The strategic plan is truly a complete picture of the organization's strategic direction. With two years under your belt, you know what works and doesn't work for your company. Your plan becomes the living document that's a true representation of your company because you've refined your process and your strategy.

With this in mind, put something down on paper and start working with it, even though you know it isn't as good as it could be. Over the course of a few years and working with an ever-evolving strategic plan, you can develop a plan that meets your expectations. See Chapter 14 for ideas on working through your implementation process and how your plan can evolve.

Start Implementing Soon Because No Plan Is Ever Complete

Your strategic plan is a work in progress. Even for those businesses that have been planning year after year, no plan is ever complete — there's always more that you could do. But don't fall into the trap that you need a complete plan before you start implementing it or you may be waiting forever. See Chapter 14 for ideas on implementation.

The reason your plan can't ever be complete is because business situations are constantly in flux. Just when you think you've got everything nailed down, something in your environment changes. Recognize the dynamic atmosphere you operate in and know that your plan can't be stagnant either. Because of this fact, your plan is about 90 percent done at all times, and give yourself permission to believe that's good enough.

Eat the Elephant One Bite at a Time

Thinking about strategic planning can be like trying to eat an elephant — it's so big, you don't know where to start. Instead of diving in, back away until you feel brave enough to tackle the beast. Consider eating the elephant one bite at a time, instead of swallowing it whole.

Use this analogy to tackle your strategic plan. Break your planning down into to realistic chunks so the tasks feel doable, and complete one part of your plan each week. Use the outline in Chapter 3 as a guide. By doing so, you can finish your plan in eight to ten weeks!

Knock Your Plan Out in One Day

If you're more of a marathon runner and less of a sprinter, consider knocking your plan out in one day. Lock the doors. Turn off the phones. Ignore your e-mail. Pull your team together for one long strategy session. And don't leave the room until the plan is done.

A couple of things can make this process go more smoothly:

- **Have a clear agenda and a timekeeper.** Move on to the next item when the time allotted is up.

- **Come prepared with your internal and external analysis data and research.** Ideally, have everyone read the material ahead of time.

- **Appoint a person to organize the plan based on the work completed.** This person should also take complete notes of the session for reference after the strategy session.

- **Take a break every one and a half to two hours.** Make sure that you're in a place that's easy to get outside for some fresh air.

- **Have a lot of snack foods and order in a good lunch.** Everyone likes to munch.

✔ **Plan some fun games.** You can only work so hard for so long, so reward your team by having fun during the day or a nice outing afterwards. You can build games into the strategic planning process. See the end of Chapter 3 for some ideas. Because your time is compressed, make sure to limit any games to 15 to 20 minutes.

Get Out of Town

For some people, shutting out the world can only happen when you leave town. If you're in this group of folks, block out a few days at your favorite getaway and get out of Dodge. Changing your surroundings helps free up your mind to think more broadly about your organization and its strategic direction.

Escaping with your whole team may not be practical; so if it isn't, take the time yourself to work on at least your mission, vision, values, and strategic objectives. After these elements are fleshed out, you can work with your staff to hammer out short-term goals and action items.

Outsource It

It's amazing how much you can accomplish in a short amount of time when you have others helping you. Enlist your business coach, a strategic planning consultant, or another advisor that you contract with to be responsible for the major portions of completing your plan. Schedule meetings every two weeks where you talk about each element of your plan, and, by the end of a few months, you'll have a completed plan.

The trick is to have your consultant or business coach create your strategic plan based on your meetings. So after each meeting, he or she completes another section of your plan based on your conversations. The person you outsource to isn't responsible for coming up with all the information.

Leave Perfection to the Accountants

You hire accountants to be perfect when they handle your books. You don't need to be such a perfectionist when you set out to complete your strategic plan. Your plan can be missing some sections or lacking dates, measures, and maybe even some goals. Some minor details may not be complete, but take a deep breath; it's okay. Your plan can still serve the purpose of providing focus and direction to your organization.

If you'd like your plan to be as complete as possible, use estimates or best guesses to fill in certain sections. Then come back to the plan in a few weeks to fill in any major gaps.

Get Everyone to Pitch In

Your team is one of your most valuable assets. Managers have a tendency to go it alone, thinking that the task at hand is only theirs to conquer. But with your strategic plan, don't think you need to put it together yourself. Get your employees to help develop the guts of your plan. Ask every team member to take a strategic objective and develop goals, measurements, targets, dead-lines, and action plans (where relevant) for their objective. See Chapter 13 for guidance.

Splitting the work up seems like less of a burden on you and also gets your staff involved. If you're worried about the end result, set the stage correctly so your team understands that the final plan is reviewed and modified by you.

Just Do It

Sometimes getting your plan done just requires a little push. So here is your push! Oh, sorry. Did that hurt? Get committed and finish your plan so you can start reaping the rewards of having a solid, intentional strategic direction for your organization. I promise you won't regret the time you spend on strategic planning. You'll realize the benefits for years to come. So, borrow some encouragement from that famous shoe slogan, and just do it!

Index

succession planning, 300
transition planning, 299–300
when to start planning, 299
expansion, geographical, 187–188
expenses
estimating, 250
projecting, 251–254
reducing with mergers and
acquisitions, 198

• F •

facilitator
benefits of use, 20
finding, 53–54
refusing to use, 333–334
running sessions yourself, 52–53
when to use, 54–55
Factiva (Web site), 206
failure
celebrating, 135
to plan, 25–26
understanding reasons for, 63
Famous Footwear, position statement
of, 217
Fannie Mae, mission statement of, 103
Fast Company (business publication), 135
FedEx, Kinko's, purchase of, 201
feedback, from customers, 149
financial assessment, purpose in strategic
plan, 37
financial performance
comparing industry numbers, 76–77
financial dynamics, understanding, 70–74
financial ratios, 70–74
liquidity, 71
risk levels, 71–72
three-year trends, 74
Trailing 12 Months (T12M), 74–76
financial ratios
accounts payable turnover, 74
current ratio, 71
debt-to-equity ratio, 71–72
description, 70
inventory turnover, 73
liquidity, 71
net profit margin, 72
productivity, 73–74

profitability, 72
quick ratio, 71
receivable turnover, 73
return on assets (ROA), 73
return on equity (ROE), 72
risk, 71–72
sales-to-assets, 73
financing
compensating balance, 255
finding correct product, 254–255
lending agreement, adjusting, 256
potential, borrowing on, 256
risk, 255–256
*Finding Information on the Internet:
A Tutorial* (University of California
Berkeley Library), 207
FISonline (Web site), 206
flexibility, importance of, 315
focus
marketing, 220–222
as roadblock to growth, 150
strategy-focused organization,
creating, 280
what to focus on, 151
Forbes Group (Web site), 322
forward planning, uncertainty
problem in, 17
foundational elements, 38
franchising, 197
Frost & Sullivan (Web site), 206
futurecasting, 55–57

• G •

Gadiesh, Orit (chairman of Bain & Co.), 18
Gates, Bill (entrepreneur), 129
General Electric Matrix, 67–69
geographical expansion, 187–188
Giant Eagle (grocery chain), 309
Girl Scouts of America (nonprofit
organization), 326
goals
action plan for, 248
cascading corporate goals to department
goals, 306–308, 309
customer, 236
establishing big, 32
measures, 240

BUSINESS, CAREERS & PERSONAL FINANCE

0-7645-5307-0

0-7645-5331-3 *†

Also available:
- Accounting For Dummies †
  0-7645-5314-3
- Business Plans Kit For Dummies †
  0-7645-5365-8
- Cover Letters For Dummies
  0-7645-5224-4
- Frugal Living For Dummies
  0-7645-5403-4
- Leadership For Dummies
  0-7645-5176-0
- Managing For Dummies
  0-7645-1771-6

- Marketing For Dummies
  0-7645-5600-2
- Personal Finance For Dummies *
  0-7645-2590-5
- Project Management For Dummies
  0-7645-5283-X
- Resumes For Dummies †
  0-7645-5471-9
- Selling For Dummies
  0-7645-5363-1
- Small Business Kit For Dummies *†
  0-7645-5093-4

HOME & BUSINESS COMPUTER BASICS

0-7645-4074-2

0-7645-3758-X

Also available:
- ACT! 6 For Dummies
  0-7645-2645-6
- iLife '04 All-in-One Desk Reference
  For Dummies
  0-7645-7347-0
- iPAQ For Dummies
  0-7645-6769-1
- Mac OS X Panther Timesaving
  Techniques For Dummies
  0-7645-5812-9
- Macs For Dummies
  0-7645-5656-8

- Microsoft Money 2004 For Dummies
  0-7645-4195-1
- Office 2003 All-in-One Desk Reference
  For Dummies
  0-7645-3883-7
- Outlook 2003 For Dummies
  0-7645-3759-8
- PCs For Dummies
  0-7645-4074-2
- TiVo For Dummies
  0-7645-6923-6
- Upgrading and Fixing PCs For Dummies
  0-7645-1665-5
- Windows XP Timesaving Techniques
  For Dummies
  0-7645-3748-2

FOOD, HOME, GARDEN, HOBBIES, MUSIC & PETS

0-7645-5295-3

0-7645-5232-5

Also available:
- Bass Guitar For Dummies
  0-7645-2487-9
- Diabetes Cookbook For Dummies
  0-7645-5230-9
- Gardening For Dummies *
  0-7645-5130-2
- Guitar For Dummies
  0-7645-5106-X
- Holiday Decorating For Dummies
  0-7645-2570-0
- Home Improvement All-in-One
  For Dummies
  0-7645-5680-0

- Knitting For Dummies
  0-7645-5395-X
- Piano For Dummies
  0-7645-5105-1
- Puppies For Dummies
  0-7645-5255-4
- Scrapbooking For Dummies
  0-7645-7208-3
- Senior Dogs For Dummies
  0-7645-5818-8
- Singing For Dummies
  0-7645-2475-5
- 30-Minute Meals For Dummies
  0-7645-2589-1

INTERNET & DIGITAL MEDIA

0-7645-1664-7

0-7645-6924-4

Also available:
- 2005 Online Shopping Directory
  For Dummies
  0-7645-7495-7
- CD & DVD Recording For Dummies
  0-7645-5956-7
- eBay For Dummies
  0-7645-5654-1
- Fighting Spam For Dummies
  0-7645-5965-6
- Genealogy Online For Dummies
  0-7645-5964-8
- Google For Dummies
  0-7645-4420-9

- Home Recording For Musicians
  For Dummies
  0-7645-1634-5
- The Internet For Dummies
  0-7645-4173-0
- iPod & iTunes For Dummies
  0-7645-7772-7
- Preventing Identity Theft For Dummies
  0-7645-7336-5
- Pro Tools All-in-One Desk Reference
  For Dummies
  0-7645-5714-9
- Roxio Easy Media Creator For Dummies
  0-7645-7131-1

* Separate Canadian edition also available
† Separate U.K. edition also available

Available wherever books are sold. For more information or to order direct: U.S. customers visit www.dummies.com or call 1-877-762-2974.
U.K. customers visit www.wileyeurope.com or call 0800 243407. Canadian customers visit www.wiley.ca or call 1-800-567-4797.

SPORTS, FITNESS, PARENTING, RELIGION & SPIRITUALITY

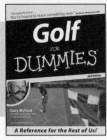

0-7645-5146-9

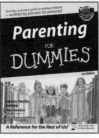

0-7645-5418-2

Also available:

- Adoption For Dummies
  0-7645-5488-3
- Basketball For Dummies
  0-7645-5248-1
- The Bible For Dummies
  0-7645-5296-1
- Buddhism For Dummies
  0-7645-5359-3
- Catholicism For Dummies
  0-7645-5391-7
- Hockey For Dummies
  0-7645-5228-7

- Judaism For Dummies
  0-7645-5299-6
- Martial Arts For Dummies
  0-7645-5358-5
- Pilates For Dummies
  0-7645-5397-6
- Religion For Dummies
  0-7645-5264-3
- Teaching Kids to Read For Dummies
  0-7645-4043-2
- Weight Training For Dummies
  0-7645-5168-X
- Yoga For Dummies
  0-7645-5117-5

TRAVEL

0-7645-5438-7

0-7645-5453-0

Also available:

- Alaska For Dummies
  0-7645-1761-9
- Arizona For Dummies
  0-7645-6938-4
- Cancún and the Yucatán For Dummies
  0-7645-2437-2
- Cruise Vacations For Dummies
  0-7645-6941-4
- Europe For Dummies
  0-7645-5456-5
- Ireland For Dummies
  0-7645-5455-7

- Las Vegas For Dummies
  0-7645-5448-4
- London For Dummies
  0-7645-4277-X
- New York City For Dummies
  0-7645-6945-7
- Paris For Dummies
  0-7645-5494-8
- RV Vacations For Dummies
  0-7645-5443-3
- Walt Disney World & Orlando For Dummies
  0-7645-6943-0

GRAPHICS, DESIGN & WEB DEVELOPMENT

0-7645-4345-8

0-7645-5589-8

Also available:

- Adobe Acrobat 6 PDF For Dummies
  0-7645-3760-1
- Building a Web Site For Dummies
  0-7645-7144-3
- Dreamweaver MX 2004 For Dummies
  0-7645-4342-3
- FrontPage 2003 For Dummies
  0-7645-3882-9
- HTML 4 For Dummies
  0-7645-1995-6
- Illustrator cs For Dummies
  0-7645-4084-X

- Macromedia Flash MX 2004 For Dummies
  0-7645-4358-X
- Photoshop 7 All-in-One Desk
  Reference For Dummies
  0-7645-1667-1
- Photoshop cs Timesaving Techniques
  For Dummies
  0-7645-6782-9
- PHP 5 For Dummies
  0-7645-4166-8
- PowerPoint 2003 For Dummies
  0-7645-3908-6
- QuarkXPress 6 For Dummies
  0-7645-2593-X

NETWORKING, SECURITY, PROGRAMMING & DATABASES

0-7645-6852-3

0-7645-5784-X

Also available:

- A+ Certification For Dummies
  0-7645-4187-0
- Access 2003 All-in-One Desk
  Reference For Dummies
  0-7645-3988-4
- Beginning Programming For Dummies
  0-7645-4997-9
- C For Dummies
  0-7645-7068-4
- Firewalls For Dummies
  0-7645-4048-3
- Home Networking For Dummies
  0-7645-42796

- Network Security For Dummies
  0-7645-1679-5
- Networking For Dummies
  0-7645-1677-9
- TCP/IP For Dummies
  0-7645-1760-0
- VBA For Dummies
  0-7645-3989-2
- Wireless All In-One Desk Reference
  For Dummies
  0-7645-7496-5
- Wireless Home Networking For Dummies
  0-7645-3910-8

HEALTH & SELF-HELP

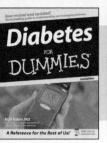

Diabetes FOR DUMMIES
2nd Edition

Alan Rubin, MD
A Reference for the Rest of Us!

0-7645-6820-5 *†

Low-Carb Dieting FOR DUMMIES

Katherine Chauncey, PhD, RD
A Reference for the Rest of Us!

0-7645-2566-2

Also available:

Alzheimer's For Dummies
0-7645-3899-3

Asthma For Dummies
0-7645-4233-8

Controlling Cholesterol For Dummies
0-7645-5440-9

Depression For Dummies
0-7645-3900-0

Dieting For Dummies
0-7645-4149-8

Fertility For Dummies
0-7645-2549-2

Fibromyalgia For Dummies
0-7645-5441-7

Improving Your Memory For Dummies
0-7645-5435-2

Pregnancy For Dummies †
0-7645-4483-7

Quitting Smoking For Dummies
0-7645-2629-4

Relationships For Dummies
0-7645-5384-4

Thyroid For Dummies
0-7645-5385-2

EDUCATION, HISTORY, REFERENCE & TEST PREPARATION

Speak Spanish — the fun and easy way!

Spanish FOR DUMMIES

A Reference for the Rest of Us!

Susana Wald

0-7645-5194-9

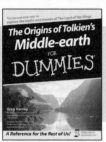

The fun and easy way to explore the myths and themes of The Lord of the Rings

The Origins of Tolkien's Middle-earth FOR DUMMIES

Greg Harvey

A Reference for the Rest of Us!

0-7645-4186-2

Also available:

Algebra For Dummies
0-7645-5325-9

British History For Dummies
0-7645-7021-8

Calculus For Dummies
0-7645-2498-4

English Grammar For Dummies
0-7645-5322-4

Forensics For Dummies
0-7645-5580-4

The GMAT For Dummies
0-7645-5251-1

Inglés Para Dummies
0-7645-5427-1

Italian For Dummies
0-7645-5196-5

Latin For Dummies
0-7645-5431-X

Lewis & Clark For Dummies
0-7645-2545-X

Research Papers For Dummies
0-7645-5426-3

The SAT I For Dummies
0-7645-7193-1

Science Fair Projects For Dummies
0-7645-5460-3

U.S. History For Dummies
0-7645-5249-X

Get smart @ dummies.com®

- **Find a full list of Dummies titles**
- **Look into loads of FREE on-site articles**
- **Sign up for FREE eTips e-mailed to you weekly**
- **See what other products carry the Dummies name**
- **Shop directly from the Dummies bookstore**
- **Enter to win new prizes every month!**

* Separate Canadian edition also available
† Separate U.K. edition also available

Available wherever books are sold. For more information or to order direct: U.S. customers visit www.dummies.com or call 1-877-762-2974.
U.K. customers visit www.wileyeurope.com or call 0800 243407. Canadian customers visit www.wiley.ca or call 1-800-567-4797.

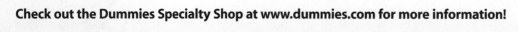

Get the industry numbers you need!

Save 15% off on over 2.5 million reports such as:

- Financial Analysis (industry-wide, small business, startup)
- Competitive Analysis
- Marketing Research (US, state and metro)
- Local Business Summary (states, metros, counties)

Coupon Code: d5kd9jze42

www.bizminer.com

(Offer valid for one time use. Not applicable for Franchise Research, Industry Data Buffet, custom work and subscription products.)

Raise Your Strategic Leadership Effectiveness to New Heights!

Take your Personal Effectiveness Inventory for $399
(A $850 value)

Using the scientifically based, cutting edge technology of Emergenetics® you will identify your personal strengths, preferences and potential limitations. The personal coaching session you receive from a trained Emergenetics® coach will provide you with efficient and powerful insights that will impact your success in implementing your strategic plan, leading your team through the strategic planning process, and amplifying overall results in your business.

Utilize the Emergenetics® Inventory process to fully understand your personal formula for success in strategic planning, communication and leadership!

Coupon Code: SPFDCOACH

www.amplitudetraining.com/PEinventory